Guide to Operatic Duets

Richard Boldrey

Pst...Inc
Dallas • Seattle

Copyright 1994 Pst ... Inc.
Library of Congress Card No.
90-061008

ISBN 1-877761-65-6

Printed in the United States of America

Copies of this book may be ordered by contacting:

Pst ... Inc.
P.O. Box 800208
Dallas, Texas 75380-0208

10-9-8-7-6-5-4-3-2-1

Guide to Operatic Duets

Contents

to my brother Robert
who once told me
that
I had more to accomplish...

Acknowledgements

Thanks to my many students, the young singers for whom this book was written.

Thanks to Jean Piatak, who started it all. Thanks to Gerard Yun, who taught me how to use a computer. Thanks to Joan Wall, Mary Dibbern, Janet Bookspan, Barbara Doscher, and Robert Spillman, who each added important guidance at various steps along the way.

Thanks to my wife, Polly Liontis, and to my children, Electra Marie Liontis and Drew Jason Boldrey, for their patience as Daddy was consumed by this project. Their love for me and their tolerance toward the computer—which for the last year has been a demanding fifth member of the family—are gifts that can never fully be repaid.

Mostly thanks to Robert Caldwell, who is more than a publisher and an editor. He is a mentor and a friend. As a mentor, he has taught, criticised, praised, guided, prodded, forced me to grow at every turn. As a friend, he is always there. I respect Robert Caldwell's genius. I am grateful for his personal warmth and love. He is the one who turned my dreams into this *Guide to Operatic Duets*.

How to use this book

Guide to Operatic Duets helps you select duets suitable for your needs. Like its companion volume, *Guide to Operatic Roles and Arias,* the information is cross-referenced for maximum usefulness and minimum flipping through the pages.

Duets
The *Duets* section is the most complete section. Each entry includes the aria, the opera (in italics), a second or common title, if there is one (in brackets), the composer and the composer's dates, and the language of the opera.

Then, set off by a bullet "•", the two roles that sing the duet are listed, followed by their general voice categories. The categories are listed in the same order as the roles, for example, in the entry *Charlotte • Werther (mezzo-soprano • tenor)*, Charlotte is the mezzo-soprano, and Werther is the tenor. Finally, set off by another bullet, "•", the general character of the duet is listed (see *Duet Categories* on page 3).

Roles are alphabetized by the first name of the main name, after articles, titles, salutations. Don José, for example, is alphabetized under José, Don; King Herod, Herod, King; Dr. Faust under Faust, Dr.; Il Conte Caramella under Caramella, Il Conte; Ann Page, under Ann Page.

The following list of salutations are placed after the main name for alphabetizing: A, An, Baron, Das, Der, Die, Doctor, Don, Donna, Dr., Duke, Ein, Eine, Emperor, Empress, Il, L', La, Lady, Le, Les, Lord, Madame, Miss, Mr. Mrs., Pope, Prince, Sir, Sultan, Superintendent, The

> *example*
>
> **A cette heure suprême**
> • *Werther* (Jules Massenet, 1842-1912), French
> • **Charlotte** • **Werther** (mezzo-soprano • tenor)
> • lyric voices
>
> **A l'autel j'allais rayonnant**
> • *Le roi d'Ys* (Edouard Lalo, 1823-1892), French
> • **Rozenn** • **Mylio** (soprano • tenor)
> • lyric voices

Roles to Duets
The *Roles to Duets* section lists the role names alphabetically. Following the role name, the opera title, the opera's second title if there is one, and the composer's last name are listed. Then, set off by a bullet "•", the other role in the duet is listed and is followed by the voice categories singing the role. Then, set off by a dash, "-", the title of the duet or duets are listed. In some instances, one role may sing several duets: all other partners, their voice categories, and duets are listed.

Adèle di Formouters, La Comtesse [Countess]
Le comte Ory (Rossini)
• **Ory, Le Comte** [Count] (soprano • tenor)
-Ah! quel respect, Madame
• **Ragonde** (soprano • mezzo-soprano)
-Dans ce séjour

Adina *L'elisir d'amore* (Donizetti)
• **Dulcamara, Dr.** (soprano • bass)
-Io son ricco e tu sei bella
-Quanto amore
• **Nemorino** (soprano • tenor)
-Chiedi all'aura lusinghiera

Voice Categories to Duets

This section allows you to locate duets for each combination of voice category—soprano • mezzo-soprano, for example. Each entry is listed under a main heading, soprano, for example, and then a sub-heading, soprano • mezzo-soprano, for example, which is underlined. Then, the duets for that combination of voices are subdivided by language. The duet name is set off in bold and the two characters that sing the role are listed in parenthesis. The title of the opera and the composer's last name appear on the next line, and then a general description of the voices that sing the duets follow.

example

---

soprano

---

soprano • soprano

ENGLISH

Begone! discharge you (Lady Elinor • Adela)
• *The Haunted Tower* (Storace)
• light voices

Hi there, dear husband
(Lucy Lockit • Polly Peachum)
• *The Beggar's Opera* (Pepusch)
• light voices

I'm bubbled! (Lucy Lockit • Polly Peachum)
• *The Beggar's Opera* (Pepusch)
• light voices

Opera to Roles

This section is a cross reference to the roles listed in this volume. It is not intended to represent a list of all of the roles that appear in the opera.

Composers to Operas

This section is a cross reference to the operas listed in this volume. It is not intended to represent a list of all of the operas by the composers.

Introduction

The duet is the most common ensemble in opera. In early French *tragédie lyrique,* from Lully to Rameau, nearly ninety percent of all opera ensembles were duets, with at least three or four per opera. In the middle 1700s in Italy, the duet was often the only ensemble in an opera, serving as the finale movement of an act—*Se viver non degg'io* (Mozart, *Mitridate*), for example. In comic opera after 1750, the only other ensemble besides the usual large finale was the requisite duet for the principal *buffa* couple. In the Classical period at the end of that century, duets became even more prevalent for both principal and secondary characters. A hundred years later, the Italian operatic duet had assumed an importance equal to the aria. The nineteenth-century Italian "grand duet"—between lovers, cohorts, rivals, or enemies—was frequently the highlight of an act.

Operatic duets are normally associated with lovers—usually soprano and tenor—such as Mimì and Rodolfo in Puccini's *La Bohème.* Composers of Italian *opera seria* in the middle 1700s wrote duets almost exclusively for the principal lovers, but the couple was usually a soprano and a male castrato (either soprano or alto). Composers of the French *opéra comique* of the same period wrote fewer duets for lovers, instead writing them to highlight dramatic situations, and nearly half of the duets were for characters of the same sex. Italian composers gradually followed the French and wrote same-sex duets, which became common in *opera seria* by the 1780s. In the nineteenth century, composers wrote duets for nearly every combination of voices, role types, and relationships, not just for lovers. Famous non-lover duets include *Mira, o Norma* (Bellini, *Norma*), *Sous le dôme épais* (Delibes, *Lakmé*), *L'amo come il fulgor del creato* (Ponchielli, *La Gioconda*), *Solenne in quest'ora* (Verdi, *La forza del destino*), and *Au fond du temple saint* (Bizet, *Les pêcheurs de perles*).

Composers wrote duets in all shapes and sizes. Some, especially for Viennese operetta and Wagner for his music dramas, wrote arias with interjections from a second character. Some decorated their duets with interjections from yet a third character. Occasionally some ended their duets as trios—*Pensa che sol per poco* (Rossini, *Elisabetta*) and *Vieni, cerchiam pe' mari* (Bellini, *Il pirata*), for example. And Wagner wrote duets that are really extended dialogues, never formally delineated duets, except possibly the great love duet in Act 2 of *Tristan und Isolde.*

History of Operatic Duets

During the 1600s, when opera was in its infancy, composers wrote duets as short pieces in simple forms. In France, for example, the binary form was the most popular. Toward the end of the century, especially in Italy, most composers wrote duets that had two short solo sections, each sung by a different character, but often to the same music, followed by the duet proper. By 1700, composers lengthened these solo sections and customarily inserted a transitional dialogue passage of alternating or overlapping phrases to introduce the final *a due* passage.

By 1730, composers in Italy wrote serious duets in the same forms as arias, the most popular being the standard AA'BAA' *da capo*. Composers in France continued to write popular binary forms or the homophonic duets of *tragédie lyrique*, in which the characters sang the same words. They only occasionally wrote *da capo* duets. In both Italy and France, however, they wrote comic duets in more flexible forms, ones that followed the flow of dialogue between the two characters.

During the Classical period in the late 1700s, the *da capo* duet of *opera seria* first gave way to a truncated AA'BA' *dal segno* form, and then was replaced by two more popular forms: ABA'C and ABC. *Se viver non degg'io* (Mozart, *Mitridate*) is a good example of the ABC duet form. In this form, each of the three sections was usually in a different key, and the normal procession of tempo in the three sections was from slow to moderate to fast, as in *Ich gehe, doch rate ich dir* (Mozart, *Die Entführung aus dem Serail*). Traditionally the last section of this form provided an opportunity for the two singers to unite in thirds or sixths, as in *Là ci darem la mano* (Mozart, *Don Giovanni*) and *Fra gli amplessi* (Mozart, *Così fan tutte*).

In the Romantic period of the early and middle 1800s, operatic duets appeared in several predictable forms, among them the single- and double-movement duets. Single-movement duets, which are rather free in form, were common outside Italy, as for example *Komm denn* (Weber, *Euryanthe*). In Italy, single-movement duets were rare apart from those of *opera buffa* or *opera semiseria*, such as *Tornami a dir che m'ami* (Donizetti, *Don Pasquale*) and *Son geloso del zefiro errante* (Bellini, *La sonnambula*). Double-movement duets either consisted of a slow *cantabile* followed by a faster *cabaletta*, or more commonly were similar to the older duet form of a dialogue section (sometimes two solos) followed by a section *a due*, such as *Va, crudele, al dio spietato* (Bellini, *Norma*) and *Anima mia!* (Verdi, *Alzira*).

The showcase duets of nineteenth-century opera were, however, the "grand duets" of the *bel canto* composers Rossini, Bellini, Donizetti, and Verdi. "Grand duets" consisted of three large movements, each movement connected to the next by a shorter transition passage. Typical "grand duets" followed the following formula:

- *Tempo d'attacco*, usually two parallel verses for the two singers, each usually fast in tempo and ending with an emphatic cadenza;

- *Transition*, usually in dialogue form, often modulating to a new key;

- *Cantabile*, usually slow, with separate texts sung jointly, the voices ultimately joining in thirds, sixths, or tenths, and ending with a combined cadenza;

- *Tempo di mezzo*, a short fast section, usually signaling a significant happening;

- *Cabaletta*, a fast section sung *a due*.

Verdi, the master of the "grand duet," often modified this form to suit the purposes of the dramatic moment.

Following are some of the best known operatic "grand duets," in chronological order: *Oui, vous l'arrachez à mon âme* (Rossini, *Guillaume Tell*, 1829), *Il pallor funesto, orrendo* (Donizetti, *Lucia di Lammermoor*, 1835), *Donna? chi sei?* (Verdi, *Nabucco*, 1842), *Fatal mia donna!* (Verdi, *Macbeth*, 1847), *Pura siccome un angelo* (Verdi, *La traviata*, 1853), *Dinnè, perchè in quest'eremo* (Verdi, *Simon Boccanegra*, 1857), and *Già nella notte densa* (Verdi, *Otello*, 1887).

Since 1850, most operatic duets have thrown over formal restraints in favor of a more episodic expression of "dialogue for two," as we find in *Das süsse Lied verhallt* (Wagner, *Lohengrin*), *Parle-moi de ma mère* (Bizet, *Carmen*), and *Mir ist die Ehre widerfahren* (Strauss, *Der Rosenkavalier*).

Duet Categories

In this volume, we have classified duets by general voice categories. Instead of being specific—*light lyric coloratura soprano* or *spinto tenor*—we have limited the duet categories to five:

- *light voices*, involving primarily soubrette or comic roles,

- *light or lyric voices*, primarily in older operas or for secondary roles,

- *lyric voices*, primarily referring to romantic leads,

- *lyric or dramatic voices*, primarily roles in grand opera, and

- *dramatic voices*, primarily heroic roles.

These five duet categories refer more to the general *quality* of voices that sing the duets than to voice *sizes*. The sizes of voice in each category may vary from composer to composer—*light* voices may be less light in a Johann Strauss operetta than in a Cimarosa *opera buffa*; *light lyric* voices in operas by Beethoven may be larger than *light lyrics* in a Haydn comic opera; *lyric* voices may be fuller in Puccini or even in Gluck than in Rossini; *lyric-dramatic* voices may be stronger in a Verdi opera than in a Monteverdi opera; *dramatic* voices in a Strauss or Wagner opera may be more heroic than in a Mozart opera.

Some operatic duets are not easily classified by voice category, because opera composers often have assigned duets to singers whose voices and characters are disparate. Smetana, in *Dalibor*, for example, wrote a duet that is sung by Milada (dramatic soprano) and Jitka (lyric soprano). Mozart, in many operas, wrote many duets for two voices of which one is heavier than the other. In *Così fan tutte*, for example, he wrote a love duet between Fiordiligi (lyric-dramatic soprano) and Ferrando (light lyric tenor). In *Don Giovanni*, he wrote duets between Donna

Anna (dramatic soprano) and Ottavio (light lyric tenor) and between Zerlina (soubrette) and Giovanni (lyric-dramatic bass-baritone).

Duets written with different voice categories pose ensemble problems that are usually taken into account when the opera is cast. A Ferrando is sought who can sing his own leggiero arias and at the same time can match the intensity of a more dramatic-voiced Fiordiligi. A Giovanni is sought who can cut a strong figure of the swashbuckling lady killer, but who at the same time can turn on the simpler charm to attract the peasant Zerlina.

In concert performances of operatic duets, the five general duet categories can be used to find voices that are more evenly matched than is often possible in performances of the opera. Light lyric voices could manage the seductive *Là ci darem la mano* between Zerlina and Giovanni, lyric voices could sing Fiordiligi's and Ferrando's *Fra gil amplessi*, whereas it would be good to find a stronger lyric-dramatic Don Ottavio to match Donna Anna in the aggressive *Fuggi, crudele, fuggi!*

The duet categories used in this volume are practical. They are intended to help singers find duet literature that is appropriate for their voices. For further and more specific information about any operatic role, the singer can consult the companion volume, *Guide to Operatic Roles and Arias.*

Duets

A cette heure suprême
- *Werther* (Jules Massenet, 1842-1912), French
- **Charlotte** • **Werther** (mezzo-soprano • tenor)
- lyric voices

A l'autel j'allais rayonnant
- *Le roi d'Ys* (Edouard Lalo, 1823-1892), French
- **Rozenn** • **Mylio** (soprano • tenor)
- lyric voices

A voti così ardente [De cet aveu si tendre]
- *La figlia del reggimento* [*La fille du régiment*] (Gaetano Donizetti, 1797-1848), Italian [French]
- **Maria** [Marie] • **Tonio** (soprano • tenor)
- light or lyric voices

Abends will ich schlafen gehn [Prayer]
- *Hänsel und Gretel* (Engelbert Humperdinck, 1854-1921), German
- **Gretel** • **Hänsel** (soprano • mezzo-soprano)
- light or lyric voices

Aber der Richtige
- *Arabella* (Richard Strauss, 1864-1949), German
- **Zdenka** • **Arabella** (soprano • soprano)
- lyric voices

Ach! du bist wieder da
- *Der Rosenkavalier* (Richard Strauss, 1864-1949), German
- **Die Feldmarschallin Fürstin Werdenberg** [Marie Thérèse] [Marschallin] • **Octavian, genannt**

Quinquin [Count Rofrano] (soprano • mezzo-soprano) Octavian is sung by either soprano or mezzo-soprano.
- lyric or dramatic voices

Ach, mich zieht's zu dir [Kissing Duet]
- *Die schöne Galathee* (Franz Suppé, 1819-1895), German
- **Galathee** • **Ganymede** (soprano • mezzo-soprano)
- light or lyric voices

Ad essi non perdono
- *Cavalleria rusticana* (Pietro Mascagni, 1863-1945), Italian
- **Santuzza** • **Alfio** (mezzo-soprano • baritone)
- dramatic voices

Adieu, mes tendres soeurs
- *La vestale* (Gaspare Spontini, 1774-1851), French
- **Julia** • **Licinius** (soprano • tenor)
- lyric or dramatic voices

Adieu, mon bien-aimé
- *Jérusalem* (Giuseppe Verdi, 1813-1901), French
- **Hélène** • **Gaston** (soprano • tenor)
- lyric or dramatic voices

Ah! ah! tout va bien
- *Pelléas et Mélisande* (Claude Debussy, 1862-1918), French
- **Mélisande** • **Goland** (mezzo-soprano • baritone)
- lyric or dramatic voices

Ah! d'immenso, estremo affetto
- *Beatrice di Tenda* (Vincenzo Bellini, 1801-1835), Italian
- **Beatrice · Orombello** (soprano · tenor)
- lyric voices

Ah! dimmi...dimmi io t'amo
- *Linda di Chamounix* (Gaetano Donizetti, 1797-1848), Italian
- **Linda · Carlo** (soprano · tenor)
- light or lyric voices

Ah! du moins à Médée
- *Médée* (Luigi Chérubini, 1760-1842), French
- **Médée · Créon** (soprano · bass)
- dramatic voices

Ah ferma!...Ah senti!
- *Paride ed Elena* (Christoph Willibald von Gluck, 1714-1787), Italian
- **Paride · Elena** (soprano · soprano) Paride, originally for soprano castrato, is sung by tenor or soprano.
- lyric voices

Ah! l'honnête homme!
- *Robert le Diable* (Giacomo Meyerbeer, 1791-1864), French
- **Raimbaut · Bertram** (tenor · bass)
- light voices

Ah mia diletta madre!
- *Alceste* (Christoph Willibald von Gluck, 1714-1787), Italian
- **Eumelo · Aspasia** (soprano · soprano)
- light voices

Ah, Mimì, tu più non torni
- *La Bohème* (Giacomo Puccini, 1858-1924), Italian
- **Rodolfo · Marcello** (tenor · baritone)
- lyric voices

Ah Minette, at last we meet in death
- *The English Cat* (Hans Werner Henze, 1926-), English
- **Minette · Tom** [Cat] (soprano · baritone)
- lyric voices

Ah! ne fuis pas encore
- *Roméo et Juliette* (Charles-François Gounod, 1812-1893), French
- **Juliette · Roméo** (soprano · tenor)
- lyric voices

Ah! parle encore
- *Mireille* (Charles-François Gounod, 1812-1893), French
- **Mireille · Vincenette** (soprano · soprano)
- lyric voices

Ah, per sempre/Pronti destrieri/Seguirti
- *La forza del destino* (Giuseppe Verdi, 1813-1901), Italian
- **Leonora · Don Alvaro** (soprano · tenor)
- dramatic voices

Ah perchè
- *Alceste* (Christoph Willibald von Gluck, 1714-1787), Italian
- **Alceste · Admeto** (soprano · tenor)
- lyric or dramatic voices

Ah perdona al primo affetto
- *La clemenza di Tito* (Wolfgang Amadeus Mozart, 1756-1791), Italian
- **Servilia · Annio** (soprano · mezzo-soprano) Annio (a pants role) can be sung by either soprano or mezzo-soprano.
- light or lyric voices

Ah! quel respect, Madame
- *Le comte Ory* (Gioachino Rossini, 1792-1868), French
- **La Comtesse Adèle di Formouters** [Countess] · **Le Comte Ory** [Count] (soprano · tenor)
- light or lyric voices

Ah! se potessi piangere
- *Belisario* (Gaetano Donizetti, 1797-1848), Italian
- **Irene · Belisario** (mezzo-soprano · baritone)
- lyric or dramatic voices

Ah! se tu vuoi fuggir
- *La Straniera* (Vincenzo Bellini, 1801-1835), Italian
- **Alaide** [La Straniera] · **Arturo** (soprano · tenor)
- lyric voices

Ah! sì, fa core e abbracciami
- *Norma* (Vincenzo Bellini, 1801-1835), Italian
- **Norma · Adalgisa** (soprano · mezzo-soprano) Adalgisa is sung by either soprano or mezzo-soprano.
- lyric voices

Ah sì, voliamo al tempio
- *Stiffelio* (Giuseppe Verdi, 1813-1901), Italian
- **Lina · Stiffelio** (soprano · tenor)
- lyric or dramatic voices

Ah! tu dei vivere/Che ti salva
- *Aida* (Giuseppe Verdi, 1813-1901), Italian
- **Amneris · Radames** (mezzo-soprano · tenor)
- dramatic voices

Ai capricci della sorte
- *L'italiana in Algeri* (Gioachino Rossini, 1792-1868), Italian
- **Isabella · Taddeo** (contralto · bass)
- light or lyric voices

Ai-je dit vrai/Ah! qu'il est loin
- *Werther* (Jules Massenet, 1842-1912), French
- **Charlotte · Werther** (mezzo-soprano · tenor)
- lyric voices

Al bel destin che attendevi
- *Linda di Chamounix* (Gaetano Donizetti, 1797-1848), Italian

- **Linda • Pierotto** (soprano • contralto)
- light or lyric voices

Al fato dan legge
- *Così fan tutte* (Wolfgang Amadeus Mozart, 1756-1791), Italian
- **Fiordiligi • Dorabella** (soprano • mezzo-soprano) Dorabella is sung by either soprano or mezzo-soprano.
- lyric voices

All'idea di quel metallo
- *Il barbiere di Siviglia* (Gioachino Rossini, 1792-1868), Italian
- **Il Conte d'Almaviva/Lindoro** [Count Almaviva] • **Figaro** (tenor • baritone)
- light voices

Als junger Liebe Lust mir verblich
- *Die Walküre* (Richard Wagner, 1813-1883), German
- **Brünnhilde • Wotan** (soprano • bass-baritone)
- dramatic voices

Amai, ma un solo istante/ Or del padre benedetta
- *Giovanna d'Arco* (Giuseppe Verdi, 1813-1901), Italian
- **Giovanna • Giacomo** (soprano • baritone)
- lyric or dramatic voices

Amaro sol per te
- *Edgar* (Giacomo Puccini, 1858-1924), Italian
- **Fidelia • Edgar** (soprano • tenor)
- lyric voices

Ami, leur rage
- *Alceste* (Christoph Willibald von Gluck, 1714-1787), French
- **Admète • Hercule** (tenor • bass)
- lyric or dramatic voices

Amore o grillo
- *Madama Butterfly* (Giacomo Puccini, 1858-1924), Italian
- **Pinkerton • Sharpless** (tenor • baritone)
- lyric or dramatic voices

And do you prefer the storm to Auntie's parlour?
- *Peter Grimes* (Benjamin Britten, 1913-1976), English
- **Peter Grimes • Captain Balstrode** (tenor • bass-baritone)
- dramatic voices

Ange adorable
- *Roméo et Juliette* (Charles-François Gounod, 1812-1893), French
- **Juliette • Roméo** (soprano • tenor)
- lyric voices

Anima mia!/Risorge ne' tuoi lumi
- *Alzira* (Giuseppe Verdi, 1813-1901), Italian

- **Alzira • Zamoro** (soprano • tenor)
- lyric or dramatic voices

Anne! Here!
- *The Rake's Progress* (Igor Stravinsky, 1882-1971), English
- **Anne Trulove • Tom Rakewell** (soprano • tenor)
- lyric voices

Apparvi alla luce [Au bruit de la guerre]
- *La figlia del reggimento* [*La fille du régiment*] (Gaetano Donizetti, 1797-1848), Italian [French]
- **Maria** [Marie] • **Sulpizio** [Sulpice] (soprano • baritone)
- light or lyric voices

Aprite, presto aprite [Escape Duet]
- *Le nozze di Figaro* (Wolfgang Amadeus Mozart, 1756-1791), Italian
- **Susanna • Cherubino** (soprano • mezzo-soprano) Cherubino is sung by either soprano or mezzo-soprano.
- lyric voices

As-tu souffert?/As-tu pleuré?
- *Mignon* (Ambroise Thomas, 1811-1896), French
- **Mignon • Lothario** (mezzo-soprano • bass)
- lyric voices

Au bonheur dont mon âme est pleine
- *Werther* (Jules Massenet, 1842-1912), French
- **Werther • Albert** (tenor • baritone)
- lyric or dramatic voices

Au bruit de la guerre [Apparvi alla luce]
- *La fille du régiment* [*La figlia del reggimento*] (Gaetano Donizetti, 1797-1848), French [Italian]
- **Marie** [Maria] • **Sulpice** [Sulpizio] (soprano • baritone)
- light or lyric voices

Au fond du temple saint
- *Les pêcheurs de perles* (Georges Bizet, 1838-1875), French
- **Nadir • Zurga** (tenor • baritone)
- lyric voices

Aux cris de la douleur [Cari figli]
- *Alceste* (Christoph Willibald von Gluck, 1714-1787), French [Italian]
- **Alceste • Admète** [Admeto] (soprano • tenor)
- lyric or dramatic voices

Avance un pas
- *Blaise et Babet* (Nicolas Dezède, c1740-1792), French
- **Babet • Blaise** (soprano • tenor)
- light voices

Avec bonté voyez ma peine
- *Robert le Diable* (Giacomo Meyerbeer, 1791-1864), French
- **Isabelle • Robert le Diable** (soprano • tenor)
- lyric voices

Avvezza al contento [Je goûtais les charmes]
- *Orfeo ed Euridice* [*Orphée et Eurydice*] (Christoph Willibald von Gluck, 1714-1787), Italian [French]
- **Euridice** [Eurydice] • **Orfeo** [Orphée] (soprano • contralto) Orfeo's role was originally for alto castrato, and is tenor in the French version. Orfeo is often sung by a mezzo-soprano.
- lyric voices

Bagnato dalle lagrime
- *Il pirata* (Vincenzo Bellini, 1801-1835), Italian
- **Imogene** • **Gualtiero** (soprano • tenor)
- lyric or dramatic voices

Baigne d'eau mes mains
- *Thaïs* (Jules Massenet, 1842-1912), French
- **Thaïs** • **Athanaël** (soprano • baritone)
- lyric or dramatic voices

Bambina, non ti crucciar
- *Adriana Lecouvreur* (Francesco Cilea, 1866-1950), Italian
- **Adriana Lecouvreur** • **Michonnet** (soprano • baritone)
- lyric or dramatic voices

Begone! discharge you
- *The Haunted Tower* (Stephen Storace, 1762-1796), English
- **Lady Elinor** • **Adela** (soprano • soprano)
- light voices

Bei jedem Walzerschritt
- *Die lustige Witwe* (Franz Lehár, 1870-1948), German
- **Hanna Glawari** • **Graf Danilo Danilowitsch** [Count Danilo] (soprano • baritone)
- light or lyric voices

Bei Männern, welche Liebe fühlen
- *Die Zauberflöte* (Wolfgang Amadeus Mozart, 1756-1791), German
- **Pamina** • **Papageno** (soprano • baritone)
- light or lyric voices

Belle nuit, ô nuit d'amour [Barcarolle]
- *Les contes d'Hoffmann* (Jacques Offenbach, 1819-1880), French
- **Nicklausse** • **Giulietta** (mezzo-soprano • mezzo-soprano) Both roles can be sung by either soprano or mezzo-soprano.
- lyric voices

Ben vi scorgo
- *La battaglia di Legnano* (Giuseppe Verdi, 1813-1901), Italian
- **Arrigo** • **Rolando** (tenor • baritone)
- lyric or dramatic voices

Bess, you is my woman
- *Porgy and Bess* (George Gershwin, 1898-1937), English
- **Bess** • **Porgy** (soprano • bass-baritone)
- dramatic voices

Bimba dagli occhi pieni di malià
- *Madama Butterfly* (Giacomo Puccini, 1858-1924), Italian
- **Cio-Cio-San** [Madama Butterfly] • **Pinkerton** (soprano • tenor)
- lyric or dramatic voices

Bleib und wache bis sie dich ruft
- *Die Frau ohne Schatten* (Richard Strauss, 1864-1949), German
- **Die Amme** [The Nurse] • **Der Kaiser** [The Emperor] (mezzo-soprano • tenor)
- dramatic voices

Blickt sein Auge doch so ehrlich
- *Martha* (Friedrich Flotow, 1812-1883), German
- **Lady Harriet Durham** • **Lyonel** (soprano • tenor)
- lyric voices

Blühenden Lebens labendes Blut
- *Götterdämmerung* (Richard Wagner, 1813-1883), German
- **Siegfried** • **Gunther** (tenor • bass-baritone)
- dramatic voices

Bocca, bocca
- *L'incoronazione di Poppea* (Claudio Monteverdi, 1567-1643), Italian
- **Nerone** • **Lucano** (mezzo-soprano • tenor) Nerone, originally for soprano castrato, is soprano or mezzo-soprano today.
- lyric voices

Brüderlein fein
- *Das Mädchen aus der Feenwelt* (Joseph Drechsler, 1782-1852), German
- **Youth** • **Fortunatus Wurzel** (soprano • tenor)
- light or lyric voices

C'était bien gentil autrefois
- *Sapho* (Jules Massenet, 1842-1912), French
- **Fanny** [Sapho] • **Irène** (soprano • mezzo-soprano)
- lyric voices

Cara non dubitar/Io ti lascio
- *Il matrimonio segreto* (Domenico Cimarosa, 1749-1801), Italian
- **Carolina** • **Paolino** (soprano • tenor)
- light voices

Cara, sarò fedele
- *Armida* (Joseph Haydn, 1732-1809), Italian
- **Armida** • **Rinaldo** (soprano • tenor)
- light or lyric voices

Cara sei tu il mio bene
- *Il barbiere di Siviglia* (Giovanni Paisiello, 1740-1816), Italian
- **Rosina** • **Il Conte di Almaviva/Lindoro** (soprano • tenor)
- light voices

Cari figli [Aux cris de la douleur]
- *Alceste* (Christoph Willibald von Gluck, 1714-1787), Italian
- **Alceste • Admeto** (soprano • tenor)
- lyric or dramatic voices

Carlo! io muoio
- *I Masnadieri* (Giuseppe Verdi, 1813-1901), Italian
- **Amalia • Massimiliano** [Count Moor] (soprano • bass)
- lyric or dramatic voices

Caro! bella! più amabile beltà
- *Giulio Cesare in Egitto* (George Frideric Handel, 1685-1759), Italian
- **Cleopatra • Giulio Cesare** (soprano • baritone) Giulio Cesare was originally written for soprano castrato.
- lyric or dramatic voices

Cat Duet [commonly known title]
- *l'Enfant et les sortilèges* (Maurice Ravel, 1875-1937), French
- **Female Cat • Tom Cat** (mezzo-soprano • baritone)
- light or lyric voices

C'è a Windsor una dama
- *Falstaff* (Giuseppe Verdi, 1813-1901), Italian
- **Falstaff • Ford** (baritone • baritone)
- lyric or dramatic voices

Ce domaine est celui des contes d'Avenel
- *La dame blanche* (Adrien Boieldieu, 1775-1834), French
- **Anna • Georges Brown/ Julien Avanel** (soprano • tenor)
- light or lyric voices

Ce que je veux
- *Hérodiade* (Jules Massenet, 1842-1912), French
- **Salomé • Jean** [John the Baptist] (soprano • tenor)
- dramatic voices

C'est à toi de trembler
- *La vestale* (Gaspare Spontini, 1774-1851), French
- **Licinius • Pontifex Maximus** (tenor • bass)
- lyric or dramatic voices

C'est le dieu de la jeunesse
- *Lakmé* (Léo Delibes, 1836-1891), French
- **Lakmé • Gérald** (soprano • tenor)
- light or lyric voices

C'est sur ce banc
- *Pénélope* (Gabriel Fauré, 1845-1924), French
- **Pénélope • Eumée** (soprano • baritone)
- lyric or dramatic voices

C'est toi! c'est moi!
- *Carmen* (Georges Bizet, 1838-1875), French
- **Carmen • Don José** (contralto • tenor)
- lyric or dramatic voices

C'était bien gentil autrefois
- *Sapho* (Jules Massenet, 1842-1912), French
- **Fanny** [Sapho] • **Irène** (soprano • mezzo-soprano)
- lyric voices

Che mai fate voi?/De qual amor [Que faites-vous donc?]
- *Don Carlo* [*Don Carlos*] (Giuseppe Verdi, 1813-1901), Italian [French]
- **Elisabetta** [Elisabeth] • **Don Carlo** [Don Carlos] (soprano • tenor)
- lyric or dramatic voices

Cheti, cheti, immantinente/ Aspetta, aspetta, cara sposina
- *Don Pasquale* (Gaetano Donizetti, 1797-1848), Italian
- **Dr. Malatesta • Don Pasquale** (baritone • bass)
- light voices

Chiedi all'aura lusinghiera
- *L'elisir d'amore* (Gaetano Donizetti, 1797-1848), Italian
- **Adina • Nemorino** (soprano • tenor)
- light voices

Chudnïy pervenets tvoren'ya [Wondrous firstling of creation]
- *Iolanta* (Pyotr Il'yich Tchaikovsky, 1840-1893), Russian
- **Iolanta • Vaudémont** (mezzo-soprano • tenor)
- lyric or dramatic voices

Cinque, dieci, venti
- *Le nozze di Figaro* (Wolfgang Amadeus Mozart, 1756-1791), Italian
- **Susanna • Figaro** (soprano • bass)
- lyric voices

Col sangue/Le minaccie/ Ah, segnasti la tua sorte
- *La forza del destino* (Giuseppe Verdi, 1813-1901), Italian
- **Don Alvaro • Don Carlo di Vargas** (tenor • baritone)
- lyric or dramatic voices

Colei Sofronia
- *Torquato Tasso* (Gaetano Donizetti, 1797-1848), Italian
- **Eleonora • Tasso** (soprano • baritone)
- lyric or dramatic voices

Colma di gioia ho l'anima
- *Alzira* (Giuseppe Verdi, 1813-1901), Italian
- **Alzira • Gusmano** (soprano • baritone)
- lyric or dramatic voices

Coloquio en la reja
- *Goyescas* (Enrique Granados, 1867-1916), Spanish
- **Rosario • Fernando** (soprano • tenor)
- lyric voices

Come frenar il pianto!
- *La gazza ladra* (Gioachino
  Rossini, 1792-1868), Italian
- **Ninetta · Fernando Villabella**
  (soprano · bass-baritone)
- light voices

Come il bacio d'un padre amoroso
- *I Masnadieri* (Giuseppe Verdi, 1813-1901), Italian
- **Carlo · Massimiliano** [Count Moor] (tenor · bass)
- lyric or dramatic voices

Come il foco allo splendore
- *L'anima del filosofo* (Joseph
  Haydn, 1732-1809), Italian
- **Euridice · Orfeo** (soprano · tenor)
- light voices

Come ti piace, imponi
- *La clemenza di Tito* (Wolfgang
  Amadeus Mozart, 1756-1791), Italian
- **Sesto · Vitellia** (mezzo-soprano · mezzo-soprano)
  Sesto was written for castrato; each role can be sung
  by soprano or mezzo-soprano.
- lyric or dramatic voices

Comment, dans ma reconnaissance/ Près du tombeau, peut-être
  [Quale o prode/ Presso alla tomba]
- *Les vêpres siciliennes* [*I vespri siciliani*] (Giuseppe
  Verdi, 1813-1901), French [Italian]
- **Hélène** [Elena] · **Henri** [Arrigo] (soprano · tenor)
- lyric or dramatic voices

Comment le dédain pourrait-il mourir?
- *Béatrice et Bénédict* (Hector
  Berlioz, 1803-1869), French
- **Béatrice · Bénédict** (mezzo-soprano · tenor)
- light or lyric voices

Contente-toi d'une victime
- *Hippolyte et Aricie* (Jean-Philippe Rameau,
  1683-1764), French
- **Tisiphone · Thésée** (tenor · bass) Tisiphone,
  tenor, was originally sung by haute-contre.
- lyric voices

Contento tu sarai [Reconciliation Duet]
- *Serva padrona, La* (Giovanni Battista
  Pergolesi, 1710-1736), Italian
- **Serpina · Uberto** (soprano · bass)
- light voices

Coughing Duet [commonly known title]
- *I filosofi immaginari* (Giovanni
  Paisiello, 1740-1816), Italian
- **Giuliano · Petronio** (baritone · bass)
- light voices

Credete alla femmine
- *Il turco in Italia* (Gioachino
  Rossini, 1792-1868), Italian
- **Fiorilla · Selim** (soprano · bass)
- light voices

Crudel! perchè finora
- *Le nozze di Figaro* (Wolfgang Amadeus
  Mozart, 1756-1791), Italian
- **Susanna · Il Conte di Almaviva** [Count]
  (soprano · baritone)
- lyric voices

Da lieg' ich! Was einem Kavalier
- *Der Rosenkavalier* (Richard
  Strauss, 1864-1949), German
- **Annina · Baron Ochs auf
  Lerchenau** (contralto · bass)
- lyric or dramatic voices

Da qual dì che t'ho veduta
- *Ernani* (Giuseppe Verdi, 1813-1901), Italian
- **Elvira · Don Carlo** (soprano · baritone)
- lyric or dramatic voices

Da tutti abbandonata
- *Maria Stuarda* (Gaetano
  Donizetti, 1797-1848), Italian
- **Maria Stuarda · Leicester** (soprano · tenor)
- lyric or dramatic voices

Dall'aule raggianti/Deh! la parola amara
- *Luisa Miller* (Giuseppe Verdi, 1813-1901), Italian
- **Federica · Rodolfo** (contralto · tenor)
- lyric or dramatic voices

Dans ce séjour
- *Le comte Ory* (Gioachino
  Rossini, 1792-1868), French
- **La Comtesse Adèle di Formouters** [Countess] ·
  Ragonde (soprano · mezzo-soprano)
- light or lyric voices

Dans la nuit où seul je veille
- *Les Huguenots* (Giacomo
  Meyerbeer, 1791-1864), French
- **Valentine · Marcel** (mezzo-soprano · bass)
- lyric voices

Dans Venise la belle [Barcarolle]
- *Le pont des soupirs* (Jacques
  Offenbach, 1819-1880), French
- **Baptiste · Cornarino Cornarini**
  [Doge of Venice] (tenor · bass)
- light voices

Darf eine nied're Magd es wagen
- *Zar und Zimmermann* (Albert
  Lortzing, 1801-1851), German
- **Marie · Ivanov** (soprano · tenor)
- lyric voices

Darf ich wohl den Worten trauen
- *Zar und Zimmermann* (Albert
  Lortzing, 1801-1851), German
- **Ivanov · Van Bett** (tenor · bass)
- light or lyric voices

Das Essen ist da
- *Tiefland* (Eugen d'Albert, 1864-1932), German
- **Marta** • **Pedro** (soprano • tenor)
- dramatic voices

Das süsse Lied verhallt
- *Lohengrin* (Richard Wagner, 1813-1883), German
- **Elsa** • **Lohengrin** (soprano • baritone)
- dramatic voices

Das Tor ist zu, Wir sind allein
- *Tiefland* (Eugen d'Albert, 1864-1932), German
- **Marta** • **Pedro** (soprano • tenor)
- dramatic voices

De cet aveu si tendre [A voti così ardente]
- *La fille du régiment* [*La figlia del reggimento*] (Gaetano Donizetti, 1797-1848), French [Italian]
- **Marie** [Maria] • **Tonio** (soprano • tenor)
- light or lyric voices

De courroux d'effroi/Ami! le coeur/Pour moi rayonne [O sdegni miei/E dolce raggio]
- *Les vêpres siciliennes* [*I vespri siciliani*] (Giuseppe Verdi, 1813-1901), French [Italian]
- **Hélène** [Elena] • **Henri** [Arrigo] (soprano • tenor)
- lyric or dramatic voices

De votre audace téméraire
- *Iphigénie en Aulide* (Christoph Willibald von Gluck, 1714-1787), French
- **Achille** • **Agamemnon** (tenor • baritone)
- lyric voices

Deh, non turbare
- *La Gioconda* (Amilcare Ponchielli, 1834-1886), Italian
- **Laura** • **Enzo** (mezzo-soprano • tenor)
- lyric or dramatic voices

Deh prendi un dolce amplesso
- *La clemenza di Tito* (Wolfgang Amadeus Mozart, 1756-1791), Italian
- **Sesto** • **Annio** (mezzo-soprano • mezzo-soprano) Annio (pants role) and Sesto (castrato) both can be sung by soprano or mezzo-soprano.
- lyric voices

Deh, scusa i trasporti
- *Elisabetta* (Gioachino Rossini, 1792-1868), Italian
- **Norfolk** • **Leicester** (tenor • tenor)
- lyric voices

Del mondo i disinganni
- *La forza del destino* (Giuseppe Verdi, 1813-1901), Italian
- **Fra Melitone** • **Guardiano** [Padre] (baritone • bass)
- lyric voices

D'Eliso in sen m'attendi
- *Lucio Silla* (Wolfgang Amadeus Mozart, 1756-1791), Italian

Giunia • **Cecilio** (soprano • mezzo-soprano) Cecilio, originally soprano castrato, is for soprano or mezzo-soprano.
- lyric voices

Delle faci festante al barlume/ Piango, perchè mi parla
- *Simon Boccanegra* (Giuseppe Verdi, 1813-1901), Italian
- **Simon Boccanegra** [The Doge of Genoa] • **Fiesco** (baritone • bass)
- lyric or dramatic voices

Den non parlare al misero/Ah! veglia, o donna
- *Rigoletto* (Giuseppe Verdi, 1813-1901), Italian
- **Gilda** • **Rigoletto** (soprano • baritone)
- lyric or dramatic voices

Depuis longtemps
- *Louise* (Gustave Charpentier, 1860-1956), French
- **Louise** • **Julien** (soprano • tenor)
- lyric voices

Der Lenz ist gekommen
- *Martha* (Friedrich Flotow, 1812-1883), German
- **Lady Harriet Durham** • **Lyonel** (soprano • tenor)
- lyric voices

Derrière ce pilier
- *Les Huguenots* (Giacomo Meyerbeer, 1791-1864), French
- **Valentine** • **Marcel** (mezzo-soprano • bass)
- lyric voices

Des chevaliers de ma patrie
- *Robert le Diable* (Giacomo Meyerbeer, 1791-1864), French
- **Robert le Diable** • **Bertram** (tenor • bass)
- lyric voices

Di pescatore ignobile
- *Lucrezia Borgia* (Gaetano Donizetti, 1797-1848), Italian
- **Lucrezia** • **Gennaro** (soprano • tenor)
- lyric or dramatic voices

Di': que' ribaldi tremano
- *Il corsaro* (Giuseppe Verdi, 1813-1901), Italian
- **Corrado** • **Seid** (tenor • baritone)
- lyric or dramatic voices

Di tue pene sparve il sogno
- *Linda di Chamounix* (Gaetano Donizetti, 1797-1848), Italian
- **Linda** • **Carlo** (soprano • tenor)
- light or lyric voices

Die Kinder sind's
- *Die tote Stadt* (Erich Wolfgang Korngold, 1897-1957), German
- **Marietta** • **Paul** (soprano • tenor)
- lyric or dramatic voices

Die Welt hat das genialste
• *Der Bettelstudent* (Carl
Millöcker, 1842-1899), German
• **Symon Rymanovicz** • **Jan** (tenor • baritone)
• light voices

Diese Liebe, plötzlich geboren
• *Capriccio* (Richard Strauss, 1864-1949), German
• **Die Gräfin [The Countess]** [Countess Madeleine] •
Flamand (soprano • tenor)
• lyric or dramatic voices

Dieser Anstand, so manierlich [Watch Duet]
• *Die Fledermaus* (Johann
Strauss, 1825-1899), German
• **Rosalinde** • **Eisenstein** (soprano • tenor)
• lyric voices

Dieu tu semas dans nos âmes
[Dio, che nell'alma infondere]
• *Don Carlos* [*Don Carlo*] (Giuseppe
Verdi, 1813-1901), French [Italian]
• **Don Carlos** [Don Carlo] • **Rodrigue** [Le Marquis de
Posa] [Rodrigo [Marchese di Posa]] (tenor • baritone)
• lyric or dramatic voices

Digli ch'è sangue italico
• *La battaglia di Legnano* (Giuseppe
Verdi, 1813-1901), Italian
• **Lida** • **Rolando** (soprano • baritone)
• lyric or dramatic voices

Dinnè, perchè in quest'eremo
Figlia! a tal nome io palpito
• *Simon Boccanegra* (Giuseppe
Verdi, 1813-1901), Italian
• **Amelia** [Maria Boccanegra] • **Simon Boccanegra**
[The Doge of Genoa] (soprano • baritone)
• lyric or dramatic voices

Dio, che mi vedi in core/Va, infelice
• *Anna Bolena* (Gaetano
Donizetti, 1797-1848), Italian
• **Anna Bolena** • **Giovanna Seymour**
(soprano • mezzo-soprano)
• lyric or dramatic voices

Dio, che nell'alma infondere
[Dieu tu semas dans nos âmes]
• *Don Carlo* [*Don Carlos*] (Giuseppe Verdi,
1813-1901), Italian [French]
• **Don Carlo** [Don Carlos] • **Rodrigo**
[Marchese di Posa] [Rodrigue [Le Marquis
de Posa]] (tenor • baritone)
• lyric or dramatic voices

Dio ti giocondi, o sposo
• *Otello* (Giuseppe Verdi, 1813-1901), Italian
• **Desdemona** • **Otello** (soprano • tenor)
• lyric or dramatic voices

Dite, che fà, dov'è
• *Tolomeo* (George Frideric
Handel, 1685-1759), Italian
• **Seleuce** • **Tolomeo** (soprano • contralto) The role
of Tolomeo was originally sung by an alto castrato.
• light or lyric voices

Dmitry! Tsarevich!
• *Boris Godunov* (Modest Petrovich
Musorgsky, 1839-1881), Russian
• **Marina** • **Dmitry** (mezzo-soprano • tenor)
• lyric or dramatic voices

Do you remember
• *Street Scene* (Kurt Weill, 1900-1950), English
• **Rose** • **Sam** (soprano • tenor)
• light or lyric voices

Dolce mia vita sei
• *Il ritorno d'Ulisse in patria* (Claudio
Monteverdi, 1567-1643), Italian
• **Melanto** • **Eurimaco** (soprano • tenor)
• light or lyric voices

Donna? chi sei?/Oh di qual'onta
aggravasi/Deh perdona
• *Nabucco* (Giuseppe Verdi, 1813-1901), Italian
• **Abigaille** • **Nabucco** (soprano • baritone)
• dramatic voices

Don't cry, mother dear
• *Amahl and the Night Visitors*
(Gian Carlo Menotti, 1911-), English
• **Amahl** • **Mother** (treble • soprano)
• light or lyric voices

D'où viens-tu?
• *Pénélope* (Gabriel Fauré, 1845-1924), French
• **Pénélope** • **Ulysse** (soprano • tenor)
• lyric or dramatic voices

Doute de la lumière
• *Hamlet* (Ambroise Thomas, 1811-1896), French
• **Ophélie** • **Hamlet** (soprano • baritone)
• lyric voices

Du! denn du bist stark
• *Elektra* (Richard Strauss, 1864-1949), German
• **Chrysothemis** • **Elektra** (soprano • soprano)
• dramatic voices

Dudu, rududu, rududu
• *Sorochinskaya yarmarka* [*The Fair at Sorochintzi*]
(Modest Petrovich Musorgsky, 1839-1881), Russian
• **Kum** • **Cherevik** (baritone • bass)
• dramatic voices

Due vaticini
• *Macbeth* (Giuseppe Verdi, 1813-1901), Italian
• **Macbeth** • **Banco** (baritone • bass)
• dramatic voices

D'un tenero amore
- *Semiramide* (Gioachino Rossini, 1792-1868), Italian
- **Arsace • Assur** (contralto • bass)
- lyric voices

Dunque io son?
- *Il barbiere di Siviglia* (Gioachino Rossini, 1792-1868), Italian
- **Rosina • Figaro** (contralto • baritone)
- light voices

Dunque, o cruda, e gloria e trono/Vieni al tempio
- *Giovanna d'Arco* (Giuseppe Verdi, 1813-1901), Italian
- **Giovanna • Carlo VII** (soprano • tenor)
- lyric or dramatic voices

E ben altro il mio sogno
- *Il Tabarro* (Giacomo Puccini, 1858-1924), Italian
- **Giorgetta • Luigi** (soprano • tenor)
- lyric or dramatic voices

E ben, per mia memoria
- *La gazza ladra* (Gioachino Rossini, 1792-1868), Italian
- **Ninetta • Pippo** (soprano • contralto)
- light voices

E deciso: tu parti
- *Zazà* (Ruggero Leoncavallo, 1857-1919), Italian
- **Zazà • Dufresne** (soprano • tenor)
- lyric voices

E il sol dell'anima/Addio, addio speranza ed anima
- *Rigoletto* (Giuseppe Verdi, 1813-1901), Italian
- **Gilda • Il Duca di Mantua** [The Duke of Mantua] (soprano • tenor)
- lyric voices

E ver?...sei d'altri?
- *La battaglia di Legnano* (Giuseppe Verdi, 1813-1901), Italian
- **Lida • Arrigo** (soprano • tenor)
- lyric or dramatic voices

Ecco l'altare
- *Andrea Chénier* (Umberto Giordano, 1867-1948), Italian
- **Maddalena • Andrea Chénier** (soprano • tenor)
- lyric or dramatic voices

Eccomi giunto inosservato e solo/A te sarà
- *Otello* (Gioachino Rossini, 1792-1868), Italian
- **Desdemona • Otello** (mezzo-soprano • tenor)
- lyric voices

Ed io pure in faccia agl'uomini/Or meco venite
- *Stiffelio* (Giuseppe Verdi, 1813-1901), Italian
- **Lina • Stankar** (soprano • baritone)
- lyric or dramatic voices

Eh, via buffone
- *Don Giovanni* (Wolfgang Amadeus Mozart, 1756-1791), Italian
- **Leporello • Don Giovanni** (bass-baritone • bass-baritone) Mozart's delineation of baritone and bass voices is very unclear.
- light or lyric voices

Ein Augenblick ist wenig
- *Ariadne auf Naxos* (Richard Strauss, 1864-1949), German
- **Zerbinetta • Der Komponist** [The Composer] (soprano • mezzo-soprano) Der Komponist is sung by either soprano or mezzo-soprano.
- lyric voices

Ein Männlein steht im Walde
- *Hänsel und Gretel* (Engelbert Humperdinck, 1854-1921), German
- **Gretel • Hänsel** (soprano • mezzo-soprano)
- light or lyric voices

Elektra! Schwester! komm mit uns!
- *Elektra* (Richard Strauss, 1864-1949), German
- **Chrysothemis • Elektra** (soprano • soprano)
- dramatic voices

Ella è morta, o sciagurato
- *I Capuleti e i Montecchi* (Vincenzo Bellini, 1801-1835), Italian
- **Romeo • Tebaldo** (mezzo-soprano • tenor)
- lyric voices

En ces lieux/Samson, ô toi, mon bien-aimé
- *Samson et Dalila* (Camille Saint-Saëns, 1835-1921), French
- **Dalila • Samson** (contralto • tenor)
- dramatic voices

Enzo Grimaldi, Principe di Santafiore
- *La Gioconda* (Amilcare Ponchielli, 1834-1886), Italian
- **Enzo • Barnaba** (tenor • baritone)
- lyric or dramatic voices

Er geht/Ja, eine Welt voll Leiden
- *Rienzi* (Richard Wagner, 1813-1883), German
- **Irene • Adriano** (soprano • mezzo-soprano)
- dramatic voices

Era d'amor l'immagine/Sul crin la rivale
- *Maria Stuarda* (Gaetano Donizetti, 1797-1848), Italian
- **Elisabetta** [Queen] **• Leicester** (soprano • tenor)
- lyric or dramatic voices

Errante sur tes pas
- *Les Troyens* (Hector Berlioz, 1803-1869), French
- **Didon • Énée** (mezzo-soprano • tenor)
- dramatic voices

Esprits de haine et de rage
- *Armide* (Christoph Willibald
  von Gluck, 1714-1787), French
- **Armide • Hidraot** (soprano • baritone)
- dramatic voices

Esprits de haine et de rage
- *Armide* (Jean-Baptiste Lully, 1632-1687), French
- **Armide • Hidraot** (soprano • baritone)
- dramatic voices

Et je sais votre nom
- *Manon* (Jules Massenet, 1842-1912), French
- **Manon • Des Grieux**
  [Le Chevalier] (soprano • tenor)
- light or lyric voices

Every wearied body/God is merciful and just
- *The Rake's Progress* (Igor Stravinsky, 1882-1971),
  English
- **Anne Trulove • Trulove** (soprano • bass)
- lyric voices

Fama! sì: l'avrete
- *Anna Bolena* (Gaetano
  Donizetti, 1797-1848), Italian
- **Giovanna Seymour • Enrico**
  [Henry VIII] (mezzo-soprano • bass)
- lyric or dramatic voices

Farewell Duet [commonly known title]
- *Oreste* (George Frideric Handel, 1685-1759), Italian
- **Ermione • Oreste** (soprano • mezzo-soprano)
  Oreste was originally written for mezzo-soprano
  castrato.
- lyric voices

Farewell for now
- *The Rake's Progress* (Igor
  Stravinsky, 1882-1971), English
- **Anne Trulove • Tom Rakewell** (soprano • tenor)
- lyric voices

Farewell my son, I am dying
  [commonly known title]
- *Boris Godunov* (Modest Petrovich
  Musorgsky, 1839-1881), Russian
- **Fyodor • Boris Godunov** (mezzo-soprano • bass)
- lyric or dramatic voices

Fatal mia donna!/Allor
  questa voce/Vieni altrove!
- *Macbeth* (Giuseppe Verdi, 1813-1901), Italian
- **Lady Macbeth • Macbeth** (soprano • baritone)
- dramatic voices

Fear no danger
- *Dido and Aeneas* (Henry
  Purcell, c1658-1695), English
- **Belinda • Second Woman**
  (soprano • mezzo-soprano)
- light voices

Florenz hat schöne Frauen
- *Boccaccio* (Franz Suppé, 1819-1895), German
- **Fiametta • Boccaccio** (soprano • mezzo-soprano)
- light voices

Forma ideal purissima/Amore, misterio celeste
- *Mefistofele* (Arrigo Boito, 1842-1918), Italian
- **Elèna** [Helen of Troy] • **Faust** (soprano • tenor)
- lyric or dramatic voices

Forse un dì conoscerete
- *La gazza ladra* (Gioachino
  Rossini, 1792-1868), Italian
- **Ninetta • Giannetto** (soprano • tenor)
- light voices

Fra gli amplessi
- *Così fan tutte* (Wolfgang Amadeus
  Mozart, 1756-1791), Italian
- **Fiordiligi • Ferrando** (soprano • tenor)
- lyric voices

Fra le tue braccia amore
- *Manon Lescaut* (Giacomo
  Puccini, 1858-1924), Italian
- **Manon Lescaut • Chevalier
  Des Grieux** (soprano • tenor)
- lyric or dramatic voices

Fuggi, crudele, fuggi!
- *Don Giovanni* (Wolfgang Amadeus
  Mozart, 1756-1791), Italian
- **Donna Anna • Don Ottavio** (soprano • tenor)
  Don Ottavio is a light lyric tenor, but Donna
  Anna is a dramatic soprano.
- lyric or dramatic voices

Fuggiam gli ardori inospiti/
  Sì: fuggiam da queste mura
- *Aïda* (Giuseppe Verdi, 1813-1901), Italian
- **Aïda • Amonasro** (soprano • baritone)
- dramatic voices

Fuyons les douceurs dangereuses
- *Armide* (Christoph Willibald
  von Gluck, 1714-1787), French
- **Danish Knight • Ubalde** (tenor • baritone)
- lyric voices

Geh'! geh'! geh'! Herz von Flandern!
- *Bastien und Bastienne* (Wolfgang Amadeus
  Mozart, 1756-1791), German
- **Bastienne • Bastien** (soprano • tenor)
- light voices

Geh' hin!
- *Bastien und Bastienne* (Wolfgang
  Amadeus Mozart, 1756-1791), German
- **Bastienne • Bastien** (soprano • tenor)
- light voices

Già nella notte densa
* *Otello* (Giuseppe Verdi, 1813-1901), Italian
* **Desdemona • Otello** (soprano • tenor)
* lyric or dramatic voices

Giorno d'orrore
* *Semiramide* (Gioachino Rossini, 1792-1868), Italian
* **Semiramide • Arsace** (soprano • contralto)
* lyric voices

Glück, das mir verlieb
* *Die tote Stadt* (Erich Wolfgang Korngold, 1897-1957), German
* **Marietta • Paul** (soprano • tenor)
* lyric or dramatic voices

Grâce au hazard
* *Le postillon de Lonjumeau* (Adolphe Adam, 1803-1856), French
* **Madeleine • Chapelou** (soprano • tenor)
* light or lyric voices

Grand Dieu! sa misère est si grande!
* *Dom Sébastien* (Gaetano Donizetti, 1797-1848), French
* **Zayda • Sébastien** (mezzo-soprano • tenor)
* lyric or dramatic voices

Gut'n Abend, Meister!
* *Die Meistersinger von Nürnberg* (Richard Wagner, 1813-1883), German
* **Eva • Hans Sachs** (soprano • baritone)
* lyric or dramatic voices

Happy we
* *Acis and Galatea* (George Frideric Handel, 1685-1759), English
* **Galatea • Acis** (soprano • tenor)
* light voices

Happy were we
* *Gloriana* (Benjamin Britten, 1913-1976), English
* **Elizabeth I • Earl of Essex** [Robert Devereux] (soprano • tenor)
* lyric or dramatic voices

Hello? Hello? Where are you, my darling?
* *The Telephone* (Gian Carlo Menotti, 1911-), English
* **Lucy • Ben** (soprano • baritone)
* light or lyric voices

Hi there, dear husband
* *The Beggar's Opera* (Johann Christoph Pepusch, 1667-1752), English
* **Lucy Lockit • Polly Peachum** (soprano • soprano)
* light voices

Hier in stillen Schatten gründen
* *Martha* (Friedrich Flotow, 1812-1883), German
* **Lady Harriet Durham • Lyonel** (soprano • tenor)
* lyric voices

Hier weilest du/Wie liebt' ich dich
* *Euryanthe* (Carl Maria von Weber, 1786-1826), German
* **Euryanthe • Adolar** (mezzo-soprano • tenor)
* dramatic voices

Hin nimm die Seele mein
* *Euryanthe* (Carl Maria von Weber, 1786-1826), German
* **Euryanthe • Adolar** (mezzo-soprano • tenor)
* dramatic voices

How dark and dreadful is this place
* *The Rake's Progress* (Igor Stravinsky, 1882-1971), English
* **Tom Rakewell • Nick Shadow** (tenor • bass-baritone)
* lyric or dramatic voices

I have a song to sing, O!
* *The Yeomen of the Guard* (Sir Arthur Sullivan, 1842-1900), English
* **Elsie Maynard • Jack Point** (soprano • baritone)
* light voices

Ich gehe, doch rate ich dir
* *Die Entführung aus dem Serail* (Wolfgang Amadeus Mozart, 1756-1791), German
* **Blonde • Osmin** (soprano • bass)
* light or lyric voices

Ich grüsse dich, du Bote
* *Ariadne auf Naxos* (Richard Strauss, 1864-1949), German
* **Prima Donna/Ariadne • Bacchus** (soprano • tenor)
* dramatic voices

Ich kenn' Ihn schon recht wohl
* *Der Rosenkavalier* (Richard Strauss, 1864-1949), German
* **Sophie • Octavian, genannt Quinquin** [Count Rofrano] (soprano • mezzo-soprano) Octavian is sung by either soprano or mezzo-soprano.
* lyric voices

Ich setz den Fall
* *Der Bettelstudent* (Carl Millöcker, 1842-1899), German
* **Laura • Symon Rymanovicz** (soprano • tenor)
* light or lyric voices

Ich will nichts hören/Träumst du Mutter?
* *Elektra* (Richard Strauss, 1864-1949), German
* **Elektra • Klytemnästra** (soprano • contralto) Klytemnästra is soprano, mezzo-soprano, or contralto.
* dramatic voices

Idolo del cor mio
- *L'incoronazione di Poppea* (Claudio Monteverdi, 1567-1643), Italian
- **Poppea** • **Nerone** (soprano • mezzo-soprano) Nerone, originally for soprano castrato, is soprano or mezzo-soprano today.
- lyric or dramatic voices

If one last doubt
- *Troilus and Cressida* (Sir William Walton, 1902-1983), English
- **Cressida** • **Troilus** [Prince] (mezzo-soprano • tenor)
- dramatic voices

Il core vi dono
- *Così fan tutte* (Wolfgang Amadeus Mozart, 1756-1791), Italian
- **Dorabella** • **Guglielmo** (mezzo-soprano • bass)
- lyric voices

Il faut nous séparer
- *Werther* (Jules Massenet, 1842-1912), French
- **Charlotte** • **Werther** (mezzo-soprano • tenor)
- lyric voices

Il grandira, car il est espagnol
- *La Périchole* (Jacques Offenbach, 1819-1880), French
- **La Périchole** • **Piquillo** (mezzo-soprano • tenor)
- light voices

Il mio garzone il piffaro sonava
- *La molinara* (Giovanni Paisiello, 1740-1816), Italian
- **Rachelina** • **Pistofolo** [Notaio] (soprano • bass)
- light or lyric voices

Il pallor funesto, orrendo/ Soffriva nel pianto languia
- *Lucia di Lammermoor* (Gaetano Donizetti, 1797-1848), Italian
- **Lucia** • **Enrico Ashton** (soprano • baritone)
- lyric voices

Il rival salvar tu dêi/Suoni la tromba intrepida
- *I Puritani* (Vincenzo Bellini, 1801-1835), Italian
- **Riccardo** • **Giorgio** (baritone • bass)
- lyric voices

Il suon dell'arpe angeliche [Conversion Duet]
- *Poliuto* (Gaetano Donizetti, 1797-1848), Italian
- **Paolina** • **Poliuto** (soprano • tenor)
- lyric or dramatic voices

I'm bubbled!
- *The Beggar's Opera* (Johann Christoph Pepusch, 1667-1752), English
- **Lucy Lockit** • **Polly Peachum** (soprano • soprano)
- light voices

In a foolish dream/What should I forgive?
- *The Rake's Progress* (Igor Stravinsky, 1882-1971), English

- **Anne Trulove** • **Tom Rakewell** (soprano • tenor)
- lyric voices

In mia man alfin tu sei
- *Norma* (Vincenzo Bellini, 1801-1835), Italian
- **Norma** • **Pollione** (soprano • tenor)
- lyric or dramatic voices

Incauta, che festi!
- *Elisabetta* (Gioachino Rossini, 1792-1868), Italian
- **Matilda** • **Leicester** (soprano • tenor)
- lyric voices

Infelice, delusa/Chi può legger nel futuro/Sull'alba
- *La forza del destino* (Giuseppe Verdi, 1813-1901), Italian
- **Leonora** • **Guardiano** [Padre] (soprano • bass)
- lyric or dramatic voices

Io non son che una povera fanciulla
- *La fanciulla del West* (Giacomo Puccini, 1858-1924), Italian
- **Minnie** • **Dick Johnson** [Ramerrez] (soprano • tenor)
- lyric or dramatic voices

Io son ricco e tu sei bella
- *L'elisir d'amore* (Gaetano Donizetti, 1797-1848), Italian
- **Adina** • **Dr. Dulcamara** (soprano • bass)
- light voices

Io son sua per l'amor
- *Adriana Lecouvreur* (Francesco Cilea, 1866-1950), Italian
- **Adriana Lecouvreur** • **La Principessa di Bouillon** [The Princess of Bouillon] (soprano • mezzo-soprano)
- lyric voices

Io t'abbraccio: è più che morte
- *Rodelinda* (George Frideric Handel, 1685-1759), Italian
- **Rodelinda** • **Bertarido** (soprano • contralto) The role of Bertarido was originally sung by an alto castrato.
- light or lyric voices

Io t'amo, Amalia/Ti scosta, o malnato
- *I Masnadieri* (Giuseppe Verdi, 1813-1901), Italian
- **Amalia** • **Francesco** (soprano • baritone)
- lyric or dramatic voices

Io ti rivedo/Ah! se un giorno
- *Maria Stuarda* (Gaetano Donizetti, 1797-1848), Italian
- **Maria Stuarda** • **Leicester** (soprano • tenor)
- lyric or dramatic voices

**Io vengo a domandar/Perduto ben/
Sotto al mio piè** [Je viens solliciter]
* *Don Carlo* [*Don Carlos*] (Giuseppe Verdi,
  1813-1901), Italian [French]
* **Elisabetta** [Elisabeth] • **Don Carlo**
  [Don Carlos] (soprano • tenor)
* lyric or dramatic voices

Irritons notre barbarie
* *Amadis* (Jean-Baptiste Lully, 1632-1687), French
* **Arcabonne** • **Arcalaus** (soprano • tenor) The role
  of Arcalaus was originally written for haute-contre.
* light or lyric voices

Ist ein Traum, kann nicht wirklich?
* *Der Rosenkavalier* (Richard
  Strauss, 1864-1949), German
* **Sophie** • **Octavian, genannt Quinquin** [Count
  Rofrano] (soprano • mezzo-soprano) Octavian is
  sung by either soprano or mezzo-soprano.
* lyric voices

Ist mein Liebster dahin
* *Die Frau ohne Schatten* (Richard
  Strauss, 1864-1949), German
* **Falcon** • **Die Kaiserin** [The Empress]
  (soprano • soprano)
* dramatic voices

Ja, seit früher Kindheit Tagen
* *Martha* (Friedrich Flotow, 1812-1883), German
* **Lyonel** • **Plumkett** (tenor • bass)
* lyric voices

J'ai gravi la montagne/La victoire facile
* *Samson et Dalila* (Camille
  Saint-Saëns, 1835-1921), French
* **Dalila** • **Le Grand Prêtre du Dagon**
  [The High Priest of Dagon] (contralto • baritone)
* dramatic voices

Jako matka [Like a mother]
* *Prodaná Nevěsta* [*The Bartered Bride*]
  (Bedřich Smetana, 1824-1884), Czech
* **Mařenka** • **Jeník** (soprano • tenor)
* lyric voices

**J'avais fait un beau rêve/Oui, voilà l'héroisme
/Au revoir** [Sogno dorato io feci!/Ma lassù]
* *Don Carlos* [*Don Carlo*] (Giuseppe Verdi,
  1813-1901), French [Italian]
* **Elisabeth** [Elisabetta] • **Don Carlos**
  [Don Carlo] (soprano • tenor)
* lyric or dramatic voices

Je crois entendre les doux compliments
* *Mignon* (Ambroise Thomas, 1811-1896), French
* **Philine** • **Wilhelm Meister** (soprano • tenor)
* light or lyric voices

Je goûtais les charmes [Avvezza al contento]
* *Orphée et Eurydice* [*Orfeo ed Euridice*] (Christoph
  Willibald von Gluck, 1714-1787), French [Italian]

* **Eurydice** [Euridice] • **Orphée** [Orfeo]
  (soprano • tenor) Orphée's role was originally
  for alto castrato in the Italian version.
* lyric voices

Je me sens, hélas, tout chose
* *L'étoile du Nord* (Emmanuel
  Chabrier, 1841-1894), French
* **Ouf** • **Siroco** (tenor • bass)
* light voices

Je ne pourrai plus sortir
* *Pelléas et Mélisande* (Claude
  Debussy, 1862-1918), French
* **Mélisande** • **Golaud** (mezzo-soprano • baritone)
* lyric or dramatic voices

Je ne souffre plus
* *Manon Lescaut* (Daniel-François-
  Esprit Auber, 1782-1871), French
* **Manon** • **Des Grieux** (soprano • tenor)
* light or lyric voices

Je suis heureuse! l'air m'enivre
* *Mignon* (Ambroise Thomas, 1811-1896), French
* **Mignon** • **Wilhelm Meister**
  (mezzo-soprano • tenor)
* lyric voices

Je vais revoir
* *Le comte Ory* (Gioachino
  Rossini, 1792-1868), French
* **Isolier** [Page] • **Le Comte Ory** [Count]
  (mezzo-soprano • tenor)
* light or lyric voices

**Je viens solliciter/O bien perdu/Que
sous mes pieds** [Io vengo a domandar]
* *Don Carlos* [*Don Carlo*] (Giuseppe
  Verdi, 1813-1901), French [Italian]
* **Elisabeth** [Elisabetta] • **Don Carlos**
  [Don Carlo] (soprano • tenor)
* lyric or dramatic voices

Je vous revois
* *Zoroastre* (Jean-Philippe
  Rameau, 1683-1764), French
* **Amélite** • **Zoroastre** (soprano • countertenor)
  Zoroastre's role was originally written for
  haute-contre.
* light or lyric voices

Jenifer, Jenifer, my darling
* *The Midsummer Marriage* (Sir
  Michael Tippett, 1905-), English
* **Jenifer** • **Mark** (soprano • tenor)
* lyric voices

Jetzt, Alter, jetzt hat es Eile!
* *Fidelio* (Ludwig von Beethoven,
  1770-1827), German
* **Don Pizarro** • **Rocco** (bass-baritone • bass)
* lyric or dramatic voices

Jetzt, Schätzchen, jetzt sind wir allein
- *Fidelio* (Ludwig von Beethoven, 1770-1827), German
- **Marzelline · Jaquino** (soprano · tenor)
- light voices

Jochanaan, ich bin verliebt
- *Salome* (Richard Strauss, 1864-1949), German
- **Salome · Jochanaan** (soprano · bass-baritone)
- dramatic voices

Joys of freedom
- *Hercules* (George Frideric Handel, 1685-1759), English
- **Iöle · Dejanira** (soprano · mezzo-soprano)
- light or lyric voices

Just think, my son [commonly known title]
- *Boris Godunov* (Modest Petrovich Musorgsky, 1839-1881), Russian
- **Grigory · Pimen** (tenor · bass)
- lyric or dramatic voices

Kannst du zweifeln
- *Die lustigen Weiber von Windsor* (Otto Nicolai, 1810-1849), German
- **Anna Reich** [Anne Page] **· Fenton** (soprano · tenor)
- light or lyric voices

Kein Andres, das mir so im Herzen loht
- *Capriccio* (Richard Strauss, 1864-1949), German
- **Clairon · Count** (contralto · baritone)
- lyric or dramatic voices

Komm denn
- *Euryanthe* (Carl Maria von Weber, 1786-1826), German
- **Eglantine · Lysiart** (mezzo-soprano · bass-baritone)
- dramatic voices
- lyric or dramatic voices

La brise est douce et parfumée
  [Chanson de Magali]
- *Mireille* (Charles-François Gounod, 1812-1893), French
- **Mireille · Vincent** (soprano · tenor)
- lyric voices

Là ci darem la mano/Andiam mio bene
- *Don Giovanni* (Wolfgang Amadeus Mozart, 1756-1791), Italian
- **Zerlina · Don Giovanni** (mezzo-soprano · bass-baritone)
- light or lyric voices

La tomba è un letto/Di rughe/ Andrem, raminghi e poveri
- *Luisa Miller* (Giuseppe Verdi, 1813-1901), Italian
- **Luisa · Miller** (soprano · baritone)
- lyric or dramatic voices

Labbra di foco
- *Falstaff* (Giuseppe Verdi, 1813-1901), Italian

- **Nannetta · Fenton** (soprano · tenor)
- light or lyric voices

Lachst du mich aus?
- *Der Rosenkavalier* (Richard Strauss, 1864-1949), German
- **Die Feldmarschallin Fürstin Werdenberg** [Marie Thérèse] [Marschallin] **· Octavian, genannt Quinquin** [Count Rofrano] (soprano · mezzo-soprano) Octavian is sung by either soprano or mezzo-soprano.
- lyric or dramatic voices

Laisse-moi contempler ton visage/ O nuit/Partez, partez
- *Faust* (Charles-François Gounod, 1812-1893), French
- **Marguerite · Faust, Dr.** (soprano · tenor)
- lyric voices

Laissez le doute dans mon âme
- *Le Cid* (Jules Massenet, 1842-1912), French
- **Infante** [Princess] **· Chimène** (soprano · soprano)
- light or lyric voices

Lakmé, c'est toi
- *Lakmé* (Léo Delibes, 1836-1891), French
- **Lakmé · Gérald** (soprano · tenor)
- light or lyric voices

L'alto retaggio non ho bramato/ O meco incolume
- *Luisa Miller* (Giuseppe Verdi, 1813-1901), Italian
- **Wurm · Il Conte di Walter** [Count] (bass · bass)
- lyric or dramatic voices

L'amo come il fulgor del creato
- *La Gioconda* (Amilcare Ponchielli, 1834-1886), Italian
- **Laura · La Gioconda** (mezzo-soprano · mezzo-soprano) The role of La Gioconda is sung by either soprano or mezzo-soprano.
- lyric or dramatic voices

L'amo! L'adoro!
- *Paride ed Elena* (Christoph Willibald von Gluck, 1714-1787), Italian
- **Elena · Paride** (soprano · tenor [soprano]) Paride, originally for soprano castrato, is sung by either tenor or soprano.
- lyric voices

L'amour est un flambeau
- *Béatrice et Bénédict* (Hector Berlioz, 1803-1869), French
- **Béatrice · Bénédict** (mezzo-soprano · tenor)
- light or lyric voices

L'amour qui brûle dans notre âme
- *La vestale* (Gaspare Spontini, 1774-1851), French
- **Julia · Licinius** (soprano · tenor)
- lyric or dramatic voices

Lascia che pianga io solo
* *Fedora* (Umberto Giordano, 1867-1948), Italian
* **La Principessa Fedora Romazoff** [Princess Fedora] • **Il Conte Loris Ipanoff** [Count Loris] (soprano • tenor)
* dramatic voices

Lass Er doch hören
* *Der Wildschütz* (Albert Lortzing, 1801-1851), German
* **Gretchen** • **Baculus** (soprano • bass)
* lyric or dramatic voices

Lasst mich hier
* *Euryanthe* (Carl Maria von Weber, 1786-1826), German
* **Euryanthe** • **Louis VI** (mezzo-soprano • bass)
* dramatic voices

**Le voilà, c'est l'infant/
Toi! mon Rodrigue! c'est toi**
* *Don Carlos* (Giuseppe Verdi, 1813-1901), French
* **Don Carlos** • **Rodrigue** [Le Marquis de Posa] (tenor • baritone)
* lyric or dramatic voices

Légères hirondelles
* *Mignon* (Ambroise Thomas, 1811-1896), French
* **Mignon** • **Lothario** (mezzo-soprano • bass)
* lyric voices

Leise, ganz leise
* *Ein Walzertraum* (Oscar Straus, 1870-1954), German
* **Niki** • **Montschi** (tenor • baritone)
* light or lyric voices

Les rendez-vous de noble compagnie
* *Le Pré aux Clercs* (Ferdinand Hérold, 1791-1833), French
* **Nicette** • **Girot** (soprano • tenor)
* light voices

L'espoir fuit de mon coeur
* *Echo et Narcisse* (Christoph Willibald von Gluck, 1714-1787), French
* **Echo** • **Cynire** (soprano • tenor)
* lyric voices

L'heure fatale est sonnée! [L'ora fatale è suonata!]
* *Don Carlos* [*Don Carlo*] (Giuseppe Verdi, 1813-1901), French [Italian]
* **Elisabeth** [Elisabetta] • **Don Carlos** [Don Carlo] (soprano • tenor)

Libiamo ne' lieti calici [Brindisi]
* *La traviata* (Giuseppe Verdi, 1813-1901), Italian
* **Violetta Valéry** • **Alfredo Germont** (soprano • tenor)
* lyric voices

Lo conosco a quegl'occhieti [Conflict Duet]
* *Serva padrona, La* (Giovanni Battista Pergolesi, 1710-1736), Italian

* **Serpina** • **Uberto** (soprano • bass)
* light voices

Lontano, lontano
* *Mefistofele* (Arrigo Boito, 1842-1918), Italian
* **Margherita** • **Faust** (soprano • tenor)
* lyric or dramatic voices

L'ora fatale è suonata! [L'heure fatale est sonnée!]
* *Don Carlo* [*Don Carlos*] (Giuseppe Verdi, 1813-1901), Italian [French]
* **Elisabetta** [Elisabeth] • **Don Carlo** [Don Carlos] (soprano • tenor)
* lyric or dramatic voices

Love has a bitter core, Vanessa
* *Vanessa* (Samuel Barber, 1910-1981), English
* **Vanessa** • **Anatol** (soprano • tenor)
* lyric or dramatic voices

Ma, chi sei?
* *Paride ed Elena* (Christoph Willibald von Gluck, 1714-1787), Italian
* **Erasto** • **Paride** (soprano • tenor) Paride, originally for soprano castrato, is sung by either tenor or soprano.
* lyric voices

Ma come puoi lasciarmi
* *La rondine* (Giacomo Puccini, 1858-1924), Italian
* **Magda** • **Ruggero** (soprano • tenor)
* lyric voices

Machen wir's den Schwalben nach
* *Die Csárdásfürstin* (Emmerich Kálmán, 1882-1953), German
* **Komtesse Stasi** [Countess Stasi] • **Edwin** (soprano • tenor) Komtesse Stasi is a soubrette.
* light or lyric voices

Mais Alice, qu'as-tu donc?
* *Robert le Diable* (Giacomo Meyerbeer, 1791-1864), French
* **Alice** • **Bertram** (mezzo-soprano • bass)
* lyric or dramatic voices

Malheureux et non coupable
* *Les vêpres siciliennes* (Giuseppe Verdi, 1813-1901), French
* **Hélène** • **Henri** (soprano • tenor)
* lyric or dramatic voices

Mars und Merkur
* *Der Barbier von Bagdad* (Peter Cornelius, 1824-1874), German
* **Nureddin** • **Abul** (tenor • bass)
* lyric or dramatic voices

Marta!...Tu mit mir, was du willst
* *Tiefland* (Eugen d'Albert, 1864-1932), German
* **Marta** • **Sebastiano** (soprano • baritone)
* dramatic voices

Me voici
- *Faust* (Charles-François
  Gounod, 1812-1893), French
- **Faust, Dr.** · **Méphistophélès** (tenor · bass)
- lyric voices

Meine Seele hüpft von Freuden
- *Zaïde* (Wolfgang Amadeus
  Mozart, 1756-1791), German
- **Zaïde** · **Gomatz** (soprano · tenor)
- light or lyric voices

Meinetwegen sollst du sterben
- *Die Entführung aus dem Serail* (Wolfgang
  Amadeus Mozart, 1756-1791), German
- **Konstanze** · **Belmonte** (soprano · tenor)
- lyric voices

Mes longs cheveux descendant
- *Pelléas et Mélisande* (Claude
  Debussy, 1862-1918), French
- **Mélisande** · **Pelléas** (mezzo-soprano · tenor)
- lyric voices

Mieux vaut mourir que rester miserable!
- *La muette de Portici* (Daniel-François-
  Esprit Auber, 1782-1871), French
- **Masniello** · **Pietro** (tenor · bass)
- lyric voices

Milostné zvířátko uděláme z vás
  [We'll make a nice little animal]
- *Prodaná Nevěsta* [*The Bartered Bride*]
  (Bedřich Smetana, 1824-1884), Czech
- **Esmeralda** · **Circus Master** (soprano · tenor)
- light voices

Mio caro ben non sospirar
- *Astarto* (Giovanni Bononcini, 1670-1747), Italian
- **Sidonia** · **Nino** (soprano · tenor)
  Originally written for castrati.
- light voices

Mir anvertraut
- *Die Frau ohne Schatten* (Richard
  Strauss, 1864-1949), German
- **Sein Weib** [Wife of Barak] ·
  Barak (soprano · bass-baritone)
- dramatic voices

**Mir ist die Ehre widerfahren/Mit Ihren Augen
  voll Tränen** [Presentation of the Rose]
- *Der Rosenkavalier* (Richard Strauss,
  1864-1949), German
- **Sophie** · **Octavian, genannt Quinquin** [Count
  Rofrano] (soprano · mezzo-soprano) Octavian is
  sung by either soprano or mezzo-soprano.
- lyric voices

**Mira, di acerbe lagrime/
  Vivrà!…Contende il giubilo**
- *Il trovatore* (Giuseppe Verdi, 1813-1901), Italian

Leonora · **Il Conte di Luna** [Count]
  (soprano · baritone)
- lyric or dramatic voices

Mira, o Norma/Sì, fino all'ore estreme
- *Norma* (Vincenzo Bellini, 1801-1835), Italian
- **Norma** · **Adalgisa** (soprano · mezzo-soprano)
  Adalgisa is sung by either soprano or mezzo-soprano.
- lyric voices

**Miserere d'un alma/Tu vedrai
  che amore in terra**
- *Il trovatore* (Giuseppe Verdi, 1813-1901), Italian
- **Leonora** · **Manrico** (soprano · tenor)
- lyric or dramatic voices

Morta al mondo
- *Maria Stuarda* (Gaetano
  Donizetti, 1797-1848), Italian
- **Elisabetta** [Queen] ·
  Maria Stuarda (soprano · soprano)
- lyric or dramatic voices

Musik ist eine heilige Kunst
- *Ariadne auf Naxos* (Richard
  Strauss, 1864-1949), German
- **Der Komponist** [The Composer] ·
  Ein Musiklehrer [A Music Master]
  (mezzo-soprano · baritone)
- lyric voices

My heart is worn with fear [commonly known title]
- *Yevgeny Onegin* [*Eugene Onegin*] (Pyotr Il'yich
  Tchaikovsky, 1840-1893), Russian
- **Tat'yana** · **Yevgeny Onegin** [Eugene Onegin]
  (soprano · baritone)
- lyric or dramatic voices

My tale shall be told both by young and by old
- *The Rake's Progress* (Igor Stravinsky,
  1882-1971), English
- **Tom Rakewell** · **Nick Shadow**
  (tenor · bass-baritone)
- lyric or dramatic voices

**Nè gustare/Voi che si larghe
  cure/Sleale! Il segreto**
- *La forza del destino* (Giuseppe
  Verdi, 1813-1901), Italian
- **Don Alvaro** · **Don Carlo
  di Vargas** (tenor · baritone)
- lyric or dramatic voices

Ne m'en veux pas d'être venue
- *Sapho* (Jules Massenet, 1842-1912), French
- **Jean** · **Fanny** [Sapho] (soprano · soprano)
  Jean's part was sung by either a tenor or
  a soprano (pants role).
- lyric voices

Ne più s'interporà
- *L'incoronazione di Poppea* (Claudio
  Monteverdi, 1567-1643), Italian

• **Poppea** • **Nerone** (soprano • mezzo-soprano)
Nerone, originally for soprano castrato, is soprano
or mezzo-soprano today.
• lyric or dramatic voices

Nein, das ist wirklich doch zu keck!
• *Die lustigen Weiber von Windsor*
(Otto Nicolai, 1810-1849), German
• **Frau Fluth** [Mrs. Ford] • **Frau Reich** [Mrs. Page]
(soprano • contralto)
• lyric voices

Nein, nein! I' trink' kein Wein
• *Der Rosenkavalier* (Richard
Strauss, 1864-1949), German
• **Octavian, genannt Quinquin** [Count Rofrano] •
Baron Ochs auf Lerchenau (soprano • bass)
• lyric or dramatic voices

Nel mirarti/Da quel dì/Vieni fra queste braccia
• *I Puritani* (Vincenzo Bellini, 1801-1835), Italian
• **Elvira** • **Arturo** (soprano • tenor)
• lyric voices

Nel veder quel tuo sembiante
• *I due supposti Conti* (Domenico
Cimarosa, 1749-1801), Italian
• **Beatrice** • **Il Conte Caramella**
[Count] (soprano • bass)
• light or lyric voices

N'espérez pas me fuir/Écoutez-moi
• *La muette de Portici* (Daniel-François-
Esprit Auber, 1782-1871), French
• **Elvire** • **Alphonse** (soprano • tenor)
• light or lyric voices

Niemand liebt dich so wie ich
• *Paganini* (Franz Lehár, 1870-1948), German
• **Anna Elisa** • **Paganini** (soprano • tenor)
• light or lyric voices

**No, d'un imene il vincolo/
Morte! Ov'io non cada**
• *La forza del destino* (Giuseppe
Verdi, 1813-1901), Italian
• **Don Alvaro** • **Don Carlo
di Vargas** (tenor • baritone)
• lyric or dramatic voices

No, no Turiddu, rimani
• *Cavalleria rusticana*
(Pietro Mascagni, 1863-1945), Italian
• **Santuzza** • **Turiddu** (soprano • tenor)
• dramatic voices

No, non temer/Se uniti negli affanni
• *Otello* (Gioachino Rossini, 1792-1868), Italian
• **Rodrigo** • **Iago** (tenor • bass-baritone) Iago was
written for either tenor or bass-baritone.
• light or lyric voices

No, tu non sai/Tornerai, ma forse spenta
• *Il corsaro* (Giuseppe Verdi, 1813-1901), Italian

• **Medora** • **Corrado** (soprano • tenor)
• lyric or dramatic voices

Noi torneremo alla romita valle
• *I Lituani* [*The Little Sweep*] (Amilcare
Ponchielli, 1834-1886), Italian
• **Aldona** • **Walter** (soprano • tenor)
• dramatic voices

Non m'inganno; al mio rivale
• *Otello* (Gioachino Rossini, 1792-1868), Italian
• **Rodrigo** • **Otello** (tenor • tenor)
• lyric voices

**Non, non morrai, chè i perfidi/
Ah! speranza dolce ancora**
• *I due Foscari* (Giuseppe Verdi, 1813-1901), Italian
• **Lucrezia Contarini** • **Jacopo Foscari**
(soprano • tenor)
• lyric or dramatic voices

**Non sai tu che se l'anima mia/
Oh qual soave brivido**
• *Un ballo in maschera* (Giuseppe
Verdi, 1813-1901), Italian
• **Amelia** • **Riccardo** (soprano • tenor)
• lyric or dramatic voices

Non sai tu che un giusto [Sais-tu que devant la tiare]
• *La favorita* [*La favorite*] (Gaetano Donizetti,
1797-1848), Italian [French]
• **Fernando** [Fernand] • **Badassare**
[Balthazar] (tenor • bass)
• lyric or dramatic voices

**Non, tu ne m'aimes pas/Là-bas,
là-bas dans la montagne**
• *Carmen* (Georges Bizet, 1838-1875), French
• **Carmen** • **Don José** (contralto • tenor)
• lyric or dramatic voices

Now close your arms
• *Troilus and Cressida* (Sir William
Walton, 1902-1983), English
• **Cressida** • **Troilus** [Prince] (mezzo-soprano • tenor)
• dramatic voices

Nuit paisible et sereine! [Nocturne Duet]
• *Béatrice et Bénédict* (Hector Berlioz,
1803-1869), French
• **Héro** • **Ursula** (soprano • mezzo-soprano)
• light voices

Nun ist die Hexe tot [Gingerbread Waltz]
• *Hänsel und Gretel* (Engelbert Humperdinck,
1854-1921), German
• **Gretel** • **Hänsel** (soprano • mezzo-soprano)
• light or lyric voices

Nur hurtig fort, nur frisch gegraben
• *Fidelio* (Ludwig von Beethoven,
1770-1827), German
• **Leonore** • **Rocco** (soprano • bass)
• lyric or dramatic voices

Nuže, milý chasníku [Now, dear young fellow]
- *Prodaná Nevěsta* [*The Bartered Bride*]
  (Bedřich Smetana, 1824-1884), Czech
- **Jeník • Kecal** (tenor • bass)
- lyric voices

O Black Swan
- *The Medium* (Gian Carlo Menotti, 1911-), English
- **Monica • Baba** [Madame Flora] (soprano •
  contralto)
- lyric voices

O cara, o cara
- *L'incoronazione di Poppea* (Claudio
  Monteverdi, 1567-1643), Italian
- **Damigella • Valletto** (soprano • tenor)
  Valletto was originally sung by a castrato.
- light voices

O che muso, che figura!
- *L'italiana in Algeri* (Gioachino
  Rossini, 1792-1868), Italian
- **Isabella • Mustafà** (contralto • bass)
- light or lyric voices

O che umor
- *Il barbiere di Siviglia* (Giovanni
  Paisiello, 1740-1816), Italian
- **Il Conte di Almaviva/
  Lindoro • Bartolo** (tenor • bass)
- light voices

**O ciel! où courez-vous?/
Tu l'as dit** [O ciel! dove vai tu?]
- *Les Huguenots* (Giacomo
  Meyerbeer, 1791-1864), French
- **Valentine • Raoul** (mezzo-soprano • tenor)
- lyric or dramatic voices

O dieu Brahma!
- *Les pêcheurs de perles*
  (Georges Bizet, 1838-1875), French
- **Leïla • Nadir** (soprano • tenor)
- lyric voices

O Dieu! de quelle ivresse
- *Les contes d'Hoffmann* (Jacques
  Offenbach, 1819-1880), French
- **Giulietta • Hoffmann** (mezzo-soprano • tenor)
- lyric or dramatic voices

O, du lieber, o du g'scheiter
- *Ein Walzertraum* (Oscar Straus,
  1870-1954), German
- **Hélène • Niki** (soprano • tenor)
- light or lyric voices

O ew'ge Nacht
- *Tristan und Isolde* (Richard
  Wagner, 1813-1883), German
- **Isolde • Tristan** (soprano • tenor)
- dramatic voices

O fatale Toison
- *Médée* (Luigi Chérubini, 1760-1842), French
- **Médée • Jason** (soprano • tenor)
- dramatic voices

O felice Mustafà/O Girello in povertà
- *Girello* (Alessandro Stradella, 1639-1682), Italian
- **Mustafà • Girello** (soprano • bass) Mustafà is a
  pants role for soprano.
- light voices

O grido di quest'anima
- *La Gioconda* (Amilcare
  Ponchielli, 1834-1886), Italian
- **Enzo • Barnaba** (tenor • baritone)
- lyric or dramatic voices

O guarda sorella
- *Così fan tutte* (Wolfgang Amadeus
  Mozart, 1756-1791), Italian
- **Fiordiligi • Dorabella** (soprano • mezzo-soprano)
  Dorabella can be sung by either mezzo-soprano or
  soprano.
- lyric voices

O! Ihr beschämt mich
- *Die lustigen Weiber von Windsor*
  (Otto Nicolai, 1810-1849), German
- **Herr Fluth** [Mr. Ford] **• Falstaff** (baritone • bass)
- lyric voices

O lumière sainte
- *Les pêcheurs de perles* (Georges
  Bizet, 1838-1875), French
- **Leïla • Nadir** (soprano • tenor)
- lyric voices

O ma Fanny, que j'aime
- *Sapho* (Jules Massenet, 1842-1912), French
- **Jean • Fanny** [Sapho] (soprano • soprano)
  Jean's part was sung by either a tenor or
  a soprano (pants role).
- lyric voices

O mia vita! O mia core
- *Il pomo d'oro* (Antonio Cesti, 1623-1669), Italian
- **Ennone • Paride** (soprano • tenor)
- light or lyric voices

O namenlose Freude!
- *Fidelio* (Ludwig von Beethoven,
  1770-1827), German
- **Leonore • Florestan** (soprano • tenor)
- dramatic voices

O nevýslovné štěstí lásky
[O the unutterable happiness]
- *Dalibor* (Bedřich Smetana, 1824-1884), Czech
- **Milada • Dalibor** (soprano • tenor)
- dramatic voices

O nuit divine
- *Roméo et Juliette* (Charles-François
  Gounod, 1812-1893), French
- **Juliette • Roméo** (soprano • tenor)
- lyric voices

O padre sospirato, o figlio desiato
- *Il ritorno d'Ulisse in patria* (Claudio
  Monteverdi, 1567-1643), Italian
- **Telemaco • Ulisse** (tenor • baritone)
  Ulisse was sung by either tenor or baritone.
- lyric voices

**O Roi! j'arrive de Flandre/Est-ce la paix que
vous donnez?** [O signor, di Fiandra arrivo]
- *Don Carlos* [*Don Carlo*] (Giuseppe Verdi,
  1813-1901), French [Italian]
- **Rodrigue** [Le Marquis de Posa] [Rodrigo [Marchese di
  Posa]] • **King Philip II** [Filippo II] (baritone • bass)
- lyric or dramatic voices

**O sdegni miei/Arrigo! ah parli a un core/E
dolce raggio** [De courroux/Pour moi rayonne]
- *I vespri siciliani* [*Les vêpres siciliennes*]
  (Giuseppe Verdi, 1813-1901), Italian [French]
- **Elena** [Hélène] • **Arrigo** [Henri] (soprano • tenor)
- lyric or dramatic voices

O signor, di Fiandra arrivo
  [O Roi! j'arrive de Flandre]
- *Don Carlo* [*Don Carlos*] (Giuseppe
  Verdi, 1813-1901), Italian [French]
- **Rodrigo** [Marchese di Posa] [Rodrigue [Le Marquis de
  Posa]] • **Filippo II** [King Philip II] (baritone • bass)
- lyric or dramatic voices

O sink' hernieder, Nacht der Liebe
- *Tristan und Isolde* (Richard Wagner,
  1813-1883), German
- **Isolde • Tristan** (soprano • tenor)
- dramatic voices

O soave fanciulla
- *La Bohème* (Giacomo Puccini, 1858-1924), Italian
- **Mimì • Rodolfo** (soprano • tenor)
- lyric voices

O statua gentilissima
- *Don Giovanni* (Wolfgang Amadeus
  Mozart, 1756-1791), Italian
- **Leporello • Don Giovanni** (bass-baritone • bass-
  baritone) Mozart's delineation of baritone and bass
  voices is unclear.
- light or lyric voices

O süsseste Wonne! seligstes Weib!
- *Die Walküre* (Richard Wagner, 1813-1883), German
- **Sieglinde • Siegmund** (soprano • tenor)
- dramatic voices

O Tanz, o Rausch
- *Die tote Stadt* (Erich Wolfgang
  Korngold, 1897-1957), German

- **Marietta • Paul** (soprano • tenor)
- lyric or dramatic voices

O Teresa, vous que j'aime plus que ma vie
- *Benvenuto Cellini* (Hector Berlioz,
  1803-1869), French
- **Teresa • Benvenuto Cellini** (soprano • tenor)
- lyric or dramatic voices

O transports, ô douce extase
- *L'africaine* (Giacomo Meyerbeer,
  1791-1864), French
- **Sélika • Vasco da Gama** (soprano • tenor)
- lyric or dramatic voices

Obbligato, ah, sì! obbligato!
- *L'elisir d'amore* (Gaetano
  Donizetti, 1797-1848), Italian
- **Nemorino • Dr. Dulcamara** (tenor • bass)
- light voices

Obey my will
- *Semele* (George Frideric
  Handel, 1685-1759), English
- **Juno • Somnus** (contralto • bass)
- lyric voices

Odio e livore!—ingrato!
- *Beatrice di Tenda* (Vincenzo
  Bellini, 1801-1835), Italian
- **Beatrice • Filippo Maria Visconti** (soprano •
  baritone)
- lyric voices

Ogni virtù più bella
- *Alceste* (Christoph Willibald
  von Gluck, 1714-1787), Italian
- **Ismene • Evandro** (soprano • tenor)
- light voices

Oh belle, a questa misera/Ah, vieni, sol morte
- *I Lombardi* (Giuseppe Verdi, 1813-1901), Italian
- **Giselda • Oronte** (soprano • tenor)
- lyric or dramatic voices

Oh! Fanny ma maîtresse/Nous irons en rêvant
- *Sapho* (Jules Massenet, 1842-1912), French
- **Jean • Fanny** [Sapho] (soprano • soprano)
  Jean's part was sung by either a tenor or a
  soprano (pants role).
- lyric voices

Oh, il Signore vi manda
- *Cavalleria rusticana* (Pietro
  Mascagni, 1863-1945), Italian
- **Santuzza • Alfio** (mezzo-soprano • tenor)
- dramatic voices

Oh Luigi! Luigi! Bada a te!
- *Il Tabarro* (Giacomo Puccini, 1858-1924), Italian
- **Giorgetta • Luigi** (soprano • tenor)
- lyric or dramatic voices

Oh qual parlar
- *Anna Bolena* (Gaetano Donizetti, 1797-1848), Italian
- **Giovanna Seymour • Enrico** [Henry VIII] (mezzo-soprano • bass)
- lyric or dramatic voices

Oh take, oh take those lips away
- *Antony and Cleopatra* (Samuel Barber, 1910-1981), English
- **Cleopatra • Antony** (soprano • bass-baritone)
- dramatic voices

On l'appelle Manon
- *Manon* (Jules Massenet, 1842-1912), French
- **Manon • Des Grieux** [Le Chevalier] (soprano • tenor)
- light or lyric voices

On—moy sokol yasnïy! [It is he, my bright falcon]
- *Knyaz' Igor'* [*Prince Igor*] (Alexander Porfir'yevich Borodin, 1833-1887), Russian
- **Yaroslavna • Igor'** (soprano • baritone)
- lyric or dramatic voices

On the banks of the sweet Garonne
- *Oberon* (Carl Maria von Weber, 1786-1826), English
- **Fatima • Sherasmin** (mezzo-soprano • baritone)
- lyric voices

One Hand, One Heart
- *West Side Story* (Leonard Bernstein, 1918-1990), English
- **Maria • Tony** (soprano • tenor)
- light or lyric voices

Onegin, I was then far younger [commonly known title]
- *Yevgeny Onegin* [*Eugene Onegin*] (Pyotr Il'yich Tchaikovsky, 1840-1893), Russian
- **Tat'yana • Yevgeny Onegin** [Eugene Onegin] (soprano • baritone)
- lyric or dramatic voices

Or dammi il braccio tuo
- *Iris* (Pietro Mascagni, 1863-1945), Italian
- **Iris • Osaka** (soprano • tenor)
- lyric or dramatic voices

Ora a noi
- *Madama Butterfly* (Giacomo Puccini, 1858-1924), Italian
- **Cio-Cio-San** [Madama Butterfly] • **Sharpless** (soprano • baritone)
- lyric or dramatic voices

Ora di morte e di vendetta
- *Macbeth* (Giuseppe Verdi, 1813-1901), Italian
- **Lady Macbeth • Macbeth** (soprano • baritone)
- dramatic voices

Ora soave
- *Andrea Chénier* (Umberto Giordano, 1867-1948), Italian
- **Maddalena • Andrea Chénier** (soprano • tenor)
- lyric or dramatic voices

Orest! Orest! Orest!
- *Elektra* (Richard Strauss, 1864-1949), German
- **Elektra • Orest** (soprano • baritone)
- dramatic voices

Ou vas-tu /Ah! Mathilde, idole de mon âme
- *Guillaume Tell* (Gioachino Rossini, 1792-1868), French
- **Arnold • Guillaume Tell** (tenor • bass)
- lyric voices

Oui, c'est moi/N'achevez pas/ Ah! ce premier baiser
- *Werther* (Jules Massenet, 1842-1912), French
- **Charlotte • Werther** (mezzo-soprano • tenor)
- lyric voices

Oui, c'est toi je t'aime
- *Faust* (Charles-François Gounod, 1812-1893), French
- **Marguerite • Faust, Dr.** (soprano • tenor)
- lyric voices

Oui, je souffre votre tendresse
- *Don Quichotte* (Jules Massenet, 1842-1912), French
- **Dulcinée • Don Quichotte** (mezzo-soprano • bass)
- lyric voices

Oui, je vous hais
- *Le roi malgré lui* (Emmanuel Chabrier, 1841-1894), French
- **Alexina • Henri de Valois** (soprano • baritone)
- lyric voices

Oui, vous l'arrachez à mon âme
- *Guillaume Tell* (Gioachino Rossini, 1792-1868), French
- **Mathilde • Arnold** (soprano • tenor)
- lyric voices

Pa-pa-pa-
- *Die Zauberflöte* (Wolfgang Amadeus Mozart, 1756-1791), German
- **Papagena • Papageno** (soprano • baritone)
- light voices

Pace, caro mio sposo
- *Una cosa rara* (Vicente Martín y Soler, 1754-1806), Italian
- **Lilla • Lubino** (soprano • bass)
- light voices

Pace e gioia sia con voi
- *Il barbiere di Siviglia* (Gioachino Rossini, 1792-1868), Italian
- **Il Conte d'Almaviva/Lindoro** [Count Almaviva] • **Bartolo** (tenor • bass)
- light voices

Pappataci!
- *L'italiana in Algeri* (Gioachino Rossini, 1792-1868), Italian
- **Lindoro • Taddeo** (tenor • bass)
- light or lyric voices

Parigi, o cara/Ah, gran Dio! morir sì giovane
- *La traviata* (Giuseppe Verdi, 1813-1901), Italian
- **Violetta Valéry • Alfredo Germont** (soprano • tenor)
- lyric voices

Parla, in tuo cor virgineo
- *Simon Boccanegra* (Giuseppe Verdi, 1813-1901), Italian
- **Amelia** [Maria Boccanegra] • **Gabriele Adorno** (soprano • tenor)
- lyric or dramatic voices

Parle-moi de ma mère
- *Carmen* (Georges Bizet, 1838-1875), French
- **Micaëla • Don José** (soprano • tenor)
- lyric voices

Pensa che sol per poco sospendo l'ira mia
- *Elisabetta* (Gioachino Rossini, 1792-1868), Italian
- **Matilda • Elisabetta** [Queen] (soprano • soprano)
- lyric voices

Per le porte
- *Imeneo* (George Frideric Handel, 1685-1759), Italian
- **Rosmene • Tirinto** (soprano • mezzo-soprano)
- light or lyric voices

Per le porte del tormento
- *Sosarme* (George Frideric Handel, 1685-1759), Italian
- **Elmira • Sosarme** (soprano • contralto) The role of Sosarme was originally sung by an alto castrato.
- light or lyric voices

Per piacere alla Signora
- *Il turco in Italia* (Gioachino Rossini, 1792-1868), Italian
- **Fiorilla • Don Geronio** (soprano • bass)
- light voices

Per queste tue manine
- *Don Giovanni* (Wolfgang Amadeus Mozart, 1756-1791), Italian
- **Zerlina • Leporello** (mezzo-soprano • baritone)
- light voices

Per te ho io nel core
- *Flaminio* (Giovanni Battista Pergolesi, 1710-1736), Italian
- **Checca • Vastiano** (soprano • bass)
- light voices

Per te ho io nel core
- *La Serva padrona* (Giovanni Battista Pergolesi, 1710-1736), Italian
- **Serpina • Uberto** (soprano • bass)
- light voices

Perchè mai cercate
- *La rondine* (Giacomo Puccini, 1858-1924), Italian
- **Magda • Ruggero** (soprano • tenor)
- lyric voices

Perchè mai, destin crudel
- *Elisabetta* (Gioachino Rossini, 1792-1868), Italian
- **Elisabetta** [Queen] • **Norfolk** (soprano • tenor)
- lyric voices

Perchè, perchè non m'ami più?/ Resta vicino a me
- *Il Tabarro* (Giacomo Puccini, 1858-1924), Italian
- **Giorgetta • Michele** (soprano • baritone)
- lyric or dramatic voices

Perdona! perdona/No, più nobile sei
- *Adriana Lecouvreur* (Francesco Cilea, 1866-1950), Italian
- **Adriana Lecouvreur • Maurizio** (soprano • tenor)
- lyric or dramatic voices

Perfides ennemis [Nemici senza cor]
- *Médée* (Luigi Chérubini, 1760-1842), French
- **Médée • Jason** (soprano • tenor)
- dramatic voices

Perigliarti ancor languente
- *Il trovatore* (Giuseppe Verdi, 1813-1901), Italian
- **Azucena • Manrico** (mezzo-soprano • tenor)
- lyric or dramatic voices

Piangi, fanciulla, piangi!
- *Rigoletto* (Giuseppe Verdi, 1813-1901), Italian
- **Gilda • Rigoletto** (soprano • baritone)
- lyric or dramatic voices

Piangi, piangi, il tuo dolore/ Maledetto il dì ch'io nacqui
- *Luisa Miller* (Giuseppe Verdi, 1813-1901), Italian
- **Luisa • Rodolfo** (soprano • tenor)
- lyric or dramatic voices

Piccolo, piccolo
- *Ein Walzertraum* (Oscar Straus, 1870-1954), German
- **Franzi • Count Lothar** (soprano • bass)
- light voices

Pietà ti prenda del mio dolore/ Alla pompa che s'appresta
- *Aïda* (Giuseppe Verdi, 1813-1901), Italian
- **Aïda • Amneris** (soprano • mezzo-soprano)
- dramatic voices

Plauso! Voce di gioia!/ Sin la tomba è a me negata
- *Belisario* (Gaetano Donizetti, 1797-1848), Italian
- **Antonina • Eutopio** (soprano • tenor)
- lyric or dramatic voices

Poca voglia di far bene
- *Sant'Alessio* (Stefano Landi, 1587-1639), Italian
- **Curtio • Martio** (soprano • soprano) Both roles may have been sung originally by castrati.
- light voices

Pour moi, je ne crains rien
- *Les pêcheurs de perles* (Georges Bizet, 1838-1875), French
- **Leïla • Zurga** (soprano • baritone)
- lyric voices

Pour mon pays/Un souffle ardent/Enfant! à mon coeur
- *Don Carlos* (Giuseppe Verdi, 1813-1901), French
- **Rodrigue** [Le Marquis de Posa] • **King Philip II** (baritone • bass)
- lyric or dramatic voices

Pour notre amour plus d'espérance/ Sur la rive étrangère
- *Guillaume Tell* (Gioachino Rossini, 1792-1868), French
- **Mathilde • Arnold** (soprano • tenor)
- lyric voices

Prender moglie!
- *Don Pasquale* (Gaetano Donizetti, 1797-1848), Italian
- **Ernesto • Don Pasquale** (tenor • bass)
- light voices

Prenderò quel brunettino
- *Così fan tutte* (Wolfgang Amadeus Mozart, 1756-1791), Italian
- **Fiordiligi • Dorabella** (soprano • mezzo-soprano) Dorabella can be sung by either soprano or mezzo-soprano.
- lyric voices

Prendi, l'anel ti dono
- *La sonnambula* (Vincenzo Bellini, 1801-1835), Italian
- **Amina • Elvino** (soprano • tenor)
- lyric voices

Présent des cieux, divine flamme
- *Zoroastre* (Jean-Philippe Rameau, 1683-1764), French
- **Amélite • Zoroastre** (soprano • countertenor) Zoroastre's role was originally written for haute-contre.
- light or lyric voices

Pretty Polly, say
- *The Beggar's Opera* (Johann Christoph Pepusch, 1667-1752), English
- **Polly Peachum • Macheath** (soprano • baritone)
- light voices

Principessa di morte/Mio fiore!
- *Turandot* (Giacomo Puccini, 1858-1924), Italian
- **Turandot • Calaf** (soprano • tenor)
- dramatic voices

Printemps revient
- *Cendrillon* (Jules Massenet, 1842-1912), French
- **Cendrillon • Pandolphe** (mezzo-soprano • bass)
- lyric voices

Prithee, pretty maiden
- *Patience* (Sir Arthur Sullivan, 1842-1900), English
- **Patience • Grosvenor** (soprano • baritone)
- light voices

Promise Duet [commonly known title]
- *The English Cat* (Hans Werner Henze, 1926-), English
- **Minette • Tom** [Cat] (soprano • baritone)
- lyric voices

Pronta io son
- *Don Pasquale* (Gaetano Donizetti, 1797-1848), Italian
- **Norina • Dr. Malatesta** (soprano • baritone)
- light voices

Pur ti miro
- *L'incoronazione di Poppea* (Claudio Monteverdi, 1567-1643), Italian
- **Poppea • Nerone** (soprano • mezzo-soprano) Nerone, originally soprano castrato, is soprano or mezzo-soprano today.
- lyric or dramatic voices

Pura siccome un angelo/ Dite alla giovine/Morro!
- *La traviata* (Giuseppe Verdi, 1813-1901), Italian
- **Violetta Valéry • Giorgio Germont** (soprano • baritone)
- lyric voices

Qual cieco fato/Del mar sul lido
- *Simon Boccanegra* (Giuseppe Verdi, 1813-1901), Italian
- **Simon Boccanegra** [The Doge of Genoa] • **Fiesco** (baritone • bass)
- lyric or dramatic voices

Qual contento
- *Orlando Paladino* (Joseph Haydn, 1732-1809), Italian
- **Angelica • Medoro** (soprano • tenor)
- light voices

Qual cor tradisti
- *Norma* (Vincenzo Bellini, 1801-1835), Italian
- **Norma • Pollione** (soprano • tenor)
- lyric or dramatic voices

Quale inchiesta!
- *Aïda* (Giuseppe Verdi, 1813-1901), Italian
- **Amneris • Radames** (mezzo-soprano • tenor)
- dramatic voices

Quale, o prode/Presso alla tomba
[Comment/Près du tombeau]
- *I vespri siciliani* [Les vêpres siciliennes] (Giuseppe Verdi, 1813-1901), Italian [French]

- **Elena** [Hélène] • **Arrigo** [Henri] (soprano • tenor)
- lyric or dramatic voices

Quand des sommets de la montagne
- *Benvenuto Cellini* (Hector Berlioz, 1803-1869), French
- **Teresa** • **Benvenuto Cellini** (soprano • tenor)
- lyric or dramatic voices

Quand j'ai quitté le château de mon père/ O mon amour [Quando le soglie paterne vareai]
- *La favorite* [*La favorita*] (Gaetano Donizetti, 1797-1848), French [Italian]
- **Léonor** [Leonora] • **Alphonse** [Alfonso] (soprano • bass)
- lyric or dramatic voices

Quand ma bonté toujours nouvelle [Quando al mio sen]
- *Les vêpres siciliennes* [*I vespri siciliani*] (Giuseppe Verdi, 1813-1901), French [Italian]
- **Henri** [Arrigo] • **Montfort** [Montforte] (tenor • baritone)
- lyric or dramatic voices

Quand nos jours s'éteindront
- *Hérodiade* (Jules Massenet, 1842-1912), French
- **Salomé** • **Jean** [John the Baptist] (soprano • tenor)
- dramatic voices

Quando al mio sen
[Quand ma bonté toujours nouvelle]
- *I vespri siciliani* [*Les vêpres siciliennes*] (Giuseppe Verdi, 1813-1901), Italian [French]
- **Arrigo** [Henri] • **Montforte** [Montfort] (tenor • baritone)
- lyric or dramatic voices

Quando di luce rosea
- *Maria Stuarda* (Gaetano Donizetti, 1797-1848), Italian
- **Maria Stuarda** • **Talbot** (soprano • bass)
- lyric or dramatic voices

Quando le soglie paterne vareai/Ah! l'alto ardor [Quand j'ai quitté/O mon amour]
- *La favorita* [*La favorite*] (Gaetano Donizetti, 1797-1848), Italian [French]
- **Leonora** [Leonor] • **Alfonso** [Alphonse] (soprano • baritone)
- lyric or dramatic voices

Quando narravi l'esule tua vita/E tu m'amavi
- *Otello* (Giuseppe Verdi, 1813-1901), Italian
- **Desdemona** • **Otello** (soprano • tenor)
- lyric or dramatic voices

Quanto amore
- *L'elisir d'amore* (Gaetano Donizetti, 1797-1848), Italian
- **Adina** • **Dr. Dulcamara** (soprano • bass)
- light voices

Quarrel Duet [commonly known title]
- *Pimpinone* (Tomaso Giovanni Albinoni, 1671-1751), Italian
- **Vespetta** • **Pimpinone** (mezzo-soprano • bass)
- light voices

Quarrel Duet [commonly known title]
- *Zaparozhets za Dunayem* [*A Cossack beyond the Danube*] (Semyon Gulak-Artemovsky, 1671-1751), Russian
- **Odarka** • **Karas** [Zaparozhets] (soprano • bass)
- lyric or dramatic voices

Que ces moments sont doux
- *Les Boréades* (Jean-Philippe Rameau, 1683-1764), French
- **Alphise** • **Abaris** (soprano • tenor) Abaris was originally written for haute-contre.
- lyric voices

Que faites-vous donc?/De quels transports/Toujours unis [Che mai fate voi?/Di qual amor]
- *Don Carlos* [*Don Carlo*] (Giuseppe Verdi, 1813-1901), French [Italian]
- **Elisabeth** [Elisabetta] • **Don Carlos** [Don Carlo] (soprano • tenor)
- lyric or dramatic voices

Que le tendre amour nous engage
- *Scylla et Glaucus* (Jean-Marie Leclair, 1697-1764), French
- **Scylla** • **Glaucus** (soprano • tenor) Glaucus was written originally for haute-contre.
- light or lyric voices

Quel tuo visetto amabile
- *Orlando Paladino* (Joseph Haydn, 1732-1809), Italian
- **Eurilla** • **Pasquale** (soprano • baritone)
- light voices

Quella ricordati
- *Semiramide* (Gioachino Rossini, 1792-1868), Italian
- **Semiramide** • **Assur** (soprano • bass)
- lyric voices

Qui chiamata m'avete?
- *La Gioconda* (Amilcare Ponchielli, 1834-1886), Italian
- **Laura** • **Alvise** (mezzo-soprano • bass)
- lyric or dramatic voices

Qui il padre ancor respira
- *Lucia di Lammermoor* (Gaetano Donizetti, 1797-1848), Italian
- **Lucia** • **Arturo** (soprano • tenor)
- lyric voices

Quoi, tous les deux
- *Le postillon de Lonjumeau* (Adolphe Adam, 1803-1856), French
- **Madeleine** • **Chapelou** (soprano • tenor)
- light or lyric voices

Ravisa qual alma
- *Il crociato in Egitto* (Giacomo Meyerbeer, 1791-1864), Italian
- **Armando · Palmide** (soprano • soprano) Armando, a pants role, was originally sung by a castrato.
- lyric or dramatic voices

Remember that I care
- *Street Scene* (Kurt Weill, 1900-1950), English
- **Rose · Sam** (soprano • tenor)
- light or lyric voices

Reviens à toi, vierge adorée
- *Les Troyens* (Hector Berlioz, 1803-1869), French
- **Cassandre · Chorèbe** (mezzo-soprano • baritone)
- dramatic voices

Rivedrai le foreste imbalsamate /Padre!...a costoro
- *Aïda* (Giuseppe Verdi, 1813-1901), Italian
- **Aïda · Amonasro** (soprano • baritone)
- dramatic voices

Rosina vezzosina
- *La vera Costanza* (Joseph Haydn, 1732-1809), Italian
- **Rosina · Errico** (soprano • tenor)
- light or lyric voices

Sa voix fait naître dans mon sein
- *Les Troyens* (Hector Berlioz, 1803-1869), French
- **Didon · Anna** (mezzo-soprano • contralto) Didon is sung by either a soprano or a mezzo-soprano.
- dramatic voices

Sai com'arde in petto mio/ Piangi, o figlia/A quel nome
- *I Puritani* (Vincenzo Bellini, 1801-1835), Italian
- **Elvira · Giorgio** (soprano • bass)
- lyric voices

Sais-tu que devant la tiare
  [Non sai tu che un giusto]
- *La favorite* [*La favorita*] (Gaetano Donizetti, 1797-1848), French [Italian]
- **Fernand** [Fernando] · **Balthazar** [Badassare] (tenor • bass)
- lyric or dramatic voices

Schelm, halt' fest!
- *Der Freischütz* (Carl Maria von Weber, 1786-1826), German
- **Agathe · Ännchen** (soprano • mezzo-soprano) Ännchen is sung by either a mezzo-soprano or a soprano.
- lyric voices

Schenkt man sich Rosen in Tirol
- *Der Vogelhändler* (Carl Zeller, 1842-1898), German
- **Electress Marie · Adam** (soprano • tenor)
- light or lyric voices

Schön wie die blaue Sommernacht
- *Giuditta* (Franz Lehár, 1870-1948), German
- **Giuditta · Octavio** (soprano • tenor)
- lyric voices

Scuoti quella fronda di ciliegio/ Tutti i fior [Flower Duet]
- *Madama Butterfly* (Giacomo Puccini, 1858-1924), Italian
- **Cio-Cio-San** [Madama Butterfly] · **Suzuki** (soprano • mezzo-soprano)
- lyric voices

Se a caso Madama
- *Le nozze di Figaro* (Wolfgang Amadeus Mozart, 1756-1791), Italian
- **Susanna · Figaro** (soprano • bass)
- lyric voices

Se fiato in corpo avete
- *Il matrimonio segreto* (Domenico Cimarosa, 1749-1801), Italian
- **Geronimo · Count Robinson** (bass • bass) Count Robinson can be sung by either baritone or bass.
- light voices

Se inclinassi a prender moglie
- *L'italiana in Algeri* (Gioachino Rossini, 1792-1868), Italian
- **Lindoro · Mustafà** (tenor • bass)
- light or lyric voices

Se la vita ancor t'è cara
- *Semiramide* (Gioachino Rossini, 1792-1868), Italian
- **Semiramide · Arsace** (soprano • contralto)
- lyric voices

Se tu mi doni un'ora
- *Mefistofele* (Arrigo Boito, 1842-1918), Italian
- **Faust · Mefistofele** (tenor • bass)
- lyric or dramatic voices

Se viver non degg'io
- *Mitridate* (Wolfgang Amadeus Mozart, 1756-1791), Italian
- **Aspasia · Sifare** (soprano • tenor) Sifare was sung by either soprano (pants role) or tenor.
- lyric voices

Secondate, aurette amiche
- *Così fan tutte* (Wolfgang Amadeus Mozart, 1756-1791), Italian
- **Ferrando · Guglielmo** (tenor • bass)
- light or lyric voices

Sei splendida e lucente
- *Manon Lescaut* (Giacomo Puccini, 1858-1924), Italian
- **Manon Lescaut · Lescaut** (soprano • baritone)
- lyric or dramatic voices

Seid la vuole/La terra, il ciel m'abborrino
- *Il corsaro* (Giuseppe Verdi, 1813-1901), Italian

- **Gulnara • Corrado** (soprano • tenor)
- lyric or dramatic voices

Sento un certo/Dolce Amor!
- *Die schweigsame Frau* (Richard
  Strauss, 1864-1949), Italian
- **Aminta • Henry Morosus** (soprano • tenor)
- lyric or dramatic voices

Serba, serba i tuoi segreti
- *La Straniera* (Vincenzo Bellini, 1801-1835), Italian
- **Alaide** [La Straniera] • **Arturo** (soprano • tenor)
- lyric voices

Serbami ognor sì fido/Alle più calde immagini
- *Semiramide* (Gioachino Rossini, 1792-1868), Italian
- **Semiramide • Arsace** (soprano • contralto)
- lyric voices

Sì, dell'ardir, degl'empi
- *Caterina Cornaro* (Gaetano
  Donizetti, 1797-1848), Italian
- **Gerardo • Lusignano** (tenor • baritone)
- lyric or dramatic voices

**Sì, fuggire: a noi non resta/
Ah! crudel d'onor ragioni**
- *I Capuleti e i Montecchi* (Vincenzo
  Bellini, 1801-1835), Italian
- **Giulietta • Romeo** (soprano • mezzo-soprano)
- lyric voices

Sì, il parto mantengo
- *La Gioconda* (Amilcare
  Ponchielli, 1834-1886), Italian
- **La Gioconda • Barnaba**
  (mezzo-soprano • baritone)
- dramatic voices

Sì, la stanchezza/Ai nostri monti
- *Il trovatore* (Giuseppe Verdi, 1813-1901), Italian
- **Azucena • Manrico** (mezzo-soprano • tenor)
- lyric or dramatic voices

Sì, pel ciel
- *Otello* (Giuseppe Verdi, 1813-1901), Italian
- **Otello • Iago** (tenor • baritone)
- dramatic voices

**Sì, quello io son, ravvisami/
Oh t'innebria nell'amplesso**
- *Attila* (Giuseppe Verdi, 1813-1901), Italian
- **Odabello • Foresto** (soprano • tenor)
- dramatic voices

Sì...sulla salma del fratello
- *La Straniera* (Vincenzo Bellini, 1801-1835), Italian
- **Arturo • Baron Valdeburgo** (tenor • bass)
- lyric voices

Si tu m'aimes, Carmen
- *Carmen* (Georges Bizet, 1838-1875), French
- **Carmen • Escamillo** (contralto • bass)
- lyric or dramatic voices

Si vous le permettiez, princes/Ulysse!
- *Pénélope* (Gabriel Fauré, 1845-1924), French
- **Pénélope • Ulysse** (soprano • tenor)
- lyric or dramatic voices

Sie ist's! Er ist's!
- *Die Verschworenen* (Franz
  Schubert, 1797-1828), German
- **Udoline • Isella** (soprano • soprano) Udoline was
  written for either tenor or soprano (pants role).
- light or lyric voices

Sie woll'n mich heiraten
- *Arabella* (Richard Strauss, 1864-1949), German
- **Arabella • Mandryka** (soprano • baritone)
- lyric or dramatic voices

Siegmund! Sieh' auf mich
- *Die Walküre* (Richard Wagner, 1813-1883), German
- **Brünnhilde • Siegmund** (soprano • tenor)
- dramatic voices

**Silvio! a quest'ora/E allor
perchè, dì, tu m'hai stregato**
- *Pagliacci* (Ruggero Leoncavallo, 1857-1919), Italian
- **Nedda • Silvio** [Campagnuolo] [A Villager]
  (soprano • baritone)
- lyric voices

S'io non moro
- *Idomeneo* (Wolfgang
  Amadeus Mozart, 1756-1791), Italian
- **Ilia • Idamante** (soprano • tenor) Idamante,
  originally castrato, is sung by tenor, soprano,
  or mezzo-soprano.
- light or lyric voices

Sirius rising as the sun's wheel
- *The Midsummer Marriage* (Sir
  Michael Tippett, 1905-), English
- **Jenifer • Mark** (soprano • tenor)
- lyric voices

Slikhalil' vï...vdokhnulil' vï
  [Have you not heard...not sighed]
- *Yevgeny Onegin* [*Eugene Onegin*] (Pyotr
  Il'yich Tchaikovsky, 1840-1893), Russian
- **Tat'yana • Ol'ga** (soprano • contralto)
- lyric or dramatic voices

So ben che difforme
- *Pagliacci* (Ruggero Leoncavallo, 1857-1919), Italian
- **Nedda • Tonio** (soprano • bass-baritone)
- lyric or dramatic voices

So geht indes hinein
- *Die lustigen Weiber von Windsor*
  (Otto Nicolai, 1810-1849), German
- **Fenton • Herr Reich** [Mr. Page] (tenor • bass)
- light or lyric voices

So jetzt hätt' ich ihn gefangen
- *Die lustigen Weiber von Windsor* (Otto Nicolai, 1810-1849), German
- **Frau Fluth** [Mrs. Ford] · **Herr Fluth** [Mr. Ford] (soprano · baritone)
- lyric voices

Soccorso, sostegno accordate/Non si pianga
- *I Capuleti e i Montecchi* (Vincenzo Bellini, 1801-1835), Italian
- **Giulietta** · **Romeo** (soprano · mezzo-soprano)
- lyric voices

Sogno dorato io feci!/Sì l'eroismo è questo/ Ma lassù [J'avais fait un beau rêve]
- *Don Carlo* [*Don Carlos*] (Giuseppe Verdi, 1813-1901), Italian [French]
- **Elisabetta** [Elisabeth] · **Don Carlo** [Don Carlos] (soprano · tenor)
- lyric or dramatic voices

Solenne in quest'ora
- *La forza del destino* (Giuseppe Verdi, 1813-1901), Italian
- **Don Alvaro** · **Don Carlo di Vargas** (tenor · baritone)
- lyric or dramatic voices

Son disperato
- *L'infedeltà delusa* (Joseph Haydn, 1732-1809), Italian
- **Vespina** · **Nanni** (soprano · bass)
- light voices

Son geloso del zefiro errante
- *La sonnambula* (Vincenzo Bellini, 1801-1835), Italian
- **Amina** · **Elvino** (soprano · tenor)
- lyric voices

Son io dinanzi al rè?/Nell'ispana suol mai l'eresia dominò [Suis-je devant le roi?]
- *Don Carlo* [*Don Carlos*] (Giuseppe Verdi, 1813-1901), Italian [French]
- **Il Grande Inquisitore** [The Grand Inquisitor] · **Filippo II** [King Philip II] (bass · bass)
- lyric or dramatic voices

Son nata a lagrimar
- *Giulio Cesare in Egitto* (George Frideric Handel, 1685-1759), Italian
- **Sesto** · **Cornelia** (mezzo-soprano · contralto) Sesto, originally a castrato, can be sung by soprano or mezzo-soprano.
- lyric voices

Son quest'occhi un stral d'Amore
- *L'incontro improvviso* (Joseph Haydn, 1732-1809), Italian
- **Rezia** · **Ali** (soprano · tenor)
- light voices

Sorgi, o padre, e la figlia rimira
- *Bianca e Fernando* (Vincenzo Bellini, 1801-1835), Italian
- **Eloisa** · **Bianca** (soprano · soprano)
- lyric voices

Sortez de l'esclavage
- *Castor et Pollux* (Jean-Philippe Rameau, 1683-1764), French
- **Telaïre** · **Pollux** (soprano · bass)
- lyric voices

Sous le dôme épais
- *Lakmé* (Léo Delibes, 1836-1891), French
- **Lakmé** · **Mallika** (soprano · mezzo-soprano)
- light or lyric voices

Speravo di trovarvi qui
- *La Bohème* (Giacomo Puccini, 1858-1924), Italian
- **Mimì** · **Marcello** (soprano · baritone)
- lyric voices

Spiegarti non poss'io
- *Idomeneo* (Wolfgang Amadeus Mozart, 1756-1791), Italian
- **Ilia** · **Idamante** (soprano · tenor) Idamante, originally castrato, is sung by tenor, soprano, or mezzo-soprano.
- light or lyric voices

Stolto! a un sol mio grido
- *I Capuleti e i Montecchi* (Vincenzo Bellini, 1801-1835), Italian
- **Romeo** · **Tebaldo** (mezzo-soprano · tenor)
- lyric voices

Suis-je devant le roi?/Dans ce beau pays [Son io dinanzi al rè?]
- *Don Carlos* [*Don Carlo*] (Giuseppe Verdi, 1813-1901), French [Italian]
- **Il Grande Inquisitore** [The Grand Inquisitor] · **King Philip II** [Filippo II] (bass · bass)
- lyric or dramatic voices

Sull'aria/Che soave zefiretto [Letter Duet]
- *Le nozze di Figaro* (Wolfgang Amadeus Mozart, 1756-1791), Italian
- **La Contessa di Almaviva** [Rosina] · **Susanna** (soprano · soprano)
- lyric voices

Sulla tomba che rinserra/ Verranno a te sull'aure
- *Lucia di Lammermoor* (Gaetano Donizetti, 1797-1848), Italian
- **Lucia** · **Edgardo** (soprano · tenor)
- lyric voices

Sur cet autel sacré
- *La vestale* (Gaspare Spontini, 1774-1851), French
- **Julia** · **Licinius** (soprano · tenor)
- lyric or dramatic voices

**Suse, liebe Suse/Brüderchen
komm tanz mit mir**
• *Hänsel und Gretel* (Engelbert Humperdinck,
1854-1921), German
• **Gretel** • **Hänsel** (soprano • mezzo-soprano)
• light or lyric voices

Suzel, buon dì/Han della porpora vivo il colore
• *L'amico Fritz* (Pietro Mascagni, 1863-1945), Italian
• **Suzel** • **Fritz Kobus** (soprano • tenor)
• lyric voices

Swan Lake Duet [commonly known title]
• *Undina* (Pyotr Il'yich Tchaikovsky, 1840-1893),
Russian
• **Undina** • **Hulbrand** (soprano • tenor)
• lyric voices

**T'abbraccio/Qual mare, qual terra/
Lassù resplendere**
• *I Masnadieri* (Giuseppe Verdi, 1813-1901), Italian
• **Amalia** • **Carlo** (soprano • tenor)
• lyric or dramatic voices

**Tardo per gli anni/Vanitosi!
che abbietti e dormenti**
• *Attila* (Giuseppe Verdi, 1813-1901), Italian
• **Ezio** • **Attila** (baritone • bass)
• dramatic voices

Tausend kleine Engel singen
• *Die Csárdásfürstin* (Emmerich
Kálmán, 1882-1953), German
• **Sylva** • **Edwin** (soprano • tenor)
• light or lyric voices

Te souvient-il du lumineux voyage [Méditation]
• *Thaïs* (Jules Massenet, 1842-1912), French
• **Thaïs** • **Athanaël** (soprano • baritone)
• lyric or dramatic voices

Ten staví se svatou skem
[This man becomes a saint]
• *Prodaná Nevěsta* [*The Bartered Bride*]
(Bedřich Smetana, 1824-1884), Czech
• **Esmeralda** • **Circus Master** (soprano • tenor)
• light voices

Thanks to this excellent device
• *The Rake's Progress* (Igor Stravinsky,
1882-1971), English
• **Tom Rakewell** • **Nick Shadow**
(tenor • bass-baritone)
• lyric or dramatic voices

The flocks shall leave the mountains
• *Acis and Galatea* (George Frideric
Handel, 1685-1759), English
• **Galatea** • **Acis** (soprano • tenor)
• light voices

The woods are green
• *The Rake's Progress* (Igor
Stravinsky, 1882-1971), English
• **Anne Trulove** • **Tom Rakewell** (soprano • tenor)
• lyric voices

Thränen, Thränen
• *Abu Hassan* (Carl Maria von
Weber, 1786-1826), German
• **Fatime** • **Abu Hassan** (soprano • tenor)
• lyric voices

Tï li Vladimir moy? [Is it you, Vladimir mine?]
• *Knyaz' Igor'* [*Prince Igor*] (Alexander Porfir'yevich
Borodin, 1833-1887), Russian
• **Konchakovna** • **Vladimir** (contralto • tenor)
• lyric or dramatic voices

Toi qui m'es apparue
• *Cendrillon* (Jules Massenet, 1842-1912), French
• **Cendrillon** • **Prince** (mezzo-soprano • tenor)
The Prince was composed for a soprano, but
today is always sung by a tenor.
• lyric voices

Toi! Vous!
• *Manon* (Jules Massenet, 1842-1912), French
• **Manon** • **Des Grieux** [Le Chevalier]
(soprano • tenor)
• light or lyric voices

Ton coeur n'a pas compris le mien
• *Les pêcheurs de perles* (Georges Bizet,
1838-1875), French
• **Leïla** • **Nadir** (soprano • tenor)
• lyric voices

Tornami a dir che m'ami
• *Don Pasquale* (Gaetano
Donizetti, 1797-1848), Italian
• **Norina** • **Ernesto** (soprano • tenor)
• light voices

Tous les deux, amoureux
• *Barbe-bleue* (Jacques Offenbach, 1819-1880), French
• **Fleurette** • **Saphir** (soprano • tenor)
• light or lyric voices

Trotze nicht
• *Euryanthe* (Carl Maria von
Weber, 1786-1826), German
• **Adolar** • **Lysiart** (tenor • bass)
• dramatic voices

Tu caro sei il dolce mio tesoro
• *Sosarme* (George Frideric
Handel, 1685-1759), Italian
• **Elmira** • **Sosarme** (soprano • contralto) The role
of Sosarme was originally sung by an alto castrato.
• light or lyric voices

Tu dall'infanzia mia
- *Le villi* (Giacomo Puccini, 1858-1924), Italian
- **Anna · Roberto** (soprano · tenor)
- lyric voices

Tu m'apristi in cor ferita
- *Il pirata* (Vincenzo Bellini, 1801-1835), Italian
- **Imogene · Ernesto** (soprano · bass)
- lyric or dramatic voices

Tu mi lasci?
- *La finta Giardiniera* (Wolfgang Amadeus Mozart, 1756-1791), Italian
- **Sandrina · Belfiore** (soprano · tenor)
- light or lyric voices

Tu pleures? Oui, de honte sur moi
- *Manon* (Jules Massenet, 1842-1912), French
- **Manon · Des Grieux** [Le Chevalier] (soprano · tenor)
- light or lyric voices

Tu por lo sai, che giudice
- *I due Foscari* (Giuseppe Verdi, 1813-1901), Italian
- **Lucrezia Contarini · Francesco Foscari** [Doge] (soprano · baritone)
- lyric or dramatic voices

Tu qui, Santuzza?
- *Cavalleria rusticana* (Pietro Mascagni, 1863-1945), Italian
- **Santuzza · Turiddu** (mezzo-soprano · tenor)
- dramatic voices

Tu sciagurato! ah! fuggi
- *Il pirata* (Vincenzo Bellini, 1801-1835), Italian
- **Imogene · Gualtiero** (soprano · tenor)
- lyric or dramatic voices

Tu sei la mia vittoria
- *Adriana Lecouvreur* (Francesco Cilea, 1866-1950), Italian
- **Adriana Lecouvreur · Maurizio** (soprano · tenor)
- lyric or dramatic voices

Tu, tu, amore?/E fascino d'amor
- *Manon Lescaut* (Giacomo Puccini, 1858-1924), Italian
- **Manon Lescaut · Chevalier Des Grieux** (soprano · tenor)
- lyric or dramatic voices

Turiddu mi tolse
- *Cavalleria rusticana* (Pietro Mascagni, 1863-1945), Italian
- **Santuzza · Alfio** (mezzo-soprano · baritone)
- dramatic voices

Tutte le feste al tempio/ Sì, vendetta, tremenda vendetta
- *Rigoletto* (Giuseppe Verdi, 1813-1901), Italian
- **Gilda · Rigoletto** (soprano · baritone)
- lyric or dramatic voices

Um in der Ehe froh zu leben
- *Fidelio* (Ludwig von Beethoven, 1770-1827), German
- **Leonore · Marzelline** (soprano · soprano) Marzelline is a soubrette-lyric; Leonore is a full dramatic.
- lyric or dramatic voices

Un buon servo del visconte
- *Linda di Chamounix* (Gaetano Donizetti, 1797-1848), Italian
- **Linda · Antonio** (soprano · bass-baritone)
- light or lyric voices

Un certo ruscelletto
- *Il mondo della luna* (Joseph Haydn, 1732-1809), Italian
- **Clarice · Ecclitico** (soprano · tenor)
- light or lyric voices

Un dì felice, eterea/De quell'amor ch'è palpito
- *La traviata* (Giuseppe Verdi, 1813-1901), Italian
- **Violetta Valéry · Alfredo Germont** (soprano · tenor)
- lyric voices

Un segreto d'importanza
- *La Cenerentola* (Gioachino Rossini, 1792-1868), Italian
- **Don Magnifico · Dandini** (bass · bass) Both roles can be sung by either baritone or bass.
- light voices

Un soave non so che
- *La Cenerentola* (Gioachino Rossini, 1792-1868), Italian
- **Cenerentola** [Angelica] · **Don Ramiro** (mezzo-soprano · tenor)
- light voices

Und du wirst mein Gebieter sein [Submission Duet]
- *Arabella* (Richard Strauss, 1864-1949), German
- **Arabella · Mandryka** (soprano · baritone)
- lyric or dramatic voices

Unheilvolle Daphne
- *Daphne* (Richard Strauss, 1864-1949), German
- **Daphne · Apollo** (soprano · tenor)
- dramatic voices

Unter ist mein Stern gegangen
- *Euryanthe* (Carl Maria von Weber, 1786-1826), German
- **Euryanthe · Eglantine** (mezzo-soprano · mezzo-soprano) Either role can be sung by either a mezzo-soprano or a soprano.
- dramatic voices

Uzh vecher, oblakov pomerknuli kraya
- *Pikovaya dama* [Pique Dame] [The Queen of Spades] (Pyotr Il'yich Tchaikovsky, 1840-1893), Russian

- **Liza** • **Milovzor** [Daphnis] [Pauline]
  (soprano • contralto)
- lyric or dramatic voices

Va, crudele, al dio spietato/Vieni in Roma
- *Norma* (Vincenzo Bellini, 1801-1835), Italian
- **Adalgisa** • **Pollione** (mezzo-soprano • tenor)
- lyric voices

Va! je t'ai pardonné/Nuit d'hyménée!/Il faut partir
- *Roméo et Juliette* (Charles-François Gounod, 1812-1893), French
- **Juliette** • **Roméo** (soprano • tenor)
- lyric voices

Ve' come gli astri stessi
- *Ernani* (Giuseppe Verdi, 1813-1901), Italian
- **Elvira** • **Ernani** (soprano • tenor)
- lyric or dramatic voices

Vedete? io son fedele
- *Manon Lescaut* (Giacomo Puccini, 1858-1924), Italian
- **Manon Lescaut** • **Chevalier Des Grieux** (soprano • tenor)
- lyric or dramatic voices

Vedi?...di morte l'angelo/O terra addio
- *Aïda* (Giuseppe Verdi, 1813-1901), Italian
- **Aïda** • **Radames** (soprano • tenor)
- lyric or dramatic voices

Vendetta d'un momento
- *La battaglia di Legnano* (Giuseppe Verdi, 1813-1901), Italian
- **Lida** • **Arrigo** (soprano • tenor)
- lyric or dramatic voices

Venti scudi
- *L'elisir d'amore* (Gaetano Donizetti, 1797-1848), Italian
- **Nemorino** • **Belcore** (tenor • baritone)
- light voices

Verdi spiaggie al lieto giorno
- *Il ritorno d'Ulisse in patria* (Claudio Monteverdi, 1567-1643), Italian
- **Eumete** • **Ulisse** (tenor • baritone)
  Ulisse was sung by either tenor or baritone.
- lyric voices

Verlässt die Kirche mich/Wohl liebst auch ich
- *Rienzi* (Richard Wagner, 1813-1883), German
- **Irene** • **Rienzi** (soprano • tenor)
- dramatic voices

V'ho ingannato!/Lassù, in cielo
- *Rigoletto* (Giuseppe Verdi, 1813-1901), Italian
- **Gilda** • **Rigoletto** (soprano • baritone)
- lyric or dramatic voices

Via resti servita
- *Le nozze di Figaro* (Wolfgang Amadeus Mozart, 1756-1791), Italian
- **Susanna** • **Marcellina** (soprano • mezzo-soprano)
  Marcellina is sung by either soprano or mezzo-soprano.
- light or lyric voices

Vicino a te s'acqueta/La nostra morte
- *Andrea Chénier* (Umberto Giordano, 1867-1948), Italian
- **Maddalena** • **Andrea Chénier** (soprano • tenor)
- lyric or dramatic voices

Viene la sera
- *Madama Butterfly* (Giacomo Puccini, 1858-1924), Italian
- **Cio-Cio-San** [Madama Butterfly] • **Pinkerton** (soprano • tenor)
- lyric or dramatic voices

Vieni a mirar la cerula/Sì, sì, dell'ara il giubilo
- *Simon Boccanegra* (Giuseppe Verdi, 1813-1901), Italian
- **Amelia** [Maria Boccanegra] • **Gabriele Adorno** (soprano • tenor)
- lyric or dramatic voices

Vieni, ah! vieni [Viens, viens, je cède éperdu]
- *La favorita* [*La favorite*] (Gaetano Donizetti, 1797-1848), Italian [French]
- **Leonora** [Leonor] • **Fernando** [Fernand] (soprano • tenor)
- lyric or dramatic voices

Vieni, appaga il tuo consorte [Viens, suis un époux]
- *Orfeo ed Euridice* [*Orphée et Eurydice*] (Christoph Willibald von Gluck, 1714-1787), Italian [French]
- **Euridice** [Eurydice] • **Orfeo** [Orphée] (soprano • contralto) Orfeo's role was originally for alto castrato, and is tenor in the French version. Orfeo is often sung by a mezzo-soprano.
- lyric voices

Vieni, cerchiam pe' mari/Taci, taci: rimorsi amari
- *Il pirata* (Vincenzo Bellini, 1801-1835), Italian
- **Imogene** • **Gualtiero** (soprano • tenor)
- lyric or dramatic voices

Vieni, Gulnara!/Sia l'istante maledetto
- *Il corsaro* (Giuseppe Verdi, 1813-1901), Italian
- **Gulnara** • **Seid** (soprano • baritone)
- lyric or dramatic voices

Viens! fuyons au bout au monde
- *Roméo et Juliette* (Charles-François Gounod, 1812-1893), French
- **Juliette** • **Roméo** (soprano • tenor)
- lyric voices

Viens, nous quitterons cette ville
- *Cendrillon* (Jules Massenet, 1842-1912), French
- **Cendrillon • Prince** (soprano • tenor) The Prince was composed for a soprano, but today is always sung by a tenor.
- lyric voices

Viens, suis un époux [Vieni, appaga il tuo consorte]
- *Orphée et Eurydice* [*Orfeo ed Euridice*] (Christoph Willibald von Gluck, 1714-1787), French [Italian]
- **Eurydice** [Euridice] • **Orphée** [Orfeo] (soprano • tenor) The role of Orphée was originally for alto castrato in the Italian.
- lyric voices

Viens, viens, je cède éperdu [Vieni, ah! vieni]
- *La favorite* [*La favorita*] (Gaetano Donizetti, 1797-1848), French [Italian]
- **Léonor** [Leonora] • **Fernand** [Fernando] (soprano • tenor)
- lyric or dramatic voices

Vincenette a votre âge
- *Mireille* (Charles-François Gounod, 1812-1893), French
- **Mireille • Vincent** (soprano • tenor)
- lyric voices

Vivat Bacchus
- *Die Entführung aus dem Serail* (Wolfgang Amadeus Mozart, 1756-1791), German
- **Pedrillo • Osmin** (tenor • bass)
- light or lyric voices

Vivere io non potrò
- *La donna del lago* (Gioachino Rossini, 1792-1868), Italian
- **Elena • Malcolm** (soprano • mezzo-soprano)
- lyric or dramatic voices

Von den edlen Kavalieren
- *Martha* (Friedrich Flotow, 1812-1883), German
- **Lady Harriet Durham • Nancy** (soprano • mezzo-soprano)
- lyric voices

Vsyo na zemle dlyz schast' ya roditsya [Everything is born for love]
- *Virineya* (Sergey Mikhaylovich Slonimsky, 1932-), Russian
- **Virineya • Pavel** (soprano • bass-baritone)
- dramatic voices

Warum hat jeder Frühling, ach, nur einen Mai?
- *Der Zarewitsch* (Franz Lehár, 1870-1948), German
- **Sonja • Der Zarewitsch** [Tsarevich] (soprano • tenor)
- light or lyric voices

Was musst' ich hören, Gott
- *Der fliegende Holländer* (Richard Wagner, 1813-1883), German
- **Senta • Erik** (soprano • tenor)
- dramatic voices

Was seh ich?/Nicht wollen die Götter
- *Daphne* (Richard Strauss, 1864-1949), German
- **Daphne • Apollo** (soprano • tenor)
- dramatic voices

Was willst du, fremder Mensch?
- *Elektra* (Richard Strauss, 1864-1949), German
- **Elektra • Orest** (soprano • baritone)
- dramatic voices

Weit über Glanz und Erdenschimmer
- *Fierrabras* (Franz Schubert, 1797-1828), German
- **Florinda • Maragond** (soprano • mezzo-soprano)
- light or lyric voices

Welch ein Geschick!/Ha! du solltest für mich sterben
- *Die Entführung aus dem Serail* (Wolfgang Amadeus Mozart, 1756-1791), German
- **Konstanze • Belmonte** (soprano • tenor)
- lyric voices

Welko! das Bild?
- *Arabella* (Richard Strauss, 1864-1949), German
- **Mandryka • Graf Waldner** [Count] (baritone • bass-baritone)
- lyric or dramatic voices

Well met, pretty maid
- *Thomas and Sally* (Thomas Augustine Arne, 1710-1778), English
- **Sally • The Squire** (soprano • tenor)
- light voices

Wenn zum Gebet
- *Der Barbier von Bagdad* (Peter Cornelius, 1824-1874), German
- **Bostana • Nureddin** (mezzo-soprano • tenor)
- lyric voices

Wer ein Liebchen hat gefunden
- *Die Entführung aus dem Serail* (Wolfgang Amadeus Mozart, 1756-1791), German
- **Belmonte • Osmin** (tenor • bass)
- light or lyric voices

We're called gondolieri
- *The Gondoliers* (Sir Arthur Sullivan, 1842-1900), English
- **Marco • Giuseppe** (tenor • baritone)
- light voices

Why does beauty bring desire?
- *The English Cat* (Hans Werner Henze, 1926-), English
- **Minette • Tom** [Cat] (soprano • baritone)
- lyric voices

Wie aus der Ferne längst vergang'n Zeiten
- *Der fliegende Holländer* (Richard Wagner, 1813-1883), German
- **Senta • Der Holländer** [The Dutchman] (soprano • baritone)
- dramatic voices

Wie dünkt mich doch die Aue heut' so schön
- *Parsifal* (Richard Wagner, 1813-1883), German
- **Parsifal • Gurnemanz** (tenor • bass)
- dramatic voices

Wie freu' ich mich
- *Die lustigen Weiber von Windsor*
  (Otto Nicolai, 1810-1849), German
- **Herr Fluth** [Mr. Ford] • **Falstaff** (baritone • bass)
- lyric voices

Wie? Hört' ich recht?
- *Der fliegende Holländer* (Richard
  Wagner, 1813-1883), German
- **Der Holländer** [The Dutchman] •
  Daland (bass-baritone • bass)
- dramatic voices

Wo ist mein Bruder?/Morgen mittag um elf
- *Capriccio* (Richard Strauss, 1864-1949), German
- **Die Gräfin** [The Countess] [Countess Madeleine] •
  Major-Domo (soprano • bass)
- lyric or dramatic voices

Wunderbar! Ja, wunderbar
- *Die tote Stadt* (Erich Wolfgang
  Korngold, 1897-1957), German
- **Marietta • Paul** (soprano • tenor)
- lyric or dramatic voices

You love him, seek to set him right
- *The Rake's Progress* (Igor Stravinsky,
  1882-1971), English
- **Anne Trulove • Baba** (soprano • mezzo-soprano)
- lyric voices

Zitto, zitto, piano, piano
- *La Cenerentola* (Gioachino
  Rossini, 1792-1868), Italian
- **Don Ramiro • Dandini** (tenor • bass)
- light voices

Známt' já jednu dívčinu
  [I know a girl who burns for you]
- *Prodaná Nevěsta* [*The Bartered Bride*]
  (Bedřich Smetana, 1824-1884), Czech
- **Mařenka • Vašek** (soprano • tenor)
- light or lyric voices

Zwei, die sich lieben, vergessen die Welt
- *Giuditta* (Franz Lehár, 1870-1948), German
- **Anita • Pierrino** (soprano • tenor)
- light voices

Roles
to
Duets

Abaris *Les Boréades* (Rameau)
(Abaris was originally written for haute-contre.)
• **Alphise** (tenor • soprano)
-Que ces moments sont doux

Abigaille *Nabucco* (Verdi)
• **Nabucco** (soprano • baritone)
-Donna? chi sei?/Oh di qual'onta
aggravasi/Deh perdona

Abu Hassan *Abu Hassan* (Weber)
• **Fatime** (tenor • soprano)
-Thränen, Thränen

Abul *Der Barbier von Bagdad* (Cornelius)
• **Nureddin** (bass • tenor)
-Mars und Merkur

Achille *Iphigénie en Aulide* (Gluck)
• **Agamemnon** (tenor • baritone)
-De votre audace téméraire

Acis *Acis and Galatea* (Handel)
• **Galatea** (tenor • soprano)
-Happy we
-The flocks shall leave the mountains

Adalgisa *Norma* (Bellini)
(Adalgisa is sung by either soprano or mezzo-soprano.)
• **Norma** (mezzo-soprano • soprano)
-Ah! sì, fa core e abbracciami
-Mira, o Norma/Sì, fino all'ore estreme

• **Pollione** (mezzo-soprano • tenor)
-Va, crudele, al dio spietato/Vieni in Roma

Adam *Der Vogelhändler* (Zeller)
• **Marie, Electress** (tenor • soprano)
-Schenkt man sich Rosen in Tirol

Adela *The Haunted Tower* (Storace)
• **Elinor, Lady** (soprano • soprano)
-Begone! discharge you

Adèle di Formouters, La Comtesse [Countess]
Le comte Ory (Rossini)
• **Ory, Le Comte** [Count] (soprano • tenor)
-Ah! quel respect, Madame
• **Ragonde** (soprano • mezzo-soprano)
-Dans ce séjour

Adina *L'elisir d'amore* (Donizetti)
• **Dulcamara, Dr.** (soprano • bass)
-Io son ricco e tu sei bella
-Quanto amore
• **Nemorino** (soprano • tenor)
-Chiedi all'aura lusinghiera

Admète [Admeto] *Alceste* (Gluck)
• **Alceste** (tenor • soprano)
-Aux cris de la douleur [Cari figli]
• **Hercule** (tenor • bass)
-Ami, leur rage

Admeto [Admète] *Alceste* (Gluck)
• **Alceste** (tenor • soprano)
-Ah perchè
-Cari figli [Aux cris de la douleur]

Adolar *Euryanthe* (Weber)
• **Euryanthe** (tenor • mezzo-soprano)
-Hier weilest du/Wie liebt' ich dich
-Hin nimm die Seele mein
• **Lysiart** (tenor • bass)
-Trotze nicht

Adriana Lecouvreur *Adriana Lecouvreur* (Cilea)
• **Maurizio** (soprano • tenor)
-Perdona! perdona/No, più nobile sei
-Tu sei la mia vittoria
• **Michonnet** (soprano • baritone)
-Bambina, non ti crucciar
• **Principessa di Bouillon, La** [The Princess
  of Bouillon](soprano • mezzo-soprano)
-Io son sua per l'amor

Adriano *Rienzi* (Wagner)
• **Irene** (mezzo-soprano • soprano)
-Er geht/Ja, eine Welt voll Leiden

Agamemnon *Iphigénie en Aulide* (Gluck)
• **Achille** (baritone • tenor)
-De votre audace téméraire

Agathe *Der Freischütz* (Weber)
• **Ännchen** (soprano • mezzo-soprano)
  (Ännchen is sung by either a
  mezzo-soprano or a soprano.)
-Schelm, halt' fest!

Aïda *Aïda* (Verdi)
• **Amneris** (soprano • mezzo-soprano)
-Pietà ti prenda del mio dolore/
  Alla pompa che s'appresta
• **Amonasro** (soprano • baritone)
-Fuggiam gli ardori inospiti/
  Sì: fuggiam da queste mura
-Rivedrai le foreste imbalsamate/Padre!...a costoro
• **Radames** (soprano • tenor)
-Vedi?...di morte l'angelo/O terra addio

Alaide [La Straniera] *La Straniera* (Bellini)
• **Arturo** (soprano • tenor)
-Ah! se tu vuoi fuggir
-Serba, serba i tuoi segreti

Albert *Werther* (Massenet)
• **Werther** (baritone • tenor)
-Au bonheur dont mon âme est pleine

Alceste *Alceste* [*Alceste*] (Gluck)
• **Admète** [Admeto] (soprano • tenor)
-Aux cris de la douleur [Cari figli]

Alceste *Alceste* [*Alceste*] (Gluck)
• **Admeto** [Admète] (soprano • tenor)
-Ah perchè
-Cari figli [Aux cris de la douleur]

Aldona *I Lituani* [*The Little Sweep*] (Ponchielli)
• **Walter** (soprano • tenor)
-Noi torneremo alla romita valle

Alexina *Le roi malgré lui* (Chabrier)
• **Henri de Valois** (soprano • baritone)
-Oui, je vous hais

Alfio *Cavalleria rusticana* (Mascagni)
• **Santuzza** (baritone • mezzo-soprano)
-Ad essi non perdono
-Oh, il Signore vi manda
-Turiddu mi tolse

Alfonso [Alphonse] *La favorita*
  [*La favorite*] (Donizetti)
• **Leonora** [Léonor] (baritone • soprano)
-Quando le soglie paterne varcai/Ah! l'alto ardor
  [Quand j'ai quitté/O mon amour]

Alfredo Germont *La traviata* (Verdi)
• **Violetta Valéry** (tenor • soprano)
-Libiamo ne' lieti calici [Brindisi]
-Parigi, o cara/Ah, gran Dio! morir sì giovane
-Un dì felice, eterea/De quell'amor ch'è palpito

Ali *L'incontro improvviso* (Haydn)
• **Rezia** (tenor • soprano)
-Son quest'occhi un stral d'Amore

Alice *Robert le Diable* (Meyerbeer)
• **Bertram** (mezzo-soprano • bass)
-Mais Alice, qu'as-tu donc?

Almaviva, Il Conte d'/Lindoro [Count Almaviva]
  Il barbiere di Siviglia (Rossini)
• **Bartolo** (tenor • bass)
-Pace e gioia sia con voi
• **Figaro** (tenor • baritone)
-All'idea di quel metallo

Almaviva, Il Conte di/Lindoro
  Il barbiere di Siviglia (Paisiello)
• **Bartolo** (tenor • bass)
-O che umor
• **Rosina** (tenor • soprano)
-Cara sei tu il mio bene

Almaviva, Il Conte di [Count]
  Le nozze di Figaro (Mozart)
• **Susanna** (baritone • soprano)
-Crudel! perchè finora

Almaviva, La Contessa di [Rosina]
  Le nozze di Figaro (Mozart)
• **Susanna** (soprano • soprano)
-Sull'aria/Che soave zefiretto [Letter Duet]

Alphise *Les Boréades* (Rameau)
• **Abaris** (soprano • tenor)
  (Abaris was originally written for haute-contre.)
-Que ces moments sont doux

Alphonse [Alfonso] *La favorite* [*La favorita*] (Donizetti)
• **Léonor** [Leonora] (bass • soprano)

-Quand j'ai quitté le château de mon père/O mon amour [Quando le soglie paterne vareai]

Alphonse *La muette de Portici* (Auber)
• **Elvire** (tenor • soprano)
-N'espérez pas me fuir/Écoutez-moi

Alvaro, Don *La forza del destino* (Verdi)
• **Carlo di Vargas, Don** (tenor • baritone)
-Col sangue/Le minaccie/Ah, segnasti la tua sorte
-Nè gustare/Voi che si larghe cure/Sleale! Il segreto
-No, d'un imene il vincolo/Morte! Ov'io non cada
-Solenne in quest'ora
• **Leonora** (tenor • soprano)
-Ah, per sempre/Pronti destrieri/Seguirti

Alvise *La Gioconda* (Ponchielli)
• **Laura** (bass • mezzo-soprano)
-Qui chiamata m'avete?

Alzira *Alzira* (Verdi)
• **Gusmano** (soprano • baritone)
-Colma di gioia ho l'anima
• **Zamoro** (soprano • tenor)
-Anima mia!/Risorge ne' tuoi lumi

Amahl *Amahl and the Night Visitors* (Menotti)
• **Mother** (treble • soprano)
-Don't cry, mother dear

Amalia *I Masnadieri* (Verdi)
• **Carlo** (soprano • tenor)
-T'abbraccio/Qual mare, qual terra/Lassù resplendere
• **Francesco** (soprano • baritone)
-Io t'amo, Amalia/Ti scosta, o malnato
• **Massimiliano** [Count Moor] (soprano • bass)
-Carlo! io muoio

Amelia *Un ballo in maschera* (Verdi)
• **Riccardo** (soprano • tenor)
-Non sai tu che se l'anima mia/Oh qual soave brivido

Amelia [Maria Boccanegra] *Simon Boccanegra* (Verdi)
• **Gabriele Adorno** (soprano • tenor)
-Parla, in tuo cor virgineo
-Vieni a mirar la cerula/Sì, sì, dell'ara il giubilo
• **Simon Boccanegra** [The Doge of Genoa] (soprano • baritone)
-Dinnè, perchè in quest'eremo/Figlia! a tal nome io palpito

Amélite *Zoroastre* (Rameau)
• **Zoroastre** (soprano • countertenor)
(Zoroastre's role was originally written for haute-contre.)
-Je vous revois
-Présent des cieux, divine flamme

Amina *La sonnambula* (Bellini)
• **Elvino** (soprano • tenor)
-Prendi, l'anel ti dono
-Son geloso del zefiro errante

Aminta *Die schweigsame Frau* (Strauss)
• **Henry Morosus** (soprano • tenor)
-Sento un certo/Dolce Amor!

Amme, Die [The Nurse] *Die Frau ohne Schatten* (Strauss)
• **Kaiser, Der** [The Emperor] (mezzo-soprano • tenor)
-Bleib und wache bis sie dich ruft

Amneris *Aïda* (Verdi)
• **Aïda** (mezzo-soprano • soprano)
-Pietà ti prenda del mio dolore/Alla pompa che s'appresta
• **Radames** (mezzo-soprano • tenor)
-Ah! tu dei vivere/Che ti salva
-Quale inchiesta!

Amonasro *Aïda* (Verdi)
• **Aïda** (baritone • soprano)
-Fuggiam gli ardori inospiti/Sì: fuggiam da queste mura
-Rivedrai le foreste imbalsamate/Padre!...a costoro

Anatol *Vanessa* (Barber)
• **Vanessa** (tenor • soprano)
-Love has a bitter core, Vanessa

Andrea Chénier *Andrea Chénier* (Giordano)
• **Maddalena** (tenor • soprano)
-Ecco l'altare
-Ora soave
-Vicino a te s'acqueta/La nostra morte

Angelica *Orlando Paladino* (Haydn)
• **Medoro** (soprano • tenor)
-Qual contento

Anita *Giuditta* (Lehár)
• **Pierrino** (soprano • tenor)
-Zwei, die sich lieben, vergessen die Welt

Anna *La dame blanche* (Boieldieu)
• **Georges Brown/Julien Avanel** (soprano • tenor)
-Ce domane est celui des contes d'Avenel

Anna *Les Troyens* (Berlioz)
• **Didon** (contralto • mezzo-soprano)
(Didon is sung by either a soprano or a mezzo-soprano.)
-Sa voix fait naître dans mon sein

Anna *Le villi* (Puccini)
• **Roberto** (soprano • tenor)
-Tu dall'infanzia mia

Anna, Donna *Don Giovanni* (Mozart)
• **Ottavio, Don** (soprano • tenor)
(Don Ottavio is a light lyric tenor, but Donna Anna is a dramatic soprano.)
-Fuggi, crudele, fuggi!

Anna Bolena *Anna Bolena* (Donizetti)
• **Giovanna Seymour** (soprano • mezzo-soprano)
-Dio, che mi vedi in core/Va, infelice

Anna Elisa *Paganini* (Lehár)
• **Paganini** (soprano • tenor)
-Niemand liebt dich so wie ich

Anna Reich [Anne Page] *Die lustigen
Weiber von Windsor* (Nicolai)
• **Fenton** (soprano • tenor)
-Kannst du zweifeln

Ännchen *Der Freischütz* (Weber)
(Ännchen is sung by either a
mezzo-soprano or a soprano.)
• **Agathe** (mezzo-soprano • soprano)
-Schelm, halt' fest!

Anne Trulove *The Rake's Progress* (Stravinsky)
• **Baba** (soprano • mezzo-soprano)
-You love him, seek to set him right
• **Tom Rakewell** (soprano • tenor)
-Anne! Here!
-Farewell for now
-In a foolish dream/What should I forgive?
-The woods are green
• **Trulove** (soprano • bass)
-Every wearied body/God is merciful and just

Annina *Der Rosenkavalier* (Strauss)
• **Ochs auf Lerchenau, Baron** (contralto • bass)
-Da lieg' ich! Was einem Kavalier

Annio *La clemenza di Tito* (Mozart)
(Annio, a pants role, can be sung
by either soprano or mezzo-soprano.)
• **Servilia** (mezzo-soprano • soprano)
-Ah perdona al primo affetto
• **Sesto** (mezzo-soprano • mezzo-soprano)
-Deh prendi un dolce amplesso

Antonina *Belisario* (Donizetti)
• **Eutopio** (soprano • tenor)
-Plauso! Voce di gioia!/Sin la tomba è a me negata

Antonio *Linda di Chamounix* (Donizetti)
• **Linda** (bass-baritone • soprano)
-Un buon servo del visconte

Antony *Antony and Cleopatra* (Barber)
• **Cleopatra** (bass-baritone • soprano)
-Oh take, oh take those lips away

Apollo *Daphne* (Strauss)
• **Daphne** (tenor • soprano)
-Unheilvolle Daphne
-Was seh ich?/Nicht wollen die Götter

Arabella *Ariadne auf Naxos* (Strauss)
• **Mandryka** (soprano • baritone)
-Sie woll'n mich heiraten
-Und du wirst mein Gebieter sein [Submission Duet]
• **Zdenka** (soprano • soprano)
-Aber der Richtige

Arcabonne *Amadis* (Lully)
• **Arcalaus** (soprano • tenor)
(The role of Arcalaus was
originally written for haute-contre.)
-Irritons notre barbarie

Arcalaus *Amadis* (Lully)
(The role of Arcalaus was
originally written for haute-contre.)
• **Arcabonne** (tenor • soprano)
-Irritons notre barbarie

Armando *Il crociato in Egitto* (Meyerbeer)
(Armando, a pants role, was
originally sung by a castrato.)
• **Palmide** (soprano • soprano)
-Ravisa qual alma

Armida *Armida* (Haydn)
• **Rinaldo** (soprano • tenor)
-Cara, sarò fedele

Armide *Armide* (Gluck)
• **Hidraot** (soprano • baritone)
-Esprits de haine et de rage

Armide *Armide* (Lully)
• **Hidraot** (soprano • baritone)
-Esprits de haine et de rage

Arnold *Guillaume Tell* (Rossini)
• **Guillaume Tell** (tenor • bass)
-Ou vas-tu /Ah! Mathilde, idole de mon âme
• **Mathilde** (tenor • soprano)
-Oui, vous l'arrachez à mon âme
-Pour notre amour plus d'espérance/
Sur la rive étrangère

Arrigo *La Battaglia di Legnano* (Verdi)
• **Lida** (tenor • soprano)
-E ver?...sei d'altri?
-Vendetta d'un momento
• **Rolando** (tenor • baritone)
-Ben vi scorgo

Arrigo [Henri] *I vespri siciliani*
[*Les vêpres siciliennes*] (Verdi)
• **Elena** [Hélène] (tenor • soprano)
-O sdegni miei/Arrigo! ah parli a un core/E dolce
raggio [De courroux/Pour moi rayonne]
-Quale, o prode/Presso alla tomba
[Comment/Près du tombeau]
• **Montforte** [Montfort] (tenor • baritone)
-Quando al mio sen [Quand ma
bonté toujours nouvelle]

Arsace *Semiramide* (Rossini)
• **Assur** (contralto • bass)
-D'un tenero amore
• **Semiramide** (contralto • soprano)
-Giorno d'orrore
-Se la vita ancor t'è cara
-Serbami ognor sì fido/Alle più calde immagini

Arturo *Lucia di Lammermoor* (Donizetti)
• **Lucia** (tenor • soprano)
-Qui il padre ancor respira

Arturo *I Puritani* (Bellini)
• **Elvira** (tenor • soprano)
-Nel mirarti/Da quel dì/Vieni fra queste braccia

Arturo *La Straniera* (Bellini)
• **Alaide** [La Straniera] (tenor • soprano)
-Ah! se tu vuoi fuggir
-Serba, serba i tuoi segreti
• **Valdeburgo, Baron** (tenor • bass)
-Sì...sulla salma del fratello

Aspasia *Alceste* (Gluck)
• **Eumelo** (soprano • soprano)
-Ah mia diletta madre!

Aspasia *Mitridate* (Mozart)
• **Sifare** (soprano • tenor)
(Sifare was sung by either
soprano (pants role) or tenor.)
-Se viver non degg'io

Assur *Semiramide* (Rossini)
• **Arsace** (bass • contralto)
-D'un tenero amore
• **Semiramide** (bass • soprano)
-Quella ricordati

Athanaël *Thaïs* (Massenet)
• **Thaïs** (baritone • soprano)
-Baigne d'eau mes mains
-Te souvient-il du lumineux voyage [Méditation]

Attila *Attila* (Verdi)
• **Ezio** (bass • baritone)
-Tardo per gli anni/Vanitosi! che abbietti e dormenti

Azucena *Il trovatore* (Verdi)
• **Manrico** (mezzo-soprano • tenor)
-Perigliarti ancor languente
-Sì, la stanchezza/Ai nostri monti

Baba [Madame Flora] *The Medium* (Menotti)
• **Monica** (contralto • soprano)
-O Black Swan

Baba *The Rake's Progress* (Stravinsky)
• **Anne Trulove** (mezzo-soprano • soprano)
-You love him, seek to set him right

Babet *Blaise et Babet* (Dezède)
• **Blaise** (soprano • tenor)
-Avance un pas

Bacchus *Ariadne auf Naxos* (Strauss)
• **Prima Donna/Ariadne** (tenor • soprano)
-Ich grüsse dich, du Bote

Baculus *Der Wildschütz* (Lortzing)
• **Gretchen** (bass • soprano)
-Lass Er doch hören

Badassare [Balthazar] *La favorita* [*La favorite*]
(Donizetti)
• **Fernando** [Fernand] (bass • tenor)
-Non sai tu che un giusto [Sais-tu que devant la tiare]

Balstrode, Captain *Peter Grimes* (Britten)
• **Peter Grimes** (bass-baritone • tenor)
-And do you prefer the storm to Auntie's parlour?

Balthazar [Badassare] *La favorite*
[*La favorita*] (Donizetti)
• **Fernand** [Fernando] (bass • tenor)
-Sais-tu que devant la tiare [Non sai tu che un giusto]

Banco *Macbeth* (Verdi)
• **Macbeth** (bass • baritone)
-Due vaticini

Baptiste *Le pont des soupirs* (Offenbach)
• **Cornarino Cornarini** [Doge of Venice] (tenor • bass)
-Dans Venise la belle [Barcarolle]

Barak *Die Frau ohne Schatten* (Strauss)
• **Weib, Sein** [Wife of Barak] (bass-baritone • soprano)
-Mir anvertraut

Barnaba *La Gioconda* (Ponchielli)
• **Enzo** (baritone • tenor)
-Enzo Grimaldi, Principe di Santafiore
-O grido di quest'anima
• **Gioconda, La** (baritone • mezzo-soprano)
-Sì, il parto mantengo

Bartolo *Il barbiere di Siviglia* (Paisiello)
• **Almaviva, Il Conte di/Lindoro** (bass • tenor)
-O che umor

Bartolo *Il barbiere di Siviglia* (Rossini)
• **Almaviva, Il Conte d'/Lindoro**
[Count Almaviva] (bass • tenor)
-Pace e gioia sia con voi

Bastien *Bastien und Bastienne* (Mozart)
• **Bastienne** (tenor • soprano)
-Geh' hin!
-Geh'! geh'! geh'! Herz von Flandern!

Bastienne *Bastien und Bastienne* (Mozart)
• **Bastien** (soprano • tenor)
-Geh' hin!
-Geh'! geh'! geh'! Herz von Flandern!

Beatrice *Beatrice di Tenda* (Bellini)
• **Filippo Maria Visconti** (soprano • baritone)
-Odio e livore!—ingrato!
• **Orombello** (soprano • tenor)
-Ah! d'immenso, estremo affetto

Béatrice *Béatrice et Bénédict* (Berlioz)
• **Bénédict** (mezzo-soprano • tenor)
-Comment le dédain pourrait-il mourir?
-L'amour est un flambeau

Beatrice *I due supposti Conti* (Cimarosa)
• **Caramella, Il Conte** [Count] (soprano • bass)
-Nel veder quel tuo sembiante

Belcore *L'elisir d'amore* (Donizetti)
• **Nemorino** (baritone • tenor)
-Venti scudi

Belfiore *La finta Giardiniera* (Mozart)
• **Sandrina** (tenor • soprano)
-Tu mi lasci?

Belinda *Dido and Aeneas* (Purcell)
• **Second Woman** (soprano • mezzo-soprano)
-Fear no danger

Belisario *Belisario* (Donizetti)
• **Irene** (baritone • mezzo-soprano)
-Ah! se potessi piangere

Belmonte *Die Entführung aus dem Serail* (Mozart)
• **Konstanze** (tenor • soprano)
-Meinetwegen sollst du sterben
-Welch ein Geschick!/Ha! du solltest für mich sterben
• **Osmin** (tenor • bass)
-Wer ein Liebchen hat gefunden

Ben *The Telephone* (Menotti)
• **Lucy** (baritone • soprano)
-Hello? Hello? Where are you, my darling?

Bénédict *Béatrice et Bénédict* (Berlioz)
• **Béatrice** (tenor • mezzo-soprano)
-Comment le dédain pourrait-il mourir?
-L'amour est un flambeau

Benvenuto Cellini *Benvenuto Cellini* (Berlioz)
• **Teresa** (tenor • soprano)
-O Teresa, vous que j'aime plus que ma vie
-Quand des sommets de la montagne

Bertarido *Rodelinda* (Handel)
(The role of Bertarido was
originally sung by an alto castrato.)
• **Rodelinda** (contralto • soprano)
-Io t'abbraccio: è più che morte

Bertram *Robert le Diable* (Meyerbeer)
• **Alice** (bass • mezzo-soprano)
-Mais Alice, qu'as-tu donc?
• **Raimbaut** (bass • tenor)
-Ah! l'honnête homme!
• **Robert le Diable** (bass • tenor)
-Des chevaliers de ma patrie

Bess *Porgy and Bess* (Gershwin)
• **Porgy** (soprano • bass-baritone)
-Bess, you is my woman

Bianca *Bianca e Fernando* (Bellini)
• **Eloisa** (soprano • soprano)
-Sorgi, o padre, e la figlia rimira

Blaise *Blaise et Babet* (Dezède)
• **Babet** (tenor • soprano)
-Avance un pas

Blonde *Die Entführung aus dem Serail* (Mozart)
• **Osmin** (soprano • bass)
-Ich gehe, doch rate ich dir

Boccaccio *Boccaccio* (Suppé)
• **Fiametta** (mezzo-soprano • soprano)
-Florenz hat schöne Frauen

Boris Godunov *Boris Godunov* (Musorgsky)
• **Fyodor** (bass • mezzo-soprano)
-Farewell my son, I am dying [commonly known title]

Bostana *Der Barbier von Bagdad* (Cornelius)
• **Nureddin** (mezzo-soprano • tenor)
-Wenn zum Gebet

Brünnhilde *Die Walküre* (Wagner)
• **Siegmund** (soprano • tenor)
-Siegmund! Sieh' auf mich
• **Wotan** (soprano • bass-baritone)
-Als junger Liebe Lust mir verblich

Calaf *Turandot* (Puccini)
• **Turandot** (tenor • soprano)
-Principessa di morte/Mio fiore!

Caramella, Il Conte [Count]
  I due supposti Conti (Cimarosa)
• **Beatrice** (bass • soprano)
-Nel veder quel tuo sembiante

Carlo *Linda di Chamounix* (Donizetti)
• **Linda** (tenor • soprano)
-Ah! dimmi...dimmi io t'amo
-Di tue pene sparve il sogno

Carlo *I Masnadieri* (Verdi)
• **Amalia** (tenor • soprano)
-T'abbraccio/Qual mare, qual terra/Lassù resplendere
• **Massimiliano** [Count Moor] (tenor • bass)
-Come il bacio d'un padre amoroso

Carlo VII *Giovanna d'Arco* (Verdi)
• **Giovanna** (tenor • soprano)
-Dunque, o cruda, e gloria e trono/Vieni al tempio

Carlo, Don [Don Carlos]
  Don Carlo [*Don Carlos*] (Verdi)
• **Elisabetta** [Elisabeth] (tenor • soprano)
-Che mai fate voi?/De qual amor
  [Que faites-vous donc?]
-Io vengo a domandar/Perduto ben/
  Sotto al mio piè [Je viens solliciter]
-L'ora fatale è suonata! [L'heure fatale est sonnée!]
-Sogno dorato io feci!/Sì l'eroismo è questo/
  Ma lassù [J'avais fait un beau rêve]
• **Rodrigo** [Marchese di Posa] [Rodrigue]
  [Le Marquis de Posa] (tenor • baritone)
-Dio, che nell'alma infondere
  [Dieu tu semas dans nos âmes]

Carlo, Don *Ernani* (Verdi)
• **Elvira** (baritone • soprano)
-Da qual dì che t'ho veduta

Carlo di Vargas, Don *La forza del destino* (Verdi)
• **Alvaro, Don** (baritone • tenor)
-Col sangue/Le minaccie/Ah, segnasti la tua sorte
-Nè gustare/Voi che si larghe cure/Sleale! Il segreto
-No, d'un imene il vincolo/Morte! Ov'io non cada
-Solenne in quest'ora

Carlos, Don [Don Carlo]
Don Carlos [*Don Carlo*] (Verdi)
• **Elisabeth** [Elisabetta] (tenor • soprano)
-J'avais fait un beau rêve/Oui, voilà l'héroisme/
Au revoir [Sogno dorato io feci!/Ma lassù]
-Je viens solliciter/O bien perdu/Que sous
mes pieds [Io vengo a domandar]
-L'heure fatale est sonnée! [L'ora fatale è suonata!]
-Que faites-vous donc?/De quels transports/
Toujours unis [Che mai fate voi?/Di qual amor]
• **Rodrigue** [Le Marquis de Posa] [Rodrigo
[Marchese di Posa]] (tenor • baritone)
-Dieu tu semas dans nos âmes
[Dio, che nell'alma infondere]
-Le voilà, c'est l'infant/Toi! mon Rodrigue! c'est toi

Carmen *Carmen* (Bizet)
• **Escamillo** (contralto • bass)
-Si tu m'aimes, Carmen
• **José, Don** (contralto • tenor)
-C'est toi! c'est moi!
-Non, tu ne m'aimes pas/Là-bas,
là-bas dans la montagne

Carolina *Il matrimonio segreto* (Cimarosa)
• **Paolino** (soprano • tenor)
-Cara non dubitar/Io ti lascio

Cassandre *Les Troyens* (Berlioz)
• **Chorèbe** (mezzo-soprano • baritone)
-Reviens à toi, vierge adorée

Cecilio *Lucio Silla* (Mozart)
(Cecilio, originally soprano castrato,
is for soprano or mezzo-soprano.)
• **Giunia** (mezzo-soprano • soprano)
-D'Eliso in sen m'attendi

Cendrillon *Cendrillon* (Massenet)
• **Pandolphe** (mezzo-soprano • bass)
-Printemps revient
• **Prince** (mezzo-soprano • tenor)
(The Prince was composed for a soprano,
but today is always sung by a tenor.)
-Toi qui m'es apparue
-Viens, nous quitterons cette ville

Cenerentola [Angelica] *La Cenerentola* (Rossini)
• **Ramiro, Don** (mezzo-soprano • tenor)
-Un soave non so che

Chapelou *Le postillon de Lonjumeau* (Adam)
• **Madeleine** (tenor • soprano)
-Grâce au hazard
-Quoi, tous les deux

Charlotte *Werther* (Massenet)
• **Werther** (mezzo-soprano • tenor)
-A cette heure suprême
-Ai-je dit vrai/Ah! qu'il est loin
-Il faut nous séparer
-Oui, c'est moi/N'achevez pas/Ah! ce premier baiser

Checca *Flaminio* (Pergolesi)
• **Vastiano** (soprano • bass)
-Per te ho io nel core

Cherevik *Sorochinskaya yarmarka*
[*The Fair at Sorochintzi*] (Musorgsky)
• **Kum** (bass • baritone)
-Dudu, rududu, rududu

Cherubino *Le nozze di Figaro* (Mozart)
(Cherubino is sung by either soprano
or mezzo-soprano.)
• **Susanna** (mezzo-soprano • soprano)
-Aprite, presto aprite [Escape Duet]

Chimène *Le Cid* (Massenet)
• **Infante** [Princess] (soprano • soprano)
-Laissez le doute dans mon âme

Chorèbe *Les Troyens* (Berlioz)
• **Cassandre** (baritone • mezzo-soprano)
-Reviens à toi, vierge adorée

Chrysothemis *Elektra* (Strauss)
• **Elektra** (soprano • soprano)
-Du! denn du bist stark
-Elektra! Schwester! komm mit uns!

Cio-Cio-San [Madama Butterfly]
Madama Butterfly (Puccini)
• **Pinkerton** (soprano • tenor)
-Bimba dagli occhi pieni di malià
-Viene la sera
• **Sharpless** (soprano • baritone)
-Ora a noi
• **Suzuki** (soprano • mezzo-soprano)
-Scuoti quella fronda di ciliegio/
Tutti i fior [Flower Duet]

Circus Master *Prodaná Nevěsta*
[*The Bartered Bride*] (Smetana)
• **Esmeralda** (tenor • soprano)
-Milostné zvířátko uděláme z vás
[We'll make a nice little animal]
-Ten staví se svatou skem [This man becomes a saint]

Clairon *Capriccio* (Strauss)
• **Count** (contralto • baritone)
-Kein Andres, das mir so im Herzen loht

Clarice *Il mondo della luna* (Haydn)
• **Ecclitico** (soprano • tenor)
-Un certo ruscelletto

Cleopatra *Antony and Cleopatra* (Barber)
• **Antony** (soprano • bass-baritone)
-Oh take, oh take those lips away

Cleopatra *Giulio Cesare in Egitto* (Handel)
• **Giulio Cesare** (soprano • baritone)
  (Giulio Cesare was originally written
  for soprano castrato.)
  -Caro! bella! più amabile beltà

Cornarino Cornarini [Doge of Venice]
  Le pont des soupirs (Offenbach)
• **Baptiste** (bass • tenor)
  -Dans Venise la belle [Barcarolle]

Cornelia *Giulio Cesare in Egitto* (Handel)
• **Sesto** (contralto • mezzo-soprano)
  (Sesto, originally a castrato, can be
  sung by soprano or mezzo-soprano.)
  -Son nata a lagrimar

Corrado *Il corsaro* (Verdi)
• **Gulnara** (tenor • soprano)
  -Seid la vuole/La terra, il ciel m'abborrino
• **Medora** (tenor • soprano)
  -No, tu non sai/Tornerai, ma forse spenta
• **Seid** (tenor • baritone)
  -Di': que' ribaldi tremano

Count *Capriccio* (Strauss)
• **Clairon** (baritone • contralto)
  -Kein Andres, das mir so im Herzen loht

Créon *Médée* (Chérubini)
• **Médée** (bass • soprano)
  -Ah! du moins à Médée

Cressida *Troilus and Cressida* (Walton)
• **Troilus** [Prince] (mezzo-soprano • tenor)
  -If one last doubt
  -Now close your arms

Curtio *Sant'Alessio* (Landi)
  (Both roles may have been sung originally by castrati.)
• **Martio** (soprano • soprano)
  -Poca voglia di far bene

Cynire *Echo et Narcisse* (Gluck)
• **Echo** (tenor • soprano)
  -L'espoir fuit de mon coeur

Daland *Der fliegende Holländer* (Wagner)
• **Holländer, Der** [The Dutchman] (bass • bass-baritone)
  -Wie? Hört' ich recht?

Dalibor *Dalibor* (Smetana)
• **Milada** (tenor • soprano)
  -O nevýslovné štěstí lásky
  [O the unutterable happiness]

Dalila *Samson et Dalila* (Saint-Saëns)
• **Grand Prêtre du Dagon, Le** [The High
  Priest of Dagon] (contralto • baritone)
  -J'ai gravi la montagne/La victoire facile
• **Samson** (contralto • tenor)
  -En ces lieux/Samson, ô toi, mon bien-aimé

Damigella *L'incoronazione di Poppea* (Monteverdi)
• **Valletto** (soprano • tenor)

(Valletto was originally sung by a castrato.)
  -O cara, o cara

Dandini *La Cenerentola* (Rossini)
• **Magnifico, Don** (bass • bass)
  (Both roles can be sung by either baritone or bass.)
  -Un segreto d'importanza
• **Ramiro, Don** (bass • tenor)
  -Zitto, zitto, piano, piano

Danilo Danilowitsch, Graf [Count Danilo]
  Die lustige Witwe (Lehár)
• **Hanna Glawari** (baritone • soprano)
  -Bei jedem Walzerschritt

Danish Knight *Armide* (Gluck)
• **Ubalde** (tenor • baritone)
  -Fuyons les douceurs dangereuses

Daphne *Daphne* (Strauss)
• **Apollo** (soprano • tenor)
  -Unheilvolle Daphne
  -Was seh ich?/Nicht wollen die Götter

Dejanira *Hercules* (Handel)
• **Iöle** (mezzo-soprano • soprano)
  -Joys of freedom

Des Grieux [Le Chevalier] *Manon* (Massenet)
• **Manon** (tenor • soprano)
  -Et je sais votre nom
  -On l'appelle Manon
  -Toi! Vous!
  -Tu pleures? Oui, de honte sur moi

Des Grieux *Manon Lescaut* (Auber)
• **Manon** (tenor • soprano)
  -Je ne souffre plus

Des Grieux, Chevalier *Manon Lescaut* (Puccini)
• **Manon Lescaut** (tenor • soprano)
  -Fra le tue braccia amore
  -Tu, tu, amore?/E fascino d'amor
  -Vedete? io son fedele

Desdemona *Otello* (Rossini)
• **Otello** (mezzo-soprano • tenor)
  -Eccomi giunto inosservato e solo/A te sarà

Desdemona *Otello* (Verdi)
• **Otello** (soprano • tenor)
  -Dio ti giocondi, o sposo
  -Già nella notte densa
  -Quando narravi l'esule tua vita/E tu m'amavi

Dick Johnson [Ramerrez]
  La fanciulla del West (Puccini)
• **Minnie** (tenor • soprano)
  -Io non son che una povera fanciulla

Didon *Les Troyens* (Berlioz)
  (Didon is sung by either a soprano or a mezzo-soprano.)
• **Anna** (mezzo-soprano • contralto)
  -Sa voix fait naître dans mon sein

- **Énée** (mezzo-soprano • tenor)
  -Errante sur tes pas

Dmitry *Boris Godunov* (Musorgsky)
- **Marina** (tenor • mezzo-soprano)
  -Dmitry! Tsarevich!

Dorabella *Così fan tutte* (Mozart)
  (Dorabella is sung by either soprano or mezzo-soprano.)
- **Fiordiligi** (mezzo-soprano • soprano)
  -Al fato dan legge
  -O guarda sorella
  -Prenderò quel brunettino
- **Guglielmo** (mezzo-soprano • bass)
  -Il core vi dono

Duca di Mantua, Il [The Duke
  of Mantua] *Rigoletto* (Verdi)
- **Gilda** (tenor • soprano)
  -E il sol dell'anima/Addio, addio speranza ed anima

Dufresne *Zazà* (Leoncavallo)
- **Zazà** (tenor • soprano)
  -E deciso: tu parti

Dulcamara, Dr. *L'elisir d'amore* (Donizetti)
- **Adina** (bass • soprano)
  -Io son ricco e tu sei bella
  -Quanto amore
- **Nemorino** (bass • tenor)
  -Obbligato, ah, sì! obbligato!

Dulcinée *Don Quichotte* (Massenet)
- **Quichotte, Don** (mezzo-soprano • bass)
  -Oui, je souffre votre tendresse

Earl of Essex [Robert Devereux] *Gloriana* (Britten)
- **Elizabeth I** (tenor • soprano)
  -Happy were we

Ecclitico *Il mondo della luna* (Haydn)
- **Clarice** (tenor • soprano)
  -Un certo ruscelletto

Echo *Echo et Narcisse* (Gluck)
- **Cynire** (soprano • tenor)
  -L'espoir fuit de mon coeur

Edgar *Edgar* (Puccini)
- **Fidelia** (tenor • soprano)
  -Amaro sol per te

Edgardo *Lucia di Lammermoor* (Donizetti)
- **Lucia** (tenor • soprano)
  -Sulla tomba che rinserra/Verranno a te sull'aure

Edwin *Die Csárdásfürstin* (Kálmán)
- **Stasi, Komtesse** [Countess Stasi] (tenor • soprano)
  (Komtesse Stasi is a soubrette.)
  -Machen wir's den Schwalben nach
- **Sylva** (tenor • soprano)
  -Tausend kleine Engel singen

Eglantine *Euryanthe* (Weber)
- **Euryanthe** (mezzo-soprano • mezzo-soprano)

  (Either role can be sung by either a
  mezzo-soprano or a soprano.)
  -Unter ist mein Stern gegangen
- **Lysiart** (mezzo-soprano • bass-baritone)
  -Komm denn

Eisenstein *Die Fledermaus* (Johann Strauss)
- **Rosalinde** (tenor • soprano)
  -Dieser Anstand, so manierlich [Watch Duet]

Elektra *Elektra* (Strauss)
- **Chrysothemis** (soprano • soprano)
  -Du! denn du bist stark
  -Elektra! Schwester! komm mit uns!
- **Klytemnästra** (soprano • contralto)
  (Klytemnästra is soprano, mezzo-
  soprano, or contralto.)
  -Ich will nichts hören/Träumst du Mutter?
- **Orest** (soprano • baritone)
  -Orest! Orest! Orest!
  -Was willst du, fremder Mensch?

Elena *La donna del lago* (Rossini)
- **Malcolm** (soprano • mezzo-soprano)
  -Vivere io non potrò

Elèna [Helen of Troy] *Mefistofele* (Boito)
- **Faust** (soprano • tenor)
  -Forma ideal purissima/Amore, misterio celeste

Elena *Paride ed Elena* (Gluck)
- **Paride** (soprano • tenor [soprano])
  (Paride, originally for soprano castrato,
  is sung by either tenor or soprano.)
  -Ah ferma!...Ah senti!
  -L'amo! L'adoro!

Elena [Hélène] *I vespri siciliani*
  [*Les vêpres siciliennes*] (Verdi)
- **Arrigo** [Henri] (soprano • tenor)
  -O sdegni miei/Arrigo! ah parli a un core/
  E dolce raggio [De courroux/Pour moi rayonne]
  -Quale, o prode/Presso alla tomba
  [Comment/Près du tombeau]

Eleonora *Torquato Tasso* (Donizetti)
- **Tasso** (soprano • baritone)
  -Colei Sofronia

Elinor, Lady *The Haunted Tower* (Storace)
- **Adela** (soprano • soprano)
  -Begone! discharge you

Elisabeth [Elisabetta] *Don Carlos* [*Don Carlo*] (Verdi)
- **Carlos, Don** [Don Carlo] (soprano • tenor)
  -J'avais fait un beau rêve/Oui, voilà l'héroisme/
  Au revoir [Sogno dorato io fei!/Ma lassù]
  -Je viens solliciter/O bien perdu/
  Que sous mes pieds [Io vengo a domandar]
  -L'heure fatale est sonnée! [L'ora fatale è suonata!]
  -Que faites-vous donc?/De quels transports/
  Toujours unis [Che mai fate voi?/Di qual amor]

Elisabetta [Elisabeth] *Don Carlo* [*Don Carlos*] (Verdi)
• **Carlo, Don** [Don Carlos] (soprano • tenor)
  -Che mai fate voi?/De qual amor
    [Que faites-vous donc?]
  -Io vengo a domandar/Perduto ben/
    Sotto al mio piè [Je viens solliciter]
  -L'ora fatale è suonata! [L'heure fatale est sonnée!]
  -Sogno dorato io feci!/Sì l'eroismo è questo/Ma lassù
    [J'avais fait un beau rêve]

Elisabetta [Queen] *Elisabetta* (Rossini)
• **Matilda** (soprano • soprano)
  -Pensa che sol per poco sospendo l'ira mia
• **Norfolk** (soprano • tenor)
  -Perchè mai, destin crudel

Elisabetta [Queen] *Maria Stuarda* (Donizetti)
• **Leicester** (soprano • tenor)
  -Era d'amor l'immagine/Sul crin la rivale
• **Maria Stuarda** (soprano • soprano)
  -Morta al mondo

Elizabeth I *Gloriana* (Britten)
• **Earl of Essex** [Robert Devereux] (soprano • tenor)
  -Happy were we

Elmira *Sosarme* (Handel)
• **Sosarme** (soprano • contralto)
  (The role of Sosarme was
    originally sung by an alto castrato.)
  -Per le porte del tormento
  -Tu caro sei il dolce mio tesoro

Eloisa *Bianca e Fernando* (Bellini)
• **Bianca** (soprano • soprano)
  -Sorgi, o padre, e la figlia rimira

Elsa *Lohengrin* (Wagner)
• **Lohengrin** (soprano • baritone)
  -Das süsse Lied verhallt

Elsie Maynard *The Yeomen of the Guard* (Sullivan)
• **Jack Point** (soprano • baritone)
  -I have a song to sing, O!

Elvino *La sonnambula* (Bellini)
• **Amina** (tenor • soprano)
  -Prendi, l'anel ti dono
  -Son geloso del zefiro errante

Elvira *Ernani* (Verdi)
• **Carlo, Don** (soprano • baritone)
  -Da qual dì che t'ho veduta
• **Ernani** (soprano • tenor)
  -Ve' come gli astri stessi

Elvira *I Puritani* (Bellini)
• **Arturo** (soprano • tenor)
  -Nel mirarti/Da quel dì/Vieni fra queste braccia
• **Giorgio** (soprano • bass)
  -Sai com'arde in petto mio/
    Piangi, o figlia/A quel nome

Elvire *La muette de Portici* (Auber)
• **Alphonse** (soprano • tenor)
  -N'espérez pas me fuir/Écoutez-moi

Énée *Les Troyens* (Berlioz)
• **Didon** (tenor • mezzo-soprano)
  -Errante sur tes pas

Ennone *Il pomo d'oro* (Cesti)
• **Paride** (soprano • tenor)
  -O mia vita! O mia core

Enrico [Henry VIII] *Anna Bolena* (Donizetti)
• **Giovanna Seymour** (bass • mezzo-soprano)
  -Fama! sì: l'avrete
  -Oh qual parlar

Enrico Ashton *Lucia di Lammermoor* (Donizetti)
• **Lucia** (baritone • soprano)
  -Il pallor funesto, orrendo/Soffriva nel pianto languia

Enzo *La Gioconda* (Ponchielli)
• **Barnaba** (tenor • baritone)
  -Enzo Grimaldi, Principe di Santafiore
  -O grido di quest'anima
• **Laura** (tenor • mezzo-soprano)
  -Deh, non turbare

Erasto *Paride ed Elena* (Gluck)
• **Paride** (soprano • tenor [soprano])
  (Paride, originally for soprano castrato,
    is sung by either tenor or soprano.)
  -Ma, chi sei?

Erik *Der fliegende Holländer* (Wagner)
• **Senta** (tenor • soprano)
  -Was musst' ich hören, Gott

Ermione *Oreste* (Handel)
• **Oreste** (soprano • mezzo-soprano)
  (Oreste was originally written
    for mezzo-soprano castrato.)
  -Farewell Duet [commonly known title]

Ernani *Ernani* (Verdi)
• **Elvira** (tenor • soprano)
  -Ve' come gli astri stessi

Ernesto *Don Pasquale* (Donizetti)
• **Norina** (tenor • soprano)
  -Tornami a dir che m'ami
• **Pasquale, Don** (tenor • bass)
  -Prender moglie!

Ernesto *Il pirata* (Bellini)
• **Imogene** (bass • soprano)
  -Tu m'apristi in cor ferita

Errico *La vera Costanza* (Haydn)
• **Rosina** (tenor • soprano)
  -Rosina vezzosina

Escamillo *Carmen* (Bizet)
• **Carmen** (bass • contralto)
  -Si tu m'aimes, Carmen

Esmeralda *Prodaná Nevěsta*
  [*The Bartered Bride*] (Smetana)
• **Circus Master** (soprano • tenor)
  -Milostné zvířátko uděláme z vás
  [We'll make a nice little animal]
  -Ten staví se svatou skem [This man becomes a saint]

Eumée *Pénélope* (Fauré)
• **Pénélope** (baritone • soprano)
  -C'est sur ce banc

Eumelo *Alceste* (Gluck)
• **Aspasia** (soprano • soprano)
  -Ah mia diletta madre!

Eumete *Il ritorno d'Ulisse in patria* (Monteverdi)
• **Ulisse** (tenor • baritone)
  (Ulisse was sung by either tenor or baritone.)
  -Verdi spiagge al lieto giorno

Euridice *L'anima del filosofo* (Haydn)
• **Orfeo** (soprano • tenor)
  -Come il foco allo splendore

Euridice [Eurydice] *Orfeo ed Euridice*
  [*Orphée et Eurydice*] (Gluck)
• **Orfeo** [Orphée] (soprano • contralto)
  (Orfeo's role was originally for alto castrato,
  and is tenor in the French version. Orfeo is often
  sung by a mezzo-soprano.)
  -Avvezza al contento [Je goûtais les charmes]
  -Vieni, appaga il tuo consorte [Viens, suis un époux]

Eurilla *Orlando Paladino* (Haydn)
• **Pasquale** (soprano • baritone)
  -Quel tuo visetto amabile

Eurimaco *Il ritorno d'Ulisse in patria* (Monteverdi)
• **Melanto** (tenor • soprano)
  -Dolce mia vita sei

Euryanthe *Euryanthe* (Weber)
• **Adolar** (mezzo-soprano • tenor)
  (Either role can be sung by either a
  mezzo-soprano or a soprano.)
  -Hier weilest du/Wie liebt' ich dich
  -Hin nimm die Seele mein
• **Eglantine** (mezzo-soprano • mezzo-soprano)
  -Unter ist mein Stern gegangen
• **Louis VI** (mezzo-soprano • bass)
  -Lasst mich hier

Eurydice [Euridice] *Orphée et Eurydice*
  [*Orfeo ed Eurydice*] (Gluck)
• **Orphée** [Orfeo] (soprano • tenor)
  (The role of Orphée was originally for
  alto castrato in the Italian version.)
  -Je goûtais les charmes [Avvezza al contento]
  -Viens, suis un époux [Vieni, appaga il tuo consorte]

Eutopio *Belisario* (Donizetti)
• **Antonina** (tenor • soprano)
  -Plauso! Voce di gioia!/Sin la tomba è a me negata

Eva *Die Meistersinger von Nürnberg* (Wagner)
• **Hans Sachs** (soprano • baritone)
  -Gut'n Abend, Meister!

Evandro *Alceste* (Gluck)
• **Ismene** (tenor • soprano)
  -Ogni virtù più bella

Ezio *Attila* (Verdi)
• **Attila** (baritone • bass)
  -Tardo per gli anni/Vanitosi! che abbietti e dormenti

Falcon *Die Frau ohne Schatten* (Strauss)
• **Kaiserin, Die** [The Empress] (soprano • soprano)
  -Ist mein Liebster dahin

Falstaff *Falstaff* (Verdi)
• **Ford** (baritone • baritone)
  -C'è a Windsor una dama

Falstaff *Die lustigen Weiber von Windsor* (Nicolai)
• **Fluth, Herr** [Mr. Ford] (bass • baritone)
  -O! Ihr beschämt mich
  -Wie freu' ich mich

Fanny [Sapho] *Sapho* (Massenet)
• **Irène** (soprano • mezzo-soprano)
  -C'était bien gentil autrefois
• **Jean** (soprano • soprano)
  (Jean's part was sung by either a
  tenor or a soprano [pants role].)
  -Ne m'en veux pas d'être venue
  -O ma Fanny, que j'aime
  -Oh! Fanny ma maîtresse/Nous irons en rêvant

Fatima *Oberon* (Weber)
• **Sherasmin** (mezzo-soprano • baritone)
  -On the banks of the sweet Garonne

Fatime *Abu Hassan* (Weber)
• **Abu Hassan** (soprano • tenor)
  -Thränen, Thränen

Faust, Dr. *Faust* (Gounod)
• **Marguerite** (tenor • soprano)
  -Laisse-moi contempler ton visage/
  O nuit/Partez, partez
  -Oui, c'est toi je t'aime
• **Méphistophélès** (tenor • bass)
  -Me voici

Faust *Mefistofele* (Boito)
• **Elèna** [Helen of Troy] (tenor • soprano)
  -Forma ideal purissima/Amore, misterio celeste
• **Margherita** (tenor • soprano)
  -Lontano, lontano
• **Mefistofele** (tenor • bass)
  -Se tu mi doni un'ora

Federica *Luisa Miller* (Verdi)
• **Rodolfo** (contralto • tenor)
  -Dall'aule raggianti/Deh! la parola amara

Fedora Romazoff, La Principessa
[Princess Fedora] *Fedora* (Giordano)
• **Loris Ipanoff, Il Conte** [Count Loris]
   (soprano • tenor)
   -Lascia che pianga io solo

Feldmarchallin Fürstin Werdenberg, Die [Marie
   Thérèse] [Marschallin] *Der Rosenkavalier* (Strauss)
• **Octavian, genannt Quinquin** [Count Rofrano]
   (soprano • mezzo-soprano)
   (Octavian is sung by either
   soprano or mezzo-soprano.)
   -Ach! du bist wieder da
   -Lachst du mich aus?

Female Cat *l'Enfant et les sortilèges* (Ravel)
• **Tom Cat** (mezzo-soprano • baritone)
   -Cat Duet [commonly known title]

Fenton *Falstaff* (Verdi)
• **Nannetta** (tenor • soprano)
   -Labbra di foco

Fenton *Die lustigen Weiber von Windsor* (Nicolai)
• **Anna Reich** [Anne Page] (tenor • soprano)
   -Kannst du zweifeln
• **Reich, Herr** [Mr. Page] (tenor • bass)
   -So geht indes hinein

Fernand [Fernando] *La favorite* [*La favorita*]
   (Donizetti)
• **Balthazar** [Badassare] (tenor • bass)
   -Sais-tu que devant la tiare [Non sai tu che un giusto]
• **Léonor** [Leonora] (tenor • soprano)
   -Viens, viens, je cède éperdu [Vieni, ah! vieni]

Fernando [Fernand] *La favorita*
   [*La favorite*] (Donizetti)
• **Badassare** [Balthazar] (tenor • bass)
   -Non sai tu che un giusto [Sais-tu que devant la tiare]
• **Leonora** [Léonor] (tenor • soprano)
   -Vieni, ah! vieni [Viens, viens, je cède éperdu]

Fernando *Goyescas* (Granados)
• **Rosario** (tenor • soprano)
   -Coloquio en la reja

Fernando Villabella *La gazza ladra* (Rossini)
• **Ninetta** (bass-baritone • soprano)
   -Come frenar il pianto!

Ferrando *Così fan tutte* (Mozart)
• **Fiordiligi** (tenor • soprano)
   -Fra gli amplessi
• **Guglielmo** (tenor • bass)
   -Secondate, aurette amiche

Fiametta *Boccaccio* (Suppé)
• **Boccaccio** (soprano • mezzo-soprano)
   -Florenz hat schöne Frauen

Fidelia *Edgar* (Puccini)
• **Edgar** (soprano • tenor)
   -Amaro sol per te

Fiesco *Simon Boccanegra* (Verdi)
• **Simon Boccanegra** [The Doge of Genoa]
   (bass • baritone)
   -Delle faci festante al barlume/Piango, perchè mi parla
   -Qual cieco fato/Del mar sul lido

Figaro *Il barbiere di Siviglia* (Rossini)
• **Almaviva, Il Conte di/Lindoro**
   [Count Almaviva] (baritone • tenor)
   -All'idea di quel metallo
• **Rosina** (baritone • contralto)
   -Dunque io son?

Figaro *Le nozze di Figaro* (Mozart)
• **Susanna** (bass • soprano)
   -Cinque, dieci, venti
   -Se a caso Madama

Filippo II [King Philip II]
   Don Carlo [*Don Carlos*] (Verdi)
• **Grande Inquisitore, Il**
   [The Grand Inquisitor] (bass • bass)
   -Son io dinanzi al rè?/Nell'ispana suol mai l'eresia
   dominò [Suis-je devant le roi?]
• **Rodrigo** [Marchese di Posa] [Rodrigue
   [Le Marquis de Posa] (bass • baritone)
   -O signor, di Fiandra arrivo
   [O Roi! j'arrive de Flandre]

Filippo Maria Visconti *Beatrice di Tenda* (Bellini)
• **Beatrice** (baritone • soprano)
   -Odio e livore!—ingrato!

Fiordiligi *Così fan tutte* (Mozart)
• **Dorabella** (soprano • mezzo-soprano)
   (Dorabella can be sung by either
   mezzo-soprano or soprano.)
   -Al fato dan legge
   -O guarda sorella
   -Prenderò quel brunettino
• **Ferrando** (soprano • tenor)
   -Fra gli amplessi

Fiorilla *Il turco in Italia* (Rossini)
• **Geronio, Don** (soprano • bass)
   -Per piacere alla Signora
• **Selim** (soprano • bass)
   -Credete alla femmine

Flamand *Capriccio* (Strauss)
• **Gräfin, Die** [The Countess] [Countess Madeleine]
   (tenor • soprano)
   -Diese Liebe, plötzlich geboren

Fleurette *Barbe-bleue* (Offenbach)
• **Saphir** (soprano • tenor)
   -Tous les deux, amoureux

Florestan *Fidelio* (Beethoven)
• **Leonore** (tenor • soprano)
   -O namenlose Freude!

Florinda *Fierrabras* (Schubert)
• **Maragond** (soprano • mezzo-soprano)
   -Weit über Glanz und Erdenschimmer

Fluth, Frau [Mrs. Ford] *Die lustigen
Weiber von Windsor* (Nicolai)
• **Fluth, Herr** [Mr. Ford] (soprano • baritone)
-So jetzt hätt' ich ihn gefangen
• **Reich, Frau** [Mrs. Page] (soprano • contralto)
-Nein, das ist wirklich doch zu keck!

Fluth, Herr [Mr. Ford] *Die lustigen
Weiber von Windsor* (Nicolai)
• **Falstaff** (baritone • bass)
-O! Ihr beschämt mich
-Wie freu' ich mich
• **Fluth, Frau** [Mrs. Ford] (baritone • soprano)
-So jetzt hätt' ich ihn gefangen

Ford *Falstaff* (Verdi)
• **Falstaff** (baritone • baritone)
-C'è a Windsor una dama

Foresto *Attila* (Verdi)
• **Odabello** (tenor • soprano)
-Sì, quello io son, ravvisami/Oh t'innebria
nell'amplesso

Fortunatus Wurzel *Das Mädchen
aus der Feenwelt* (Drechsler)
• **Youth** (tenor • soprano)
-Brüderlein fein

Francesco *I Masnadieri* (Verdi)
• **Amalia** (baritone • soprano)
-Io t'amo, Amalia/Ti scosta, o malnato

Francesco Foscari [Doge] *I due Foscari* (Verdi)
• **Lucrezia Contarini** (baritone • soprano)
-Tu por lo sai, che giudice

Franzi *Ein Walzertraum* (Straus)
• **Lothar, Count** (soprano • bass)
-Piccolo, piccolo

Fritz Kobus *L'amico Fritz* (Mascagni)
• **Suzel** (tenor • soprano)
-Suzel, buon dì/Han della porpora vivo il colore

Fyodor *Boris Godunov* (Musorgsky)
• **Boris Godunov** (mezzo-soprano • bass)
-Farewell my son, I am dying [commonly known title]

Gabriele Adorno *Simon Boccanegra* (Verdi)
• **Amelia** [Maria Boccanegra] (tenor • soprano)
-Parla, in tuo cor virgineo
-Vieni a mirar la cerula/Sì, sì, dell'ara il giubilo

Galatea *Acis and Galatea* (Handel)
• **Acis** (soprano • tenor)
-Happy we
-The flocks shall leave the mountains

Galathee *Die schöne Galathee* (Suppé)
• **Ganymede** (soprano • mezzo-soprano)
-Ach, mich zieht's zu dir [Kissing Duet]

Ganymede *Die schöne Galathee* (Suppé)
• **Galathee** (mezzo-soprano • soprano)
-Ach, mich zieht's zu dir [Kissing Duet]

Gaston *Jérusalem* (Verdi)
• **Hélène** (tenor • soprano)
-Adieu, mon bien-aimé

Gennaro *Lucrezia Borgia* (Donizetti)
• **Lucrezia** (tenor • soprano)
-Di pescatore ignobile

Georges Brown/Julien Avanel
La dame blanche (Boieldieu)
• **Anna** (tenor • soprano)
-Ce domaine est celui des contes d'Avenel

Gérald *Lakmé* (Delibes)
• **Lakmé** (tenor • soprano)
-C'est le dieu de la jeunesse
-Lakmé, c'est toi

Gerardo *Caterina Cornaro* (Donizetti)
• **Lusignano** (tenor • baritone)
-Sì, dell'ardir, degl'empi

Geronimo *Il matrimonio segreto* (Cimarosa)
• **Robinson, Count** (bass • bass)
(Count Robinson can be sung
by either baritone or bass.)
-Se fiato in corpo avete

Geronio, Don *Il turco in Italia* (Rossini)
• **Fiorilla** (bass • soprano)
-Per piacere alla Signora

Giacomo *Giovanna d'Arco* (Verdi)
• **Giovanna** (baritone • soprano)
-Amai, ma un solo istante/Or del padre benedetta

Giannetto *La gazza ladra* (Rossini)
• **Ninetta** (tenor • soprano)
-Forse un dì conoscerete

Gilda *Rigoletto* (Verdi)
• **Duca di Mantua, Il** [The Duke
of Mantua] (soprano • tenor)
-E il sol dell'anima/Addio, addio speranza ed anima
• **Rigoletto** (soprano • baritone)
-Den non parlare al misero/Ah! veglia, o donna
-Piangi, fanciulla, piangi!
-Tutte le feste al tempio/
Sì, vendetta, tremenda vendetta
-V'ho ingannato!/Lassù, in cielo

Gioconda, La *La Gioconda* (Ponchielli)
(The role of La Gioconda is sung by
either soprano or mezzo-soprano.)
• **Barnaba** (mezzo-soprano • baritone)
-Sì, il parto mantengo
• **Laura** (mezzo-soprano • mezzo-soprano)
-L'amo come il fulgor del creato

Giorgetta *Il Tabarro* (Puccini)
• **Luigi** (soprano • tenor)
  -E ben altro il mio sogno
  -Oh Luigi! Luigi! Bada a te!
• **Michele** (soprano • baritone)
  -Perchè, perchè non m'ami più?/Resta vicino a me

Giorgio *I Puritani* (Bellini)
• **Elvira** (bass • soprano)
  -Sai com'arde in petto mio/
    Piangi, o figlia/A quel nome
• **Riccardo** (bass • baritone)
  -Il rival salvar tu dêi/Suoni la tromba intrepida

Giorgio Germont *La traviata* (Verdi)
• **Violetta Valéry** (baritone • soprano)
  -Pura siccome un angelo/Dite alla giovine/Morro!

Giovanna *Giovanna d'Arco* (Verdi)
• **Carlo VII** (soprano • tenor)
  -Dunque, o cruda, e gloria e trono/Vieni al tempio
• **Giacomo** (soprano • baritone)
  -Amai, ma un solo istante/Or del padre benedetta

Giovanna Seymour *Anna Bolena* (Donizetti)
• **Anna Bolena** (mezzo-soprano • soprano)
  -Dio, che mi vedi in core/Va, infelice
• **Enrico** [Henry VIII] (mezzo-soprano • bass)
  -Fama! sì: l'avrete
  -Oh qual parlar

Giovanni, Don *Don Giovanni* (Mozart)
  (Mozart's delineation of baritone
    and bass voices is very unclear.)
• **Leporello** (bass-baritone • bass-baritone)
  -Eh, via buffone
  -O statua gentilissima
• **Zerlina** (bass-baritone • mezzo-soprano)
  -Là ci darem la mano/Andiam mio bene

Girello *Girello* (Stradella)
• **Mustafà** (bass • soprano)
  (Mustafà is a pants role for soprano.)
  -O felice Mustafà/O Girello in povertà

Girot *Le Pré aux Clercs* (Hérold)
• **Nicette** (tenor • soprano)
  -Les rendez-vous de noble compagnie

Giselda *I Lombardi* (Verdi)
• **Oronte** (soprano • tenor)
  -Oh belle, a questa misera/Ah, vieni, sol morte

Giuditta *Giuditta* (Lehár)
• **Octavio** (soprano • tenor)
  -Schön wie die blaue Sommernacht

Giuliano *I filosofi immaginari* (Paisiello)
• **Petronio** (baritone • bass)
  -Coughing Duet [commonly known title]

Giulietta *I Capuleti e i Montecchi* (Bellini)
• **Romeo** (soprano • mezzo-soprano)

-Sì, fuggire; a noi non resta/Ah! crudel d'onor ragioni
-Soccorso, sostegno accordate/Non si pianga

Giulietta *Les contes d'Hoffmann* (Offenbach)
• **Hoffmann** (mezzo-soprano • tenor)
  -O Dieu! de quelle ivresse
• **Nicklausse** (mezzo-soprano • mezzo-soprano)
  (Both roles can be sung by either
    soprano or mezzo-soprano.)
  -Belle nuit, ô nuit d'amour [Barcarolle]

Giulio Cesare *Giulio Cesare in Egitto* (Handel)
  (Giulio Cesare was originally
    written for soprano castrato.)
• **Cleopatra** (baritone • soprano)
  -Caro! bella! più amabile beltà

Giunia *Lucio Silla* (Mozart)
• **Cecilio** (soprano • mezzo-soprano)
  (Cecilio, originally soprano castrato,
    is for soprano or mezzo-soprano.)
  -D'Eliso in sen m'attendi

Giuseppe *The Gondoliers* (Sullivan)
• **Marco** (baritone • tenor)
  -We're called gondolieri

Glaucus *Scylla et Glaucus* (Leclair)
  (Glaucus was written originally for haute-contre.)
• **Scylla** (tenor • soprano)
  -Que le tendre amour nous engage

Golaud *Pelléas et Mélisande* (Debussy)
• **Mélisande** (baritone • mezzo-soprano)
  -Ah! ah! tout va bien
  -Je ne pourrai plus sortir

Gomatz *Zaïde* (Mozart)
• **Zaïde** (tenor • soprano)
  -Meine Seele hüpft von Freuden

Gräfin, Die [The Countess] [Countess Madeleine]
  Capriccio (Strauss)
• **Flamand** (soprano • tenor)
  -Diese Liebe, plötzlich geboren
• **Major-Domo** (soprano • bass)
  -Wo ist mein Bruder?/Morgen mittag um elf

Grand Prêtre du Dagon, Le [The High Priest
  of Dagon] *Samson et Dalila* (Saint-Saëns)
• **Dalila** (baritone • contralto)
  -J'ai gravi la montagne/La victoire facile

Grande Inquisitore, Il [The Grand Inquisitor]
  Don Carlo [Don Carlos] (Verdi)
• **Filippo II** [King Philip II] (bass • bass)
  -Son io dinanzi al rè?/Nell'ispana suol mai
    l'eresia dominò [Suis-je devant le roi?]
• **Philip II, King** [Filippo II] (bass • bass)
  -Suis-je devant le roi?/Dans ce beau pays
    [Son io dinanzi al rè?]

Gretchen *Der Wildschütz* (Lortzing)
• **Baculus** (soprano • bass)
  -Lass Er doch hören

Gretel *Hänsel und Gretel* (Humperdinck)
• **Hänsel** (soprano • mezzo-soprano)
 -Abends will ich schlafen gehn [Prayer]
 -Ein Männlein steht im Walde
 -Nun ist die Hexe tot [Gingerbread Waltz]
 -Suse, liebe Suse/Brüderchen komm tanz mit mir

Grigory *Boris Godunov* (Musorgsky)
• **Pimen** (tenor • bass)
 -Just think, my son [commonly known title]

Grosvenor *Patience* (Sullivan)
• **Patience** (baritone • soprano)
 -Prithee, pretty maiden

Gualtiero *Il pirata* (Bellini)
• **Imogene** (tenor • soprano)
 -Bagnato dalle lagrime
 -Tu sciagurato! ah! fuggi
 -Vieni, cerchiam pe' mari/Taci, taci: rimorsi amari

Guardiano [Padre] *La forza del destino* (Verdi)
• **Leonora** (bass • soprano)
 -Infelice, delusa/Chi può legger nel futuro/Sull'alba
• **Melitone, Fra** (bass • baritone)
 -Del mondo i disinganni

Guglielmo *Così fan tutte* (Mozart)
• **Dorabella** (bass • mezzo-soprano)
 -Il core vi dono
• **Ferrando** (bass • tenor)
 -Secondate, aurette amiche

Guillaume Tell *Guillaume Tell* (Rossini)
• **Arnold** (bass • tenor)
 -Ou vas-tu /Ah! Mathilde, idole de mon âme

Gulnara *Il corsaro* (Verdi)
• **Corrado** (soprano • tenor)
 -Seid la vuole/La terra, il ciel m'abborrino
• **Seid** (soprano • baritone)
 -Vieni, Gulnara!/Sia l'istante maledetto

Gunther *Götterdämmerung* (Wagner)
• **Siegfried** (bass-baritone • tenor)
 -Blühenden Lebens labendes Blut

Gurnemanz *Parsifal* (Wagner)
• **Parsifal** (bass • tenor)
 -Wie dünkt mich doch die Aue heut' so schön

Gusmano *Alzira* (Verdi)
• **Alzira** (baritone • soprano)
 -Colma di gioia ho l'anima

Hamlet *Hamlet* (Thomas)
• **Ophélie** (baritone • soprano)
 -Doute de la lumière

Hanna Glawari *Die lustige Witwe* (Lehár)
• **Danilo Danilowitsch, Graf** [Count Danilo]
 (soprano • baritone)
 -Bei jedem Walzerschritt

Hans Sachs *Die Meistersinger von Nürnberg* (Wagner)
• **Eva** (baritone • soprano)
 -Gut'n Abend, Meister!

Hänsel *Hänsel und Gretel* (Humperdinck)
• **Gretel** (mezzo-soprano • soprano)
 -Abends will ich schlafen gehn [Prayer]
 -Ein Männlein steht im Walde
 -Nun ist die Hexe tot [Gingerbread Waltz]
 -Suse, liebe Suse/Brüderchen komm tanz mit mir

Harriet Durham, Lady *Martha* (Flotow)
• **Lyonel** (soprano • tenor)
 -Blickt sein Auge doch so ehrlich
 -Der Lenz ist gekommen
 -Hier in stillen Schatten gründen
• **Nancy** (soprano • mezzo-soprano)
 -Von den edlen Kavalieren

Hélène *Jérusalem* (Verdi)
• **Gaston** (soprano • tenor)
 -Adieu, mon bien-aimé

Hélène [Elena] *Les Vêpres Siciliennes*
 [*I Vespri Siciliani*] (Verdi)
• **Henri** [Arrigo] (soprano • tenor)
 -Comment, dans ma reconnaissance/Près du tombeau,
  peut-être [Quale o prode/ Presso alla tomba]
 -De courroux d'effroi/Ami! le coeur/Pour moi
  rayonne [O sdegni miei/E dolce raggio]
 -Malheureux et non coupable

Hélène *Ein Walzertraum* (Straus)
• **Niki** (soprano • tenor)
 -O, du lieber, o du g'scheiter

Henri [Arrigo] *Les vêpres siciliennes*
 [*I vespri siciliani*] (Verdi)
• **Hélène** [Elena] (tenor • soprano)
 -Comment, dans ma reconnaissance/Près du tombeau,
  peut-être [Quale o prode/ Presso alla tomba]
 -De courroux d'effroi/Ami! le coeur/Pour moi
  rayonne [O sdegni miei/E dolce raggio]
 -Malheureux et non coupable
• **Montfort** [Montforte] (tenor • baritone)
 -Quand ma bonté toujours nouvelle
  [Quando al mio sen]

Henri de Valois *Le roi malgré lui* (Chabrier)
• **Alexina** (baritone • soprano)
 -Oui, je vous hais

Henry Morosus *Die schweigsame Frau* (Strauss)
• **Aminta** (tenor • soprano)
 -Sento un certo/Dolce Amor!

Hercule *Alceste* (Gluck)
• **Admète** (bass • tenor)
 -Ami, leur rage

Héro *Béatrice et Bénédict* (Berlioz)
• **Ursula** (soprano • mezzo-soprano)
 -Nuit paisible et sereine! [Nocturne Duet]

Hidraot *Armide* (Gluck)
• **Armide** (baritone • soprano)
 -Esprits de haine et de rage

Hidraot *Armide* (Lully)
• **Armide** (baritone • soprano)
 -Esprits de haine et de rage

Hoffmann *Les contes d'Hoffmann* (Offenbach)
• **Giulietta** (tenor • mezzo-soprano)
 -O Dieu! de quelle ivresse

Holländer, Der [The Dutchman]
 Der fliegende Holländer (Wagner)
• **Daland** (bass-baritone • bass)
 -Wie? Hört' ich recht?
• **Senta** (baritone • soprano)
 -Wie aus der Ferne längst vergang'n Zeiten

Hulbrand *Undina* (Tchaikovsky)
• **Undina** (tenor • soprano)
 -Swan Lake Duet [commonly known title]

Iago *Otello* (Rossini)
 (Iago was written for either tenor or bass-baritone.)
• **Rodrigo** (bass-baritone • tenor)
 -No, non temer/Se uniti negli affanni

Iago *Otello* (Verdi)
• **Otello** (baritone • tenor)
 -Sì, pel ciel

Idamante *Idomeneo* (Mozart)
 (Idamante, originally castrato, is sung by tenor,
 soprano, or mezzo-soprano.)
• **Ilia** (tenor • soprano)
 -S'io non moro
 -Spiegarti non poss'io

Igor' *Knyaz' Igor'* [*Prince Igor*] (Borodin)
• **Yaroslavna** (baritone • soprano)
 -On—moy sokol yasnïy! [It is he, my bright falcon]

Ilia *Idomeneo* (Mozart)
• **Idamante** (soprano • tenor)
 (Idamante, originally castrato, is sung by tenor,
 soprano, or mezzo-soprano.)
 -S'io non moro
 -Spiegarti non poss'io

Imogene *Il pirata* (Bellini)
• **Ernesto** (soprano • bass)
 -Tu m'apristi in cor ferita
• **Gualtiero** (soprano • tenor)
 -Bagnato dalle lagrime
 -Tu sciagurato! ah! fuggi
 -Vieni, cerchiam pe' mari/Taci, taci: rimorsi amari

Infante [Princess] *Le Cid* (Massenet)
• **Chimène** (soprano • soprano)
 -Laissez le doute dans mon âme

Iolanta *Iolanta* (Tchaikovsky)
• **Vaudémont** (mezzo-soprano • tenor)
 -Chudnïy pervenets tvoren'ya
 [Wondrous firstling of creation]

Iöle *Hercules* (Handel)
• **Dejanira** (soprano • mezzo-soprano)
 -Joys of freedom

Irene *Belisario* (Donizetti)
• **Belisario** (mezzo-soprano • baritone)
 -Ah! se potessi piangere

Irene *Rienzi* (Wagner)
• **Adriano** (soprano • mezzo-soprano)
 -Er geht/Ja, eine Welt voll Leiden
• **Rienzi** (soprano • tenor)
 -Verlässt die Kirche mich/Wohl liebst auch ich

Irène *Sapho* (Massenet)
• **Fanny** [Sapho] (mezzo-soprano • soprano)
 -C'était bien gentil autrefois

Iris *Iris* (Mascagni)
• **Osaka** (soprano • tenor)
 -Or dammi il braccio tuo

Isabella *L'italiana in Algeri* (Rossini)
• **Mustafà** (contralto • bass)
 -O che muso, che figura!
• **Taddeo** (contralto • bass)
 -Ai capricci della sorte

Isabelle *Robert le Diable* (Meyerbeer)
• **Robert le Diable** (soprano • tenor)
 -Avec bonté voyez ma peine

Isella *Die Verschworenen* (Schubert)
• **Udoline** (soprano • soprano)
 (Udoline was written for either
 tenor or soprano [pants role].)
 -Sie ist's! Er ist's!

Ismene *Alceste* (Gluck)
• **Evandro** (soprano • tenor)
 -Ogni virtù più bella

Isolde *Tristan und Isolde* (Wagner)
• **Tristan** (soprano • tenor)
 -O ew'ge Nacht
 -O sink' hernieder, Nacht der Liebe

Isolier [Page] *Le comte Ory* (Rossini)
• **Ory, Le Comte** [Count] (mezzo-soprano • tenor)
 -Je vais revoir

Ivanov *Zar und Zimmermann* (Lortzing)
• **Marie** (tenor • soprano)
 -Darf eine nied're Magd es wagen
• **Van Bett** (tenor • bass)
 -Darf ich wohl den Worten trauen

Jack Point *The Yeomen of the Guard* (Sullivan)
• **Elsie Maynard** (baritone • soprano)
 -I have a song to sing, O!

Jacopo Foscari *I due Foscari* (Verdi)
• **Lucrezia Contarini** (tenor • soprano)
 -Non, non morrai, chè i perfidi/
  Ah! speranza dolce ancora

Jan *Der Bettelstudent* (Millöcker)
• **Symon Rymanovicz** (baritone • tenor)
-Die Welt hat das genialste

Jaquino *Fidelio* (Beethoven)
• **Marzelline** (tenor • soprano)
-Jetzt, Schätzchen, jetzt sind wir allein

Jason *Médée* (Chérubini)
• **Médée** (tenor • soprano)
-O fatale Toison
-Perfides ennemis [Nemici senza cor]

Jean [John the Baptist] *Hérodiade* (Massenet)
• **Salomé** (tenor • soprano)
-Ce que je veux
-Quand nos jours s'éteindront

Jean *Sapho* (Massenet)
(Jean's part was sung by either a
tenor or a soprano (pants role).)
• **Fanny** [Sapho] (soprano • soprano)
-Ne m'en veux pas d'être venue
-O ma Fanny, que j'aime
-Oh! Fanny ma maîtresse/Nous irons en rêvant

Jenifer *The Midsummer Marriage* (Tippett)
• **Mark** (soprano • tenor)
-Jenifer, Jenifer, my darling
-Sirius rising as the sun's wheel

Jeník *Prodaná Nevěsta* [*The Bartered Bride*] (Smetana)
• **Kecal** (tenor • bass)
-Nuže, milý chasníku [Now, dear young fellow]
• **Mařenka** (tenor • soprano)
-Jako matka [Like a mother]

Jochanaan *Salome* (Strauss)
• **Salome** (bass-baritone • soprano)
-Jochanaan, ich bin verliebt

José, Don *Carmen* (Bizet)
• **Carmen** (tenor • contralto)
-C'est toi! c'est moi!
-Non, tu ne m'aimes pas/Là-bas,
là-bas dans la montagne
• **Micaëla** (tenor • soprano)
-Parle-moi de ma mère

Julia *La vestale* (Spontini)
• **Licinius** (soprano • tenor)
-Adieu, mes tendres soeurs
-L'amour qui brûle dans notre âme
-Sur cet autel sacré

Julien *Louise* (Charpentier)
• **Louise** (tenor • soprano)
-Depuis longtemps

Juliette *Roméo et Juliette* (Gounod)
• **Roméo** (soprano • tenor)
-Ah! ne fuis pas encore
-Ange adorable
-O nuit divine

-Va! je t'ai pardonné/Nuit d'hyménée!/Il faut partir
-Viens! fuyons au bout au monde

Juno *Semele* (Handel)
• **Somnus** (contralto • bass)
-Obey my will

Kaiser, Der [The Emperor]
Die Frau ohne Schatten (Strauss)
• **Amme, Die** [The Nurse] (tenor • mezzo-soprano)
-Bleib und wache bis sie dich ruft

Kaiserin, Die [The Empress]
Die Frau ohne Schatten (Strauss)
• **Falcon** (soprano • soprano)
-Ist mein Liebster dahin

Karas [Zaparozhets] *Zaparozhets za Dunayem*
[*A Cossack beyond the Danube*] (Gulak-Artemovsky)
• **Odarka** (bass • soprano)
-Quarrel Duet [commonly known title]

Kecal *Prodaná Nevěsta* [*The Bartered Bride*] (Smetana)
• **Jeník** (bass • tenor)
-Nuže, milý chasníku [Now, dear young fellow]

Klytemnästra *Elektra* (Strauss)
(Klytemnästra is soprano, mezzo-soprano, or contralto.)
• **Elektra** (contralto • soprano)
-Ich will nichts hören/Träumst du Mutter?

Komponist, Der [The Composer]
Ariadne auf Naxos (Strauss)
(Der Komponist is sung by either
soprano or mezzo-soprano.)
• **Musiklehrer, Ein** [A Music Master]
(mezzo-soprano • baritone)
-Musik ist eine heilige Kunst
• **Zerbinetta** (mezzo-soprano • soprano)
-Ein Augenblick ist wenig

Konchakovna *Knyaz' Igor'* [*Prince Igor*] (Borodin)
• **Vladimir** (contralto • tenor)
-Tï li Vladimir moy? [Is it you, Vladimir mine?]

Konstanze *Die Entführung aus dem Serail* (Mozart)
• **Belmonte** (soprano • tenor)
-Meinetwegen sollst du sterben
-Welch ein Geschick!/Ha! du solltest für mich sterben

Kum *Sorochinskaya yarmarka*
[*The Fair at Sorochintzï*] (Musorgsky)
• **Cherevik** (baritone • bass)
-Dudu, rududu, rududu

Lakmé *Lakmé* (Delibes)
• **Gérald** (soprano • tenor)
-C'est le dieu de la jeunesse
-Lakmé, c'est toi
• **Mallika** (soprano • mezzo-soprano)
-Sous le dôme épais

Laura *Der Bettelstudent* (Millöcker)
• **Symon Rymanovicz** (soprano • tenor)
-Ich setz den Fall

Laura *La Gioconda* (Ponchielli)
- **Alvise** (mezzo-soprano • bass)
 -Qui chiamata m'avete?
- **Enzo** (mezzo-soprano • tenor)
 -Deh, non turbare
- **Gioconda, La** (mezzo-soprano • mezzo-soprano)
 (The role of La Gioconda is sung by
 either soprano or mezzo-soprano.)
 -L'amo come il fulgor del creato

Leicester *Elisabetta* (Rossini)
- **Matilda** (tenor • soprano)
 -Incauta, che festi!
- **Norfolk** (tenor • tenor)
 -Deh, scusa i trasporti

Leicester *Maria Stuarda* (Donizetti)
- **Elisabetta** [Queen] (tenor • soprano)
 -Era d'amor l'immagine/Sul crin la rivale
- **Maria Stuarda** (tenor • soprano)
 -Da tutti abbandonata
 -Io ti rivedo/Ah! se un giorno

Leïla *Les pêcheurs de perles* (Bizet)
- **Nadir** (soprano • tenor)
 -O dieu Brahma!
 -O lumière sainte
 -Ton coeur n'a pas compris le mien
- **Zurga** (soprano • baritone)
 -Pour moi, je ne crains rien

Léonor [Leonora] *La favorite* [*La favorita*] (Donizetti)
- **Alphonse** [Alfonso] (soprano • bass)
 -Quand j'ai quitté le château de mon père/O mon
 amour [Quando le soglie paterne vareai]
- **Fernand** [Fernando] (soprano • tenor)
 -Viens, viens, je cède éperdu [Vieni, ah! vieni]

Leonora [Léonor] *La favorita* [*La favorite*] (Donizetti)
- **Alfonso** [Alphonse] (soprano • baritone)
 -Quando le soglie paterne vareai/Ah! l'alto ardor
 [Quand j'ai quitté/O mon amour]
- **Fernando** [Fernand] (soprano • tenor)
 -Vieni, ah! vieni [Viens, viens, je cède éperdu]

Leonora *La forza del destino* (Verdi)
- **Alvaro, Don** (soprano • tenor)
 -Ah, per sempre/Pronti destrieri/Seguirti
- **Guardiano** [Padre] (soprano • bass)
 -Infelice, delusa/Chi può legger nel futuro/Sull'alba

Leonora *Il trovatore* (Verdi)
- **Luna, Il Conte di** [Count] (soprano • baritone)
 -Mira, di acerbe lagrime/Vivrà!...Contende il giubilo
- **Manrico** (soprano • tenor)
 -Miserere d'un alma/Tu vedrai che amore in terra

Leonore *Fidelio* (Beethoven)
- **Florestan** (soprano • tenor)
 -O namenlose Freude!
- **Marzelline** (soprano • soprano)
 (Marzelline is a soubrette-lyric;

Leonore is a full dramatic.)
 -Um in der Ehe froh zu leben
- **Rocco** (soprano • bass)
 -Nur hurtig fort, nur frisch gegraben

Leporello *Don Giovanni* (Mozart)
 (Mozart's delineation of baritone
 and bass voices is unclear.)
- **Giovanni, Don** (bass-baritone • bass-baritone)
 -Eh, via buffone
 -O statua gentilissima
- **Zerlina** (baritone • mezzo-soprano)
 -Per queste tue manine

Lescaut *Manon Lescaut* (Puccini)
- **Manon Lescaut** (baritone • soprano)
 -Sei splendida e lucente

Licinius *La vestale* (Spontini)
- **Julia** (tenor • soprano)
 -Adieu, mes tendres soeurs
 -L'amour qui brûle dans notre âme
 -Sur cet autel sacré
- **Pontifex Maximus** (tenor • bass)
 -C'est à toi de trembler

Lida *La battaglia di Legnano* (Verdi)
- **Arrigo** (soprano • tenor)
 -E ver?...sei d'altri?
 -Vendetta d'un momento
- **Rolando** (soprano • baritone)
 -Digli ch'è sangue italico

Lilla *Una cosa rara* (Martín y Soler)
- **Lubino** (soprano • bass)
 -Pace, caro mio sposo

Lina *Stiffelio* (Verdi)
- **Stankar** (soprano • baritone)
 -Ed io pure in faccia agl'uomini/Or meco venite
- **Stiffelio** (soprano • tenor)
 -Ah sì, voliamo al tempio

Linda *Linda di Chamounix* (Donizetti)
- **Antonio** (soprano • bass-baritone)
 -Un buon servo del visconte
- **Carlo** (soprano • tenor)
 -Ah! dimmi...dimmi io t'amo
 -Di tue pene sparve il sogno
- **Pierotto** (soprano • contralto)
 -Al bel destin che attendevi

Lindoro *L'italiana in Algeri* (Rossini)
- **Mustafà** (tenor • bass)
 -Se inclinassi a prender moglie
- **Taddeo** (tenor • bass)
 -Pappataci!

Liza *Pikovaya dama* [*Pique Dame*]
 [*The Queen of Spades*] (Tchaikovsky)
- **Milovzor** [Daphnis] [Pauline] (soprano • contralto)
 -Uzh vecher, oblakov pomerknuli kraya

Lohengrin *Lohengrin* (Wagner)
• **Elsa** (baritone • soprano)
  -Das süsse Lied verhallt

Loris Ipanoff, Il Conte
  [Count Loris] *Fedora* (Giordano)
• **Fedora Romazoff, La Principessa**
  [Princess Fedora] (tenor • soprano)
  -Lascia che pianga io solo

Lothar, Count *Ein Walzertraum* (Straus)
• **Franzi** (bass • soprano)
  -Piccolo, piccolo

Lothario *Mignon* (Thomas)
• **Mignon** (bass • mezzo-soprano)
  -As-tu souffert?/As-tu pleuré?
  -Légères hirondelles

Louis VI *Euryanthe* (Weber)
• **Euryanthe** (bass • mezzo-soprano)
  -Lasst mich hier

Louise *Louise* (Charpentier)
• **Julien** (soprano • tenor)
  -Depuis longtemps

Lubino *Una cosa rara* (Martín y Soler)
• **Lilla** (bass • soprano)
  -Pace, caro mio sposo

Lucano *L'incoronazione di Poppea* (Monteverdi)
• **Nerone** (tenor • mezzo-soprano)
  (Nerone, originally for soprano castrato,
    is soprano or mezzo-soprano today.)
  -Bocca, bocca

Lucia *Lucia di Lammermoor* (Donizetti)
• **Arturo** (soprano • tenor)
  -Qui il padre ancor respira
• **Edgardo** (soprano • tenor)
  -Sulla tomba che rinserra/Verranno a te sull'aure
• **Enrico Ashton** (soprano • baritone)
  -Il pallor funesto, orrendo/Soffriva nel pianto languia

Lucrezia *Lucrezia Borgia* (Donizetti)
• **Gennaro** (soprano • tenor)
  -Di pescatore ignobile

Lucrezia Contarini *I due Foscari* (Verdi)
• **Francesco Foscari** [Doge] (soprano • baritone)
  -Tu por lo sai, che giudice
• **Jacopo Foscari** (soprano • tenor)
  -Non, non morrai, chè i perfidi/
    Ah! speranza dolce ancora

Lucy *The Telephone* (Menotti)
• **Ben** (soprano • baritone)
  -Hello? Hello? Where are you, my darling?

Lucy Lockit *The Beggar's Opera* (Pepusch)
• **Polly Peachum** (soprano • soprano)
  -Hi there, dear husband
  -I'm bubbled!

Luigi *Il Tabarro* (Puccini)
• **Giorgetta** (tenor • soprano)
  -E ben altro il mio sogno
  -Oh Luigi! Luigi! Bada a te!

Luisa *Luisa Miller* (Verdi)
• **Miller** (soprano • baritone)
  -La tomba è un letto/Di rughe/
    Andrem, raminghi e poveri
• **Rodolfo** (soprano • tenor)
  -Piangi, piangi, il tuo dolore/
    Maledetto il dì ch'io nacqui

Luna, Il Conte di [Count] *Il trovatore* (Verdi)
• **Leonora** (baritone • soprano)
  -Mira, di acerbe lagrime/Vivrà!...Contende il giubilo

Lusignano *Caterina Cornaro* (Donizetti)
• **Gerardo** (baritone • tenor)
  -Sì, dell'ardir, degl'empi

Lyonel *Martha* (Flotow)
• **Harriet Durham, Lady** (tenor • soprano)
  -Blickt sein Auge doch so ehrlich
  -Der Lenz ist gekommen
  -Hier in stillen Schatten gründen
• **Plumkett** (tenor • bass)
  -Ja, seit früher Kindheit Tagen

Lysiart *Euryanthe* (Weber)
• **Adolar** (bass • tenor)
  -Trotze nicht
• **Eglantine** (bass-baritone • mezzo-soprano)
  -Komm denn

Macbeth *Macbeth* (Verdi)
• **Banco** (baritone • bass)
  -Due vaticini
• **Macbeth, Lady** (baritone • soprano)
  -Fatal mia donna!/Allor questa voce/Vieni altrove!
  -Ora di morte e di vendetta

Macbeth, Lady *Macbeth* (Verdi)
• **Macbeth** (soprano • baritone)
  -Fatal mia donna!/Allor questa voce/Vieni altrove!
  -Ora di morte e di vendetta

Macheath *The Beggar's Opera* (Pepusch)
• **Polly Peachum** (baritone • soprano)
  -Pretty Polly, say

Maddalena *Andrea Chénier* (Giordano)
• **Andrea Chénier** (soprano • tenor)
  -Ecco l'altare
  -Ora soave
  -Vicino a te s'acqueta/La nostra morte

Madeleine *Le postillon de Lonjumeau* (Adam)
• **Chapelou** (soprano • tenor)
  -Grâce au hazard
  -Quoi, tous les deux

Magda *La rondine* (Puccini)
• **Ruggero** (soprano • tenor)
-Ma come puoi lasciarmi
-Perchè mai cercate

Magnifico, Don *La Cenerentola* (Rossini)
(Both roles can be sung by either baritone or bass.)
• **Dandini** (bass • bass)
-Un segreto d'importanza

Major-Domo *Capriccio* (Strauss)
• **Gräfin, Die** [The Countess] [Countess
Madeleine] (bass • soprano)
-Wo ist mein Bruder?/Morgen mittag um elf

Malatesta, Dr. *Don Pasquale* (Donizetti)
• **Norina** (baritone • soprano)
-Pronta io son
• **Pasquale, Don** (baritone • bass)
-Cheti, cheti, immantinente/
Aspetta, aspetta, cara sposina

Malcolm *La donna del lago* (Rossini)
• **Elena** (mezzo-soprano • soprano)
-Vivere io non potrò

Mallika *Lakmé* (Delibes)
• **Lakmé** (mezzo-soprano • soprano)
-Sous le dôme épais

Mandryka *Arabella* (Strauss)
• **Arabella** (baritone • soprano)
-Sie woll'n mich heiraten
-Und du wirst mein Gebieter sein [Submission Duet]
• **Waldner, Graf** [Count] (baritone • bass-baritone)
-Welko! das Bild?

Manon *Manon* (Massenet)
• **Des Grieux** [Le Chevalier] (soprano • tenor)
-Et je sais votre nom
-On l'appelle Manon
-Toi! Vous!
-Tu pleures? Oui, de honte sur moi

Manon *Manon Lescaut* (Auber)
• **Des Grieux** (soprano • tenor)
-Je ne souffre plus

Manon Lescaut *Manon Lescaut* (Puccini)
• **Des Grieux, Chevalier** (soprano • tenor)
-Fra le tue braccia amore
-Tu, tu, amore?/E fascino d'amor
-Vedete? io son fedele
• **Lescaut** (soprano • baritone)
-Sei splendida e lucente

Manrico *Il trovatore* (Verdi)
• **Azucena** (tenor • mezzo-soprano)
-Perigliarti ancor languente
-Sì, la stanchezza/Ai nostri monti
• **Leonora** (tenor • soprano)
-Miserere d'un alma/Tu vedrai che amore in terra

Maragond *Fierrabras* (Schubert)
• **Florinda** (mezzo-soprano • soprano)
-Weit über Glanz und Erdenschimmer

Marcel *Les Huguenots* (Meyerbeer)
• **Valentine** (bass • mezzo-soprano)
-Dans la nuit où seul je veille
-Derrière ce pilier

Marcellina *Le nozze di Figaro* (Mozart)
(Marcellina is sung by either
soprano or mezzo-soprano.)
• **Susanna** (mezzo-soprano • soprano)
-Via resti servita

Marcello *La Bohème* (Puccini)
• **Mimì** (baritone • soprano)
-Speravo di trovarvi qui
• **Rodolfo** (baritone • tenor)
-Ah, Mimì, tu più non torni

Marco *The Gondoliers* (Sullivan)
• **Giuseppe** (tenor • baritone)
-We're called gondolieri

Mařenka *Prodaná Nevěsta*
[*The Bartered Bride*] (Smetana)
• **Jeník** (soprano • tenor)
-Jako matka [Like a mother]
• **Vašek** (soprano • tenor)
-Známť já jednu dívčinu
[I know a girl who burns for you]

Margherita *Mefistofele* (Boito)
• **Faust** (soprano • tenor)
-Lontano, lontano

Marguerite *Faust* (Gounod)
• **Faust, Dr.** (soprano • tenor)
-Laisse-moi contempler ton
visage/O nuit/Partez, partez
-Oui, c'est toi je t'aime

Maria [Marie] *La Fille du régiment*
[*La figlia del reggimento*] (Donizetti)
• **Sulpizio** [Sulpice] (soprano • baritone)
-Apparvi alla luce [Au bruit de la guerre]

Maria *West Side Story* (Bernstein)
• **Tony** (soprano • tenor)
-One Hand, One Heart

Maria Stuarda *Maria Stuarda* (Donizetti)
• **Elisabetta** [Queen] (soprano • soprano)
-Morta al mondo
• **Leicester** (soprano • tenor)
-Da tutti abbandonata
-Io ti rivedo/Ah! se un giorno
• **Talbot** (soprano • bass)
-Quando di luce rosea
• **Tonio** (soprano • tenor)
-A voti così ardente [De cet aveu si tendre]

Marie [Maria] *La fille du régiment*
   [*La figlia del reggimento*] (Donizetti)
• **Sulpice** [Sulpizio] (soprano • baritone)
   -Au bruit de la guerre [Apparvi alla luce]
• **Tonio** (soprano • tenor)
   -De cet aveu si tendre [A voti così ardente]

Marie *Zar und Zimmermann* (Lortzing)
• **Ivanov** (soprano • tenor)
   -Darf eine nied're Magd es wagen

Marie, Electress *Der Vogelhändler* (Zeller)
• **Adam** (soprano • tenor)
   -Schenkt man sich Rosen in Tirol

Marietta *Die tote Stadt* (Korngold)
• **Paul** (soprano • tenor)
   -Die Kinder sind's
   -Glück, das mir verlieb
   -O Tanz, o Rausch
   -Wunderbar! Ja, wunderbar

Marina *Boris Godunov* (Musorgsky)
• **Dmitry** (mezzo-soprano • tenor)
   -Dmitry! Tsarevich!

Mark *The Midsummer Marriage* (Tippett)
• **Jenifer** (tenor • soprano)
   -Jenifer, Jenifer, my darling
   -Sirius rising as the sun's wheel

Marta *Tiefland* (Albert)
• **Pedro** (soprano • tenor)
   -Das Essen ist da
   -Das Tor ist zu, Wir sind allein
• **Sebastiano** (soprano • baritone)
   -Marta!...Tu mit mir, was du willst

Martio *Sant'Alessio* (Landi)
   (Both roles may have been sung originally by castrati.)
• **Curtio** (soprano • soprano)
   -Poca voglia di far bene

Marzelline *Fidelio* (Beethoven)
• **Jaquino** (soprano • tenor)
   -Jetzt, Schätzchen, jetzt sind wir allein
• **Leonore** (soprano • soprano)
   (Marzelline is a soubrette-lyric;
     Leonore is a full dramatic.)
   -Um in der Ehe froh zu leben

Masniello *La muette de Portici* (Auber)
• **Pietro** (tenor • bass)
   -Mieux vaut mourir que rester miserable!

Massimiliano [Count Moor] *I Masnadieri* (Verdi)
• **Amalia** (bass • soprano)
   -Carlo! io muoio
• **Carlo** (bass • tenor)
   -Come il bacio d'un padre amoroso

Mathilde *Guillaume Tell* (Rossini)
• **Arnold** (soprano • tenor)
   -Oui, vous l'arrachez à mon âme

   -Pour notre amour plus d'espérance/
    Sur la rive étrangère

Matilda *Elisabetta* (Rossini)
• **Elisabetta** [Queen] (soprano • soprano)
   -Pensa che sol per poco sospendo l'ira mia
• **Leicester** (soprano • tenor)
   -Incauta, che festi!

Maurizio *Adriana Lecouvreur* (Cilea)
• **Adriana Lecouvreur** (tenor • soprano)
   -Perdona! perdona/No, più nobile sei
   -Tu sei la mia vittoria

Médée *Médée* (Chérubini)
• **Créon** (soprano • bass)
   -Ah! du moins à Médée
• **Jason** (soprano • tenor)
   -O fatale Toison
   -Perfides ennemis [Nemici senza cor]

Medora *Il corsaro* (Verdi)
• **Corrado** (soprano • tenor)
   -No, tu non sai/Tornerai, ma forse spenta

Medoro *Orlando Paladino* (Haydn)
• **Angelica** (tenor • soprano)
   -Qual contento

Mefistofele *Mefistofele* (Boito)
• **Faust** (bass • tenor)
   -Se tu mi doni un'ora

Melanto *Il ritorno d'Ulisse in patria* (Monteverdi)
• **Eurimaco** (soprano • tenor)
   -Dolce mia vita sei

Mélisande *Pelléas et Mélisande* (Debussy)
• **Golaud** (mezzo-soprano • baritone)
   -Ah! ah! tout va bien
   -Je ne pourrai plus sortir
• **Pelléas** (mezzo-soprano • tenor)
   -Mes longs cheveux descendant

Melitone, Fra *La forza del destino* (Verdi)
• **Guardiano** [Padre] (baritone • bass)
   -Del mondo i disinganni

Méphisthophélès *Faust* (Gounod)
• **Faust, Dr.** (bass • tenor)
   -Me voici

Micaëla *Carmen* (Bizet)
• **José, Don** (soprano • tenor)
   -Parle-moi de ma mère

Michele *Il Tabarro* (Puccini)
• **Giorgetta** (baritone • soprano)
   -Perchè, perchè non m'ami più?/Resta vicino a me

Michonnet *Adriana Lecouvreur* (Cilea)
• **Adriana Lecouvreur** (baritone • soprano)
   -Bambina, non ti crucciar

Mignon *Mignon* (Thomas)
• **Lothario** (mezzo-soprano • bass)
  -As-tu souffert?/As-tu pleuré?
  -Légères hirondelles
• **Wilhelm Meister** (mezzo-soprano • tenor)
  -Je suis heureuse! l'air m'enivre

Milada *Dalibor* (Smetana)
• **Dalibor** (soprano • tenor)
  -O nevýslovné štěstí lásky
   [O the unutterable happiness]

Miller *Luisa Miller* (Verdi)
• **Luisa** (baritone • soprano)
  -La tomba è un letto/Di rughe/
   Andrem, raminghi e poveri

Milovzor [Daphnis] [Pauline] *Pikovaya dama*
   [*Pique Dame*] [*The Queen of Spades*] (Tchaikovsky)
• **Liza** (contralto • soprano)
  -Uzh vecher, oblakov pomerknuli kraya

Mimì *La Bohème* (Puccini)
• **Marcello** (soprano • baritone)
  -Speravo di trovarvi qui
• **Rodolfo** (soprano • tenor)
  -O soave fanciulla

Minette *The English Cat* (Henze)
• **Tom** [Cat] (soprano • baritone)
  -Ah Minette, at last we meet in death
  -Promise Duet [commonly known title]
  -Why does beauty bring desire?

Minnie *La fanciulla del West* (Puccini)
• **Dick Johnson** [Ramerrez] (soprano • tenor)
  -Io non son che una povera fanciulla

Mireille *Mireille* (Gounod)
• **Vincenette** (soprano • soprano)
  -Ah! parle encore
• **Vincent** (soprano • tenor)
  -La brise est douce et parfumée [Chanson de Magali]
  -Vincenette a votre âge

Monica *The Medium* (Menotti)
• **Baba** [Madame Flora] (soprano • contralto)
  -O Black Swan

Montfort [Montforte] *Les vêpres siciliennes*
   [*I vespri siciliani*] (Verdi)
• **Henri** [Arrigo] (baritone • tenor)
  -Quand ma bonté toujours nouvelle
   [Quando al mio sen]

Montforte [Montfort] *I vespri siciliani*
   [*Les vêpres siciliennes*] (Verdi)
• **Arrigo** [Henri] (baritone • tenor)
  -Quando al mio sen [Quand ma
   bonté toujours nouvelle]

Montschi *Ein Walzertraum* (Straus)
• **Niki** (baritone • tenor)
  -Leise, ganz leise

Mother *Amahl and the Night Visitors* (Menotti)
• **Amahl** (soprano • treble)
  -Don't cry, mother dear

Musiklehrer, Ein [A Music Master]
   Ariadne auf Naxos (Strauss)
• **Komponist, Der** [The Composer]
   (baritone • mezzo-soprano)
  -Musik ist eine heilige Kunst

Mustafà *Girello* (Stradella)
   (Mustafà is a pants role for soprano.)
• **Girello** (soprano • bass)
  -O felice Mustafà/O Girello in povertà

Mustafà *L'italiana in Algeri* (Rossini)
• **Isabella** (bass • contralto)
  -O che muso, che figura!
• **Lindoro** (bass • tenor)
  -Se inclinassi a prender moglie

Mylio *Le roi d'Ys* (Lalo)
• **Rozenn** (tenor • soprano)
  -A l'autel j'allais rayonnant

Nabucco *Nabucco* (Verdi)
• **Abigaille** (baritone • soprano)
  -Donna? chi sei?/Oh di qual'onta
   aggravasi/Deh perdona

Nadir *Les pêcheurs de perles* (Bizet)
• **Leïla** (tenor • soprano)
  -O dieu Brahma!
  -O lumière sainte
  -Ton coeur n'a pas compris le mien
• **Zurga** (tenor • baritone)
  -Au fond du temple saint

Nancy *Martha* (Flotow)
• **Harriet Durham, Lady** (mezzo-soprano • soprano)
  -Von den edlen Kavalieren

Nannetta *Falstaff* (Verdi)
• **Fenton** (soprano • tenor)
  -Labbra di foco

Nanni *L'infedeltà delusa* (Haydn)
• **Vespina** (bass • soprano)
  -Son disperato

Nedda *Pagliacci* (Leoncavallo)
• **Silvio** [Campagnuolo] [A Villager] (soprano • baritone)
  -Silvio! a quest'ora/E allor perchè, dì, tu m'hai stregato
• **Tonio** (soprano • bass-baritone)
  -So ben che difforme

Nemorino *L'elisir d'amore* (Donizetti)
• **Adina** (tenor • soprano)
  -Chiedi all'aura lusinghiera
• **Belcore** (tenor • baritone)
  -Venti scudi
• **Dulcamara, Dr.** (tenor • bass)
  -Obbligato, ah, sì! obbligato!

Nerone *L'incoronazione di Poppea* (Monteverdi)
(Nerone, originally for soprano castrato,
is soprano or mezzo-soprano today.)
• **Lucano** (mezzo-soprano • tenor)
-Bocca, bocca
• **Poppea** (mezzo-soprano • soprano)
-Idolo del cor mio
-Ne più s'interporà
-Pur ti miro

Nicette *Le Pré aux Clercs* (Hérold)
• **Girot** (soprano • tenor)
-Les rendez-vous de noble compagnie

Nick Shadow *The Rake's Progress* (Stravinsky)
• **Tom Rakewell** (bass-baritone • tenor)
-How dark and dreadful is this place
-My tale shall be told both by young and by old
-Thanks to this excellent device

Nicklausse *Les contes d'Hoffmann* (Offenbach)
(Both roles can be sung by either
soprano or mezzo-soprano.)
• **Giulietta** (mezzo-soprano • mezzo-soprano)
-Belle nuit, ô nuit d'amour [Barcarolle]

Niki *Ein Walzertraum* (Straus)
• **Hélène** (tenor • soprano)
-O, du lieber, o du g'scheiter
• **Montschi** (tenor • baritone)
-Leise, ganz leise

Ninetta *La gazza ladra* (Rossini)
• **Fernando Villabella** (soprano • bass-baritone)
-Come frenar il pianto!
• **Giannetto** (soprano • tenor)
-Forse un dì conoscerete
• **Pippo** (soprano • contralto)
-E ben, per mia memoria

Nino *Astarto* (Bononcini)
(Originally written for castrati.)
• **Sidonia** (tenor • soprano)
-Mio caro ben non sospirar

Norfolk *Elisabetta* (Rossini)
• **Elisabetta** [Queen] (tenor • soprano)
-Perchè mai, destin crudel
• **Leicester** (tenor • tenor)
-Deh, scusa i trasporti

Norina *Don Pasquale* (Donizetti)
• **Ernesto** (soprano • tenor)
-Tornami a dir che m'ami
• **Malatesta, Dr.** (soprano • baritone)
-Pronta io son

Norma *Norma* (Bellini)
• **Adalgisa** (soprano • mezzo-soprano)
(Adalgisa is sung by either
soprano or mezzo-soprano.)
-Ah! sì, fa core e abbracciami
-Mira, o Norma/Sì, fino all'ore estreme

• **Pollione** (soprano • tenor)
-In mia man alfin tu sei
-Qual cor tradisti

Nureddin *Der Barbier von Bagdad* (Cornelius)
• **Abul** (tenor • bass)
-Mars und Merkur
• **Bostana** (tenor • mezzo-soprano)
-Wenn zum Gebet

Ochs auf Lerchenau, Baron
Der Rosenkavalier (Strauss)
• **Annina** (bass • contralto)
-Da lieg' ich! Was einem Kavalier
• **Octavian, genannt Quinquin**
[Count Rofrano] (bass • soprano)
-Nein, nein! I' trink' kein Wein

Octavian, genannt Quinquin
[Count Rofrano] *Der Rosenkavalier* (Strauss)
(Octavian is sung by either soprano or mezzo-soprano.)
• **Feldmarschallin Fürstin Werdenberg, Die** [Marie
Thérèse] [Marschallin] (mezzo-soprano • soprano)
-Ach! du bist wieder da
-Lachst du mich aus?
• **Ochs auf Lerchenau, Baron** (soprano • bass)
-Nein, nein! I' trink' kein Wein
• **Sophie** (mezzo-soprano • soprano)
-Ich kenn' Ihn schon recht wohl
-Ist ein Traum, kann nicht wirklich?
-Mir ist die Ehre widerfahren/Mit Ihren Augen voll
Tränen [Presentation of the Rose]

Octavio *Giuditta* (Lehár)
• **Giuditta** (tenor • soprano)
-Schön wie die blaue Sommernacht

Odabello *Attila* (Verdi)
• **Foresto** (soprano • tenor)
-Sì, quello io son, ravvisami/
Oh t'innebria nell'amplesso

Odarka *Zaparozhets za Dunayem* [A Cossack
beyond the Danube] (Gulak-Artemovsky)
• **Karas** [Zaparozhets] (soprano • bass)
-Quarrel Duet [commonly known title]

Ol'ga *Yevgeny Onegin* [Eugene Onegin] (Tchaikovsky)
• **Tat'yana** (contralto • soprano)
-Slikhalil' vï...vdokhnulil' vï [Have you not
heard...not sighed]

Ophélie *Hamlet* (Thomas)
• **Hamlet** (soprano • baritone)
-Doute de la lumière

Orest *Elektra* (Strauss)
• **Elektra** (baritone • soprano)
-Orest! Orest! Orest!
-Was willst du, fremder Mensch?

Oreste *Oreste* (Handel)
(Oreste was originally written
for mezzo-soprano castrato.)
• **Ermione** (mezzo-soprano • soprano)
-Farewell Duet [commonly known title]

Orfeo *L'anima del filosofo* (Haydn)
• **Euridice** (tenor • soprano)
-Come il foco allo splendore

Orfeo *Orfeo ed Euridice* [*Orphée et Eurydice*] (Gluck)
(Orfeo's role was originally for alto castrato,
and is tenor in the French version. Orfeo is
often sung by a mezzo-soprano.)
• **Euridice** [Eurydice] (contralto • soprano)
-Avvezza al contento [Je goûtais les charmes]
-Vieni, appaga il tuo consorte [Viens, suis un époux]

Orombello *Beatrice di Tenda* (Bellini)
• **Beatrice** (tenor • soprano)
-Ah! d'immenso, estremo affetto

Oronte *I Lombardi* (Verdi)
• **Giselda** (tenor • soprano)
-Oh belle, a questa misera/Ah, vieni, sol morte

Orphée [Orfeo] *Orphée et Eurydice*
[*Orfeo ed Euridice*] (Gluck)
(The role of Orphée was originally
for alto castrato in the Italian version.)
• **Eurydice** [Euridice] (tenor • soprano)
-Je goûtais les charmes [Avvezza al contento]
-Viens, suis un époux [Vieni, appaga il tuo consorte]

Ory, Le Comte [Count] *Le comte Ory* (Rossini)
• **Adèle di Formouters, La Comtesse** [Countess]
(tenor • soprano)
-Ah! quel respect, Madame
• **Isolier** [Page] (tenor • mezzo-soprano)
-Je vais revoir

Osaka *Iris* (Mascagni)
• **Iris** (tenor • soprano)
-Or dammi il braccio tuo

Osmin *Die Entführung aus dem Serail* (Mozart)
• **Belmonte** (bass • tenor)
-Wer ein Liebchen hat gefunden
• **Blonde** (bass • soprano)
-Ich gehe, doch rate ich dir
• **Pedrillo** (bass • tenor)
-Vivat Bacchus

Otello *Otello* (Rossini)
• **Desdemona** (tenor • mezzo-soprano)
-Eccomi giunto inosservato e solo/A te sarà
• **Rodrigo** (tenor • tenor)
-Non m'inganno; al mio rivale

Otello *Otello* (Verdi)
• **Desdemona** (tenor • soprano)
-Dio ti giocondi, o sposo
-Già nella notte densa
-Quando narravi l'esule tua vita/E tu m'amavi

• **Iago** (tenor • baritone)
-Sì, pel ciel

Ottavio, Don *Don Giovanni* (Mozart)
(Don Ottavio is a light lyric tenor,
but Donna Anna is a dramatic soprano.)
• **Anna, Donna** (tenor • soprano)
-Fuggi, crudele, fuggi!

Ouf *L'étoile du Nord* (Chabrier)
• **Siroco** (tenor • bass)
-Je me sens, hélas, tout chose

Paganini *Paganini* (Lehár)
• **Anna Elisa** (tenor • soprano)
-Niemand liebt dich so wie ich

Palmide *Il crociato in Egitto* (Meyerbeer)
• **Armando** (soprano • soprano)
(Armando, a pants role, was
originally sung by a castrato.)
-Ravisa qual alma

Pamina *Die Zauberflöte* (Mozart)
• **Papageno** (soprano • baritone)
-Bei Männern, welche Liebe fühlen

Pandolphe *Cendrillon* (Massenet)
• **Cendrillon** (bass • mezzo-soprano)
-Printemps revient

Paolina *Poliuto* (Donizetti)
• **Poliuto** (soprano • tenor)
-Il suon dell'arpe angeliche [Conversion Duet]

Paolino *Il matrimonio segreto* (Cimarosa)
• **Carolina** (tenor • soprano)
-Cara non dubitar/Io ti lascio

Papagena *Die Zauberflöte* (Mozart)
• **Papageno** (soprano • baritone)
-Pa-pa-pa-

Papageno *Die Zauberflöte* (Mozart)
• **Pamina** (baritone • soprano)
-Bei Männern, welche Liebe fühlen
• **Papagena** (baritone • soprano)
-Pa-pa-pa-

Paride *Paride ed Elena* (Gluck)
(Paride, originally for soprano castrato,
is sung by tenor or soprano.)
• **Elena** (tenor [soprano] • soprano)
-Ah ferma!...Ah senti!
-L'amo! L'adoro!
• **Erasto** (tenor • soprano)
-Ma, chi sei?

Paride *Il pomo d'oro* (Cesti)
• **Ennone** (tenor • soprano)
-O mia vita! O mia core

Parsifal *Parsifal* (Wagner)
• **Gurnemanz** (tenor • bass)
-Wie dünkt mich doch die Aue heut' so schön

Pasquale *Orlando Paladino* (Haydn)
• **Eurilla** (baritone • soprano)
  -Quel tuo visetto amabile

Pasquale, Don *Don Pasquale* (Donizetti)
• **Ernesto** (bass • tenor)
  -Prender moglie!
• **Malatesta, Dr.** (bass • baritone)
  -Cheti, cheti, immantinente/
  Aspetta, aspetta, cara sposina

Patience *Patience* (Sullivan)
• **Grosvenor** (soprano • baritone)
  -Prithee, pretty maiden

Paul *Die tote Stadt* (Korngold)
• **Marietta** (tenor • soprano)
  -Die Kinder sind's
  -Glück, das mir verlieb
  -O Tanz, o Rausch
  -Wunderbar! Ja, wunderbar

Pavel *Virineya* (Slonimsky)
• **Virineya** (bass-baritone • soprano)
  -Vsyo na zemle dlyz schast' ya roditsya
  [Everything is born for love]

Pedrillo *Die Entführung aus dem Serail* (Mozart)
• **Osmin** (tenor • bass)
  -Vivat Bacchus

Pedro *Tiefland* (Albert)
• **Marta** (tenor • soprano)
  -Das Essen ist da
  -Das Tor ist zu, Wir sind allein

Pelléas *Pelléas et Mélisande* (Debussy)
• **Mélisande** (tenor • mezzo-soprano)
  -Mes longs cheveux descendant

Pénélope *Pénélope* (Fauré)
• **Eumée** (soprano • baritone)
  -C'est sur ce banc
• **Ulysse** (soprano • tenor)
  -D'où viens-tu?
  -Si vous le permettiez, princes/Ulysse!

Périchole, La *La Périchole* (Offenbach)
• **Piquillo** (mezzo-soprano • tenor)
  -Il grandira, car il est espagnol

Peter Grimes *Peter Grimes* (Britten)
• **Balstrode, Captain** (tenor • bass-baritone)
  -And do you prefer the storm to Auntie's parlour?

Petronio *I filosofi immaginari* (Paisiello)
• **Giuliano** (bass • baritone)
  -Coughing Duet [commonly known title]

Philine *Mignon* (Thomas)
• **Wilhelm Meister** (soprano • tenor)
  -Je crois entendre les doux compliments

Philip II, King [Filippo II]
  Don Carlos [*Don Carlo*] (Verdi)
• **Grande Inquisitore, Il**
  [The Grand Inquisitor] (bass • bass)
  -Suis-je devant le roi?/Dans ce beau pays
  [Son io dinanzi al rè?]
• **Rodrigue** [Le Marquis de Posa] [Rodrigo
  [Marchese di Posa]] (bass • baritone)
  -O Roi! j'arrive de Flandre/Est-ce la paix que vous
  donnez? [O signor, di Fiandra arrivo]
  -Pour mon pays/Un souffle ardent/
  Enfant! à mon coeur

Pierotto *Linda di Chamounix* (Donizetti)
• **Linda** (contralto • soprano)
  -Al bel destin che attendevi

Pierrino *Giuditta* (Lehár)
• **Anita** (tenor • soprano)
  -Zwei, die sich lieben, vergessen die Welt

Pietro *La muette de Portici* (Auber)
• **Masniello** (bass • tenor)
  -Mieux vaut mourir que rester miserable!

Pimen *Boris Godunov* (Musorgsky)
• **Grigory** (bass • tenor)
  -Just think, my son [commonly known title]

Pimpinone *Pimpinone* (Albinoni)
• **Vespetta** (bass • mezzo-soprano)
  -Quarrel Duet [commonly known title]

Pinkerton *Madama Butterfly* (Puccini)
• **Cio-Cio-San** [Madama Butterfly] (tenor • soprano)
  -Bimba dagli occhi pieni di malià
  -Viene la sera
• **Sharpless** (tenor • baritone)
  -Amore o grillo

Pippo *La gazza ladra* (Rossini)
• **Ninetta** (contralto • soprano)
  -E ben, per mia memoria

Piquillo *La Périchole* (Offenbach)
• **Périchole, La** (tenor • mezzo-soprano)
  -Il grandira, car il est espagnol

Pistofolo [Notaio] *La molinara* (Paisiello)
• **Rachelina** (bass • soprano)
  -Il mio garzone il piffaro sonava

Pizarro, Don *Fidelio* (Beethoven)
• **Rocco** (bass-baritone • bass)
  -Jetzt, Alter, jetzt hat es Eile!

Plumkett *Martha* (Flotow)
• **Lyonel** (bass • tenor)
  -Ja, seit früher Kindheit Tagen

Poliuto *Poliuto* (Donizetti)
• **Paolina** (tenor • soprano)
  -Il suon dell'arpe angeliche [Conversion Duet]

Pollione *Norma* (Bellini)
• **Adalgisa** (tenor • mezzo-soprano)
  -Va, crudele, al dio spietato/Vieni in Roma
• **Norma** (tenor • soprano)
  -In mia man alfin tu sei
  -Qual cor tradisti

Pollux *Castor et Pollux* (Rameau)
• **Telaïre** (bass • soprano)
  -Sortez de l'esclavage

Polly Peachum *The Beggar's Opera* (Pepusch)
• **Lucy Lockit** (soprano • soprano)
  -Hi there, dear husband
  -I'm bubbled!
• **Macheath** (soprano • baritone)
  -Pretty Polly, say

Pontifex Maximus *La vestale* (Spontini)
• **Licinius** (bass • tenor)
  -C'est à toi de trembler

Poppea *L'incoronazione di Poppea* (Monteverdi)
• **Nerone** (soprano • mezzo-soprano)
  (Nerone, originally for soprano castrato,
    is soprano or mezzo-soprano today.)
  -Idolo del cor mio
  -Ne più s'interporà
  -Pur ti miro

Porgy *Porgy and Bess* (Gershwin)
• **Bess** (bass-baritone • soprano)
  -Bess, you is my woman

Prima Donna/Ariadne *Ariadne auf Naxos* (Strauss)
• **Bacchus** (soprano • tenor)
  -Ich grüsse dich, du Bote

Prince *Cendrillon* (Massenet)
  (The Prince was composed for a soprano,
  but today is always sung by a tenor.)
• **Cendrillon** (tenor • mezzo-soprano)
  -Toi qui m'es apparue
  -Viens, nous quitterons cette ville

Principessa di Bouillon, La
  [The Princess of Bouillon]
  Adriana Lecouvreur (Cilea)
• **Adriana Lecouvreur** (mezzo-soprano • soprano)
  -Io son sua per l'amor

Quichotte, Don *Don Quichotte* (Massenet)
• **Dulcinée** (bass • mezzo-soprano)
  -Oui, je souffre votre tendresse

Rachelina *La molinara* (Paisiello)
• **Pistofolo** [Notaio] (soprano • bass)
  -Il mio garzone il piffaro sonava

Radames *Aïda* (Verdi)
• **Aïda** (tenor • soprano)
  -Vedi?...di morte l'angelo/O terra addio
• **Amneris** (tenor • mezzo-soprano)
  -Ah! tu dei vivere/Che ti salva
  -Quale inchiesta!

Ragonde *Le comte Ory* (Rossini)
• **Adèle di Formouters, La Comtesse** [Countess]
  (mezzo-soprano • soprano)
  -Dans ce séjour

Raimbaut *Robert le Diable* (Meyerbeer)
• **Bertram** (tenor • bass)
  -Ah! l'honnête homme!

Ramiro, Don *La Cenerentola* (Rossini)
• **Cenerentola** [Angelica] (tenor • mezzo-soprano)
  -Un soave non so che
• **Dandini** (tenor • bass)
  -Zitto, zitto, piano, piano

Raoul *Les Huguenots* (Meyerbeer)
• **Valentine** (tenor • mezzo-soprano)
  -O ciel! où courez-vous?/Tu l'as dit
  [O ciel! dove vai tu?]

Reich, Frau [Mrs. Page] *Die lustigen*
  Weiber von Windsor (Nicolai)
• **Fluth, Frau** [Mrs. Ford] (contralto • soprano)
  -Nein, das ist wirklich doch zu keck!

Reich, Herr [Mr. Page] *Die lustigen*
  Weiber von Windsor (Nicolai)
• **Fenton** (bass • tenor)
  -So geht indes hinein

Rezia *L'incontro improvviso* (Haydn)
• **Ali** (soprano • tenor)
  -Son quest'occhi un stral d'Amore

Riccardo *Un ballo in maschera* (Verdi)
• **Amelia** (tenor • soprano)
  -Non sai tu che se l'anima mia/Oh qual soave brivido

Riccardo *I Puritani* (Bellini)
• **Giorgio** (baritone • bass)
  -Il rival salvar tu dêi/Suoni la tromba intrepida

Rienzi *Rienzi* (Wagner)
• **Irene** (tenor • soprano)
  -Verlässt die Kirche mich/Wohl liebst auch ich

Rigoletto *Rigoletto* (Verdi)
• **Gilda** (baritone • soprano)
  -Den non parlare al misero/Ah! veglia, o donna
  -Piangi, fanciulla, piangi!
  -Tutte le feste al tempio/
    Sì, vendetta, tremenda vendetta
  -V'ho ingannato!/Lassù, in cielo

Rinaldo *Armida* (Haydn)
• **Armida** (tenor • soprano)
  -Cara, sarò fedele

Robert le Diable *Robert le Diable* (Meyerbeer)
• **Bertram** (tenor • bass)
  -Des chevaliers de ma patrie
• **Isabelle** (tenor • soprano)
  -Avec bonté voyez ma peine

Roberto *Le villi* (Puccini)
• **Anna** (tenor • soprano)
-Tu dall'infanzia mia

Robinson, Count *Il matrimonio segreto* (Cimarosa)
(Count Robinson can be sung
by either baritone or bass.)
• **Geronimo** (bass • bass)
-Se fiato in corpo avete

Rocco *Fidelio* (Beethoven)
• **Leonore** (bass • soprano)
-Nur hurtig fort, nur frisch gegraben
• **Pizarro, Don** (bass • bass-baritone)
-Jetzt, Alter, jetzt hat es Eile!

Rodelinda *Rodelinda* (Handel)
• **Bertarido** (soprano • contralto)
(The role of Bertarido was
originally sung by an alto castrato.)
-Io t'abbraccio: è più che morte

Rodolfo *La Bohème* (Puccini)
• **Marcello** (tenor • baritone)
-Ah, Mimì, tu più non torni
• **Mimì** (tenor • soprano)
-O soave fanciulla

Rodolfo *Luisa Miller* (Verdi)
• **Federica** (tenor • contralto)
-Dall'aule raggianti/Deh! la parola amara
• **Luisa** (tenor • soprano)
-Piangi, piangi, il tuo dolore/
Maledetto il dì ch'io nacqui

Rodrigo [Marchese di Posa] [Rodrigue [Le Marquis
de Posa] *Don Carlo* [*Don Carlos*] (Verdi)
• **Carlo, Don** [Don Carlos] (baritone • tenor)
-Dio, che nell'alma infondere
[Dieu tu semas dans nos âmes]
• **Filippo II** [King Philip II] (baritone • bass)
-O signor, di Fiandra arrivo
[O Roi! j'arrive de Flandre]

Rodrigo *Otello* (Rossini)
• **Iago** (tenor • bass-baritone)
(Iago was written for either tenor or bass-baritone.)
-No, non temer/Se uniti negli affanni
• **Otello** (tenor • tenor)
-Non m'inganno; al mio rivale

Rodrigue [Le Marquis de Posa] [Rodrigo [Marchese
di Posa]] *Don Carlos* [*Don Carlo*] (Verdi)
• **Carlos, Don** [Don Carlo] (baritone • tenor)
-Dieu tu semas dans nos âmes
[Dio, che nell'alma infondere]
-Le voilà, c'est l'infant/Toi! mon Rodrigue! c'est toi
• **Philip II, King** [Filippo II] (baritone • bass)
-O Roi! j'arrive de Flandre/Est-ce la paix que
vous donnez? [O signor, di Fiandra arrivo]
-Pour mon pays/Un souffle ardent/
Enfant! à mon coeur

Rolando *La battaglia di Legnano* (Verdi)
• **Arrigo** (baritone • tenor)
-Ben vi scorgo
• **Lida** (baritone • soprano)
-Digli ch'è sangue italico

Romeo *I Capuleti e i Montecchi* (Bellini)
• **Giulietta** (mezzo-soprano • soprano)
-Sì, fuggire: a noi non resta/Ah! crudel d'onor ragioni
-Soccorso, sostegno accordate/Non si pianga
• **Tebaldo** (mezzo-soprano • tenor)
-Ella è morta, o sciagurato
-Stolto! a un sol mio grido

Roméo *Roméo et Juliette* (Gounod)
• **Juliette** (tenor • soprano)
-Ah! ne fuis pas encore
-Ange adorable
-O nuit divine
-Va! je t'ai pardonné/Nuit d'hyménée!/Il faut partir
-Viens! fuyons au bout au monde

Rosalinde *Die Fledermaus* (Johann Strauss)
• **Eisenstein** (soprano • tenor)
-Dieser Anstand, so manierlich [Watch Duet]

Rosario *Goyescas* (Granados)
• **Fernando** (soprano • tenor)
-Coloquio en la reja

Rose *Street Scene* (Weill)
• **Sam** (soprano • tenor)
-Do you remember
-Remember that I care

Rosina *Il barbiere di Siviglia* (Paisiello)
• **Almaviva, Il Conte di/Lindoro** (soprano • tenor)
-Cara sei tu il mio bene

Rosina *Il barbiere di Siviglia* (Rossini)
• **Figaro** (contralto • baritone)
-Dunque io son?

Rosina *La vera Costanza* (Haydn)
• **Errico** (soprano • tenor)
-Rosina vezzosina

Rosmene *Imeneo* (Handel)
• **Tirinto** (soprano • mezzo-soprano)
-Per le porte

Rozenn *Le roi d'Ys* (Lalo)
• **Mylio** (soprano • tenor)
-A l'autel j'allais rayonnant

Ruggero *La rondine* (Puccini)
• **Magda** (tenor • soprano)
-Ma come puoi lasciarmi
-Perchè mai cercate

Sally *Thomas and Sally* (Arne)
• **Squire, The** (soprano • tenor)
-Well met, pretty maid

Salomé *Hérodiade* (Massenet)
• **Jean** [John the Baptist] (soprano • tenor)
  -Ce que je veux
  -Quand nos jours s'éteindront

Salome *Salome* (Strauss)
• **Jochanaan** (soprano • bass-baritone)
  -Jochanaan, ich bin verliebt

Sam *Street Scene* (Weill)
• **Rose** (tenor • soprano)
  -Do you remember
  -Remember that I care

Samson *Samson et Dalila* (Saint-Saëns)
• **Dalila** (tenor • contralto)
  -En ces lieux/Samson, ô toi, mon bien-aimé

Sandrina *La finta Giardiniera* (Mozart)
• **Belfiore** (soprano • tenor)
  -Tu mi lasci?

Santuzza *Cavalleria rusticana* (Mascagni)
• **Alfio** (mezzo-soprano • baritone)
  -Ad essi non perdono
  -Oh, il Signore vi manda
  -Turiddu mi tolse
• **Turiddu** (soprano • tenor)
  -No, no Turiddu, rimani
  -Tu qui, Santuzza?

Saphir *Barbe-bleue* (Offenbach)
• **Fleurette** (tenor • soprano)
  -Tous les deux, amoureux

Scylla *Scylla et Glaucus* (Leclair)
• **Glaucus** (soprano • tenor)
  (Glaucus was written originally for haute-contre.)
  -Que le tendre amour nous engage

Sebastiano *Tiefland* (Albert)
• **Marta** (baritone • soprano)
  -Marta!...Tu mit mir, was du willst

Sébastien *Dom Sébastien* (Donizetti)
• **Zayda** (tenor • mezzo-soprano)
  -Grand Dieu! sa misère est si grande!

Second Woman *Dido and Aeneas* (Purcell)
• **Belinda** (mezzo-soprano • soprano)
  -Fear no danger

Seid *Il corsaro* (Verdi)
• **Corrado** (baritone • tenor)
  -Di': que' ribaldi tremano
• **Gulnara** (baritone • soprano)
  -Vieni, Gulnara!/Sia l'istante maledetto

Seleuce *Tolomeo* (Handel)
• **Tolomeo** (soprano • contralto)
  (The role of Tolomeo was
  originally sung by an alto castrato.)
  -Dite, che fà, dov'è
  -Io t'abbraccio: è più che morte

Sélika *L'africaine* (Meyerbeer)
• **Vasco da Gama** (soprano • tenor)
  -O transports, ô douce extase

Selim *Il turco in Italia* (Rossini)
• **Fiorilla** (bass • soprano)
  -Credete alla femmine

Semiramide *Semiramide* (Rossini)
• **Arsace** (soprano • contralto)
  -Giorno d'orrore
  -Se la vita ancor t'è cara
  -Serbami ognor sì fido/Alle più calde immagini
• **Assur** (soprano • bass)
  -Quella ricordati

Senta *Der fliegende Holländer* (Wagner)
• **Erik** (soprano • tenor)
  -Was musst' ich hören, Gott
• **Holländer, Der** [The Dutchman] (soprano • baritone)
  -Wie aus der Ferne längst vergang'n Zeiten

Serpina *Serva padrona, La* (Pergolesi)
• **Uberto** (soprano • bass)
  -Contento tu sarai [Reconciliation Duet]
  -Lo conosco a quegl'occhieti [Conflict Duet]
  -Per te ho io nel core

Servilia *La clemenza di Tito* (Mozart)
• **Annio** (soprano • mezzo-soprano)
  (Annio [a pants role] can be sung by
  either soprano or mezzo-soprano.)
  -Ah perdona al primo affetto

Sesto *La clemenza di Tito* (Mozart)
• **Annio** (mezzo-soprano • mezzo-soprano)
  (Annio [a pants role] can be sung by
  either soprano or mezzo-soprano.)
  -Deh prendi un dolce amplesso
• **Vitellia** (mezzo-soprano • mezzo-soprano)
  -Come ti piace, imponi

Sesto *Giulio Cesare in Egitto* (Handel)
  (Sesto, originally a castrato, can be
  sung by soprano or mezzo-soprano.)
• **Cornelia** (mezzo-soprano • contralto)
  -Son nata a lagrimar

Sharpless *Madama Butterfly* (Puccini)
• **Cio-Cio-San** [Madama Butterfly] (baritone • soprano)
  -Ora a noi
• **Pinkerton** (baritone • tenor)
  -Amore o grillo

Sherasmin *Oberon* (Weber)
• **Fatima** (baritone • mezzo-soprano)
  -On the banks of the sweet Garonne

Sidonia *Astarto* (Bononcini)
  (Originally written for castrati.)
• **Nino** (soprano • tenor)
  -Mio caro ben non sospirar

Siegfried *Götterdämmerung* (Wagner)
• **Gunther** (tenor • bass-baritone)
  -Blühenden Lebens labendes Blut

Sieglinde *Die Walküre* (Wagner)
• **Siegmund** (soprano • tenor)
  -O süsseste Wonne! seligstes Weib!

Siegmund *Die Walküre* (Wagner)
• **Brünnhilde** (tenor • soprano)
  -Siegmund! Sieh' auf mich
• **Sieglinde** (tenor • soprano)
  -O süsseste Wonne! seligstes Weib!

Sifare *Mitridate* (Mozart)
  (Sifare was sung by either soprano (pants role) or tenor.)
• **Aspasia** (tenor • soprano)
  -Se viver non degg'io

Silvio [Campagnuolo] [A Villager]
  Pagliacci (Leoncavallo)
• **Nedda** (baritone • soprano)
  -Silvio! a quest'ora/E allor perchè, dì, tu m'hai stregato

Simon Boccanegra [The Doge of Genoa]
  Simon Boccanegra (Verdi)
• **Amelia** [Maria Boccanegra] (baritone • soprano)
  -Dinnè, perchè in quest'eremo/
  Figlia! a tal nome io palpito
• **Fiesco** (baritone • bass)
  -Delle faci festante al barlume/Piango, perchè mi parla
  -Qual cieco fato/Del mar sul lido

Siroco *L'étoile du Nord* (Chabrier)
• **Ouf** (bass • tenor)
  -Je me sens, hélas, tout chose

Somnus *Semele* (Handel)
• **Juno** (bass • contralto)
  -Obey my will

Sonja *Der Zarewitsch* (Lehár)
• **Zarewitsch, Der** [Tsarevich] (soprano • tenor)
  -Warum hat jeder Frühling, ach, nur einen Mai?

Sophie *Der Rosenkavalier* (Strauss)
• **Octavian, genannt Quinquin** [Count Rofrano]
  (soprano • mezzo-soprano)
  (Octavian is sung by either
  soprano or mezzo-soprano.)
  -Ich kenn' Ihn schon recht wohl
  -Ist ein Traum, kann nicht wirklich?
  -Mir ist die Ehre widerfahren/Mit Ihren
  Augen voll Tränen [Presentation of the Rose]

Sosarme *Sosarme* (Handel)
  (The role of Sosarme was originally
  sung by an alto castrato.)
• **Elmira** (contralto • soprano)
  -Per le porte del tormento
  -Tu caro sei il dolce mio tesoro

Squire, The *Thomas and Sally* (Arne)
• **Sally** (tenor • soprano)
  -Well met, pretty maid

Stankar *Stiffelio* (Verdi)
• **Lina** (baritone • soprano)
  -Ed io pure in faccia agl'uomini/Or meco venite

Stasi, Komtesse [Countess Stasi]
  Die Csárdásfürstin (Kálmán)
  (Komtesse Stasi is a soubrette.)
• **Edwin** (soprano • tenor)
  -Machen wir's den Schwalben nach

Stiffelio *Stiffelio* (Verdi)
• **Lina** (tenor • soprano)
  -Ah sì, voliamo al tempio

Sulpice [Sulpizio] *La fille du régiment*
  [*La figlia del reggimento*] (Donizetti)
• **Marie** [Maria] (baritone • soprano)
  -Au bruit de la guerre [Apparvi alla luce]

Sulpizio [Sulpice] *La figlia del reggimento*
  [*La fille du régiment*] (Donizetti)
• **Maria** [Marie] (baritone • soprano)
  -Apparvi alla luce [Au bruit de la guerre]

Susanna *Le nozze di Figaro* (Mozart)
• **Cherubino** (soprano • mezzo-soprano)
  (Cherubino is sung by either
  soprano or mezzo-soprano.)
  -Aprite, presto aprite [Escape Duet]
• **Almaviva, Il Conte di** [Count] (soprano • baritone)
  -Crudel! perchè finora
• **Almaviva, La Contessa di** [Rosina]
  (soprano • soprano)
  -Sull'aria/Che soave zefiretto [Letter Duet]
• **Figaro** (soprano • bass)
  -Cinque, dieci, venti
  -Se a caso Madama
• **Marcellina** (soprano • mezzo-soprano)
  (Marcellina is sung by either
  soprano or mezzo-soprano.)
  -Via resti servita

Suzel *L'amico Fritz* (Mascagni)
• **Fritz Kobus** (soprano • tenor)
  -Suzel, buon dì/Han della porpora vivo il colore

Suzuki *Madama Butterfly* (Puccini)
• **Cio-Cio-San** [Madama Butterfly]
  (mezzo-soprano • soprano)
  -Scuoti quella fronda di ciliegio/
  Tutti i fior [Flower Duet]

Sylva *Die Csárdásfürstin* (Kálmán)
• **Edwin** (soprano • tenor)
  -Tausend kleine Engel singen

Symon Rymanovicz *Der Bettelstudent* (Millöcker)
• **Jan** (tenor • baritone)
  -Die Welt hat das genialste
• **Laura** (tenor • soprano)
  -Ich setz den Fall

Taddeo *L'italiana in Algeri* (Rossini)
• **Isabella** (bass • contralto)
 -Ai capricci della sorte
• **Lindoro** (bass • tenor)
 -Pappataci!

Talbot *Maria Stuarda* (Donizetti)
• **Maria Stuarda** (bass • soprano)
 -Quando di luce rosea

Tasso *Torquato Tasso* (Donizetti)
• **Eleonora** (baritone • soprano)
 -Colei Sofronia

Tat'yana *Yevgeny Onegin*
 [*Eugene Onegin*] (Tchaikovsky)
• **Ol'ga** (soprano • contralto)
 -Slikhalil' vï...vdokhnulil' vï
 [Have you not heard...not sighed]
• **Yevgeny Onegin** [Eugene Onegin]
 (soprano • baritone)
 -My heart is worn with fear [commonly known title]
 -Onegin, I was then far younger
 [commonly known title]

Tebaldo *I Capuleti e i Montecchi* (Bellini)
• **Romeo** (tenor • mezzo-soprano)
 -Ella è morta, o sciagurato
 -Stolto! a un sol mio grido

Telaïre *Castor et Pollux* (Rameau)
• **Pollux** (soprano • bass)
 -Sortez de l'esclavage

Telemaco *Il ritorno d'Ulisse in patria* (Monteverdi)
• **Ulisse** (tenor • baritone)
 (Ulisse was sung by either tenor or baritone.)
 -O padre sospirato, o figlio desiato

Teresa *Benvenuto Cellini* (Berlioz)
• **Benvenuto Cellini** (soprano • tenor)
 -O Teresa, vous que j'aime plus que ma vie
 -Quand des sommets de la montagne

Thaïs *Thaïs* (Massenet)
• **Athanaël** (soprano • baritone)
 -Baigne d'eau mes mains
 -Te souvient-il du lumineux voyage [Méditation]

Thésée *Hippolyte et Aricie* (Rameau)
• **Tisiphone** (bass • tenor)
 (Tisiphone, tenor, was originally
 sung by haute-contre.)
 -Contente-toi d'une victime

Tirinto *Imeneo* (Handel)
• **Rosmene** (mezzo-soprano • soprano)
 -Per le porte

Tisiphone *Hippolyte et Aricie* (Rameau)
 (Tisiphone, tenor, was originally
 sung by haute-contre.)
• **Thésée** (tenor • bass)
 -Contente-toi d'une victime

Tolomeo *Tolomeo* (Handel)
 (The role of Tolomeo was originally
 sung by an alto castrato.)
• **Seleuce** (contralto • soprano)
 -Dite, che fà, dov'è
 -Io t'abbraccio: è più che morte

Tom [Cat] *The English Cat* (Henze)
• **Minette** (baritone • soprano)
 -Ah Minette, at last we meet in death
 -Promise Duet [commonly known title]
 -Why does beauty bring desire?

Tom Cat *l'Enfant et les sortilèges* (Ravel)
• **Female Cat** (baritone • mezzo-soprano)
 -Cat Duet [commonly known title]

Tom Rakewell *The Rake's Progress* (Stravinsky)
• **Anne Trulove** (tenor • soprano)
 -Anne! Here!
 -Farewell for now
 -In a foolish dream/What should I forgive?
 -The woods are green
• **Nick Shadow** (tenor • bass-baritone)
 -How dark and dreadful is this place
 -My tale shall be told both by young and by old
 -Thanks to this excellent device

Tonio *La figlia del reggimento*
 [*La fille du régiment*] (Donizetti)
• **Maria** [Marie] (tenor • soprano)
 -A voti così ardente [De cet aveu si tendre]

Tonio *La fille du régiment*
 [*La figlia del reggimento*] (Donizetti)
• **Marie** [Maria] (tenor • soprano)
 -De cet aveu si tendre [A voti così ardente]

Tonio *Pagliacci* (Leoncavallo)
• **Nedda** (bass-baritone • soprano)
 -So ben che difforme

Tony *West Side Story* (Bernstein)
• **Maria** (tenor • soprano)
 -One Hand, One Heart

Tristan *Tristan und Isolde* (Wagner)
• **Isolde** (tenor • soprano)
 -O ew'ge Nacht
 -O sink' hernieder, Nacht der Liebe

Troilus [Prince] *Troilus and Cressida* (Walton)
• **Cressida** (tenor • mezzo-soprano)
 -If one last doubt
 -Now close your arms

Trulove *The Rake's Progress* (Stravinsky)
• **Anne Trulove** (bass • soprano)
 -Every wearied body/God is merciful and just

Turandot *Turandot* (Puccini)
• **Calaf** (soprano • tenor)
 -Principessa di morte/Mio fiore!

Turiddu *Cavalleria rusticana* (Mascagni)
• **Santuzza** (tenor • soprano)
-No, no Turiddu, rimani
-Tu qui, Santuzza?

Ubalde *Armide* (Gluck)
• **Danish Knight** (baritone • tenor)
-Fuyons les douceurs dangereuses

Uberto *Serva padrona, La* (Pergolesi)
• **Serpina** (bass • soprano)
-Contento tu sarai [Reconciliation Duet]
-Lo conosco a quegl'occhieti [Conflict Duet]
-Per te ho io nel core

Udoline *Die Verschworenen* (Schubert)
(Udoline was written for either
tenor or soprano (pants role).)
• **Isella** (soprano • soprano)
-Sie ist's! Er ist's!

Ulisse *Il ritorno d'Ulisse in patria* (Monteverdi)
(Ulisse was sung by either tenor or baritone.)
• **Eumete** (baritone • tenor)
-Verdi spiaggie al lieto giorno
• **Telemaco** (baritone • tenor)
-O padre sospirato, o figlio desiato

Ulysse *Pénélope* (Fauré)
• **Pénélope** (tenor • soprano)
-D'où viens-tu?
-Si vous le permettiez, princes/Ulysse!

Undina *Undina* (Tchaikovsky)
• **Hulbrand** (soprano • tenor)
-Swan Lake Duet [commonly known title]

Ursula *Béatrice et Bénédict* (Berlioz)
• **Héro** (mezzo-soprano • soprano)
-Nuit paisible et sereine! [Nocturne Duet]

Valdeburgo, Baron *La Straniera* (Bellini)
• **Arturo** (bass • tenor)
-Sì...sulla salma del fratello

Valentine *Les Huguenots* (Meyerbeer)
• **Marcel** (mezzo-soprano • bass)
-Dans la nuit où seul je veille
-Derrière ce pilier
• **Raoul** (mezzo-soprano • tenor)
-O ciel! où courez-vous?/
Tu l'as dit [O ciel! dove vai tu?]

Valletto *L'incoronazione di Poppea* (Monteverdi)
(Valletto was originally sung by a castrato.)
• **Damigella** (tenor • soprano)
-O cara, o cara

Van Bett *Zar und Zimmermann* (Lortzing)
• **Ivanov** (bass • tenor)
-Darf ich wohl den Worten trauen

Vanessa *Vanessa* (Barber)
• **Anatol** (soprano • tenor)
-Love has a bitter core, Vanessa

Vasco da Gama *L'africaine* (Meyerbeer)
• **Sélika** (tenor • soprano)
-O transports, ô douce extase

Vašek *Prodaná Nevěsta* [*The Bartered Bride*] (Smetana)
• **Mařenka** (tenor • soprano)
-Známť já jednu dívčinu
[I know a girl who burns for you]

Vastiano *Flaminio* (Pergolesi)
• **Checca** (bass • soprano)
-Per te ho io nel core

Vaudémont *Iolanta* (Tchaikovsky)
• **Iolanta** (tenor • mezzo-soprano)
-Chudnïy pervenets tvoren'ya
[Wondrous firstling of creation]

Vespetta *Pimpinone* (Albinoni)
• **Pimpinone** (mezzo-soprano • bass)
-Quarrel Duet [commonly known title]

Vespina *L'infedeltà delusa* (Haydn)
• **Nanni** (soprano • bass)
-Son disperato

Vincenette *Mireille* (Gounod)
• **Mireille** (soprano • soprano)
-Ah! parle encore

Vincent *Mireille* (Gounod)
• **Mireille** (tenor • soprano)
-La brise est douce et parfumée [Chanson de Magali]
-Vincenette a votre âge

Violetta Valéry *La traviata* (Verdi)
• **Alfredo Germont** (soprano • tenor)
-Libiamo ne' lieti calici [Brindisi]
-Parigi, o cara/Ah, gran Dio! morir sì giovane
-Un dì felice, eterea/De quell'amor ch'è palpito
• **Giorgio Germont** (soprano • baritone)
-Pura siccome un angelo/Dite alla giovine/Morro!

Virineya *Virineya* (Slonimsky)
• **Pavel** (soprano • bass-baritone)
-Vsyo na zemle dlyz schast' ya roditsya
[Everything is born for love]

Vitellia *La clemenza di Tito* (Mozart)
(Sesto was written for castrato; each role
can be sung by soprano or mezzo-soprano.)
• **Sesto** (mezzo-soprano • mezzo-soprano)
-Come ti piace, imponi

Vladimir *Knyaz' Igor'* [*Prince Igor*] (Borodin)
• **Konchakovna** (tenor • contralto)
-Tï li Vladimir moy? [Is it you, Vladimir mine?]

Waldner, Graf [Count] *Arabella* (Strauss)
• **Mandryka** (bass-baritone • baritone)
-Welko! das Bild?

Walter *I Lituani* [*The Little Sweep*] (Ponchielli)
• **Aldona** (tenor • soprano)
-Noi torneremo alla romita valle

Walter, Il Conte di [Count] *Luisa Miller* (Verdi)
• **Wurm** (bass • bass)
   -L'alto retaggio non ho bramato/O meco incolume

Weib, Sein [Wife of Barak]
   Die Frau ohne Schatten (Strauss)
• **Barak** (soprano • bass-baritone)
   -Mir anvertraut

Werther *Werther* (Massenet)
• **Albert** (tenor • baritone)
   -Au bonheur dont mon âme est pleine
• **Charlotte** (tenor • mezzo-soprano)
   -A cette heure suprême
   -Ai-je dit vrai/Ah! qu'il est loin
   -Il faut nous séparer
   -Oui, c'est moi/N'achevez pas/Ah! ce premier baiser

Wilhelm Meister *Mignon* (Thomas)
• **Mignon** (tenor • mezzo-soprano)
   -Je suis heureuse! l'air m'enivre
• **Philine** (tenor • soprano)
   -Je crois entendre les doux compliments

Wotan *Die Walküre* (Wagner)
• **Brünnhilde** (bass-baritone • soprano)
   -Als junger Liebe Lust mir verblich

Wurm *Luisa Miller* (Verdi)
• **Walter, Il Conte di** [Count] (bass • bass)
   -L'alto retaggio non ho bramato/O meco incolume

Yaroslavna *Knyaz' Igor'* [*Prince Igor*] (Borodin)
• **Igor'** (soprano • baritone)
   -On—moy sokol yasnïy! [It is he, my bright falcon]

Yevgeny Onegin [Eugene Onegin] *Yevgeny Onegin*
   [*Eugene Onegin*] (Tchaikovsky)
• **Tat'yana** (baritone • soprano)
   -My heart is worn with fear [commonly known title]
   -Onegin, I was then far younger
   [commonly known title]

Youth *Das Mädchen aus der Feenwelt* (Drechsler)
• **Fortunatus Wurzel** (soprano • tenor)
   -Brüderlein fein

Zaïde *Zaïde* (Mozart)
• **Gomatz** (soprano • tenor)
   -Meine Seele hüpft von Freuden

Zamoro *Alzira* (Verdi)
• **Alzira** (tenor • soprano)
   -Anima mia!/Risorge ne' tuoi lumi

Zarewitsch, Der [Tsarevich] *Der Zarewitsch* (Lehár)
• **Sonja** (tenor • soprano)
   -Warum hat jeder Frühling, ach, nur einen Mai?

Zayda *Dom Sébastien* (Donizetti)
• **Sébastien** (mezzo-soprano • tenor)
   -Grand Dieu! sa misère est si grande!

Zazà *Zazà* (Leoncavallo)
• **Dufresne** (soprano • tenor)
   -E deciso: tu parti

Zdenka *Arabella* (Strauss)
• **Arabella** (soprano • soprano)
   -Aber der Richtige

Zerbinetta *Ariadne auf Naxos* (Strauss)
• **Komponist, Der** [The Composer]
   (soprano • mezzo-soprano) (Der Komponist
   is sung by either soprano or mezzo-soprano.)
   -Ein Augenblick ist wenig

Zerlina *Don Giovanni* (Mozart)
• **Giovanni, Don** (mezzo-soprano • bass-baritone)
   -Là ci darem la mano/Andiam mio bene
• **Leporello** (mezzo-soprano • baritone)
   -Per queste tue manine

Zoroastre *Zoroastre* (Rameau)
   (Zoroastre's role was originally
   written for haute-contre.)
• **Amélite** (countertenor • soprano)
   -Je vous revois
   -Présent des cieux, divine flamme

Zurga *Les pêcheurs de perles* (Bizet)
• **Leïla** (baritone • soprano)
   -Pour moi, je ne crains rien
• **Nadir** (baritone • tenor)
   -Au fond du temple saint

Voice Categories to Duets

---

treble

treble • soprano

ENGLISH

Don't cry, mother dear (Amahl • Mother)
• *Amahl and the Night Visitors* (Menotti)
• light or lyric voices

---

soprano

soprano • soprano

ENGLISH

Begone! discharge you (Lady Elinor • Adela)
• *The Haunted Tower* (Storace)
• light voices

Hi there, dear husband
(Lucy Lockit • Polly Peachum)
• *The Beggar's Opera* (Pepusch)
• light voices

I'm bubbled! (Lucy Lockit • Polly Peachum)
• *The Beggar's Opera* (Pepusch)
• light voices

FRENCH

Ah! parle encore (Mireille • Vincenette)
• *Mireille* (Gounod)
• lyric voices

Laissez le doute dans mon âme
(Infante [Princess] • Chimène)
• *Le Cid* (Massenet)
• light or lyric voices

Ne m'en veux pas d'être venue
(Jean • Fanny [Sapho])
(Jean's part was sung by either a
tenor or a soprano [pants role].)
• *Sapho* (Massenet)
• lyric voices

O ma Fanny, que j'aime (Jean • Fanny [Sapho])
(Jean's part was sung by either a
tenor or a soprano [pants role].)
• *Sapho* (Massenet)
• lyric voices

**Oh! Fanny ma maîtresse/Nous irons
en rêvant** (Jean • Fanny [Sapho])
(Jean's part was sung by either a
tenor or a soprano [pants role].)
• *Sapho* (Massenet)
• lyric voices

GERMAN

Aber der Richtige (Zdenka • Arabella)
• *Arabella* (Strauss)
• lyric voices

Du! denn du bist stark (Chrysothemis • Elektra)
• *Elektra* (Strauss)
• dramatic voices

Elektra! Schwester! komm mit uns!
  (Chrysothemis • Elektra)
• *Elektra* (Strauss)
• dramatic voices

Ist mein Liebster dahin
  (Falcon • Die Kaiserin [The Empress])
• *Die Frau ohne Schatten* (Strauss)
• dramatic voices

Sie ist's! Er ist's! (Udoline • Isella)
  (Udoline was written for either
  tenor or soprano [pants role].)
• *Die Verschworenen* (Schubert)
• light or lyric voices

Um in der Ehe froh zu leben
  (Leonore • Marzelline)
  (Marzelline is a soubrette-lyric;
  Leonore is a full dramatic.)
• *Fidelio* (Beethoven)
• lyric or dramatic voices

ITALIAN

Ah ferma!...Ah senti! (Paride • Elena)
  (Paride, originally written for soprano
  castrato, is sung by tenor or soprano.)
• *Paride ed Elena* (Gluck)
• lyric voices

Ah mia diletta madre! (Eumelo • Aspasia)
• *Alceste* (Gluck)
• light voices

L'amo! L'adoro! (Elena • Paride)
  (Paride, originally written for soprano castrato,
  is sung by either tenor or soprano.)
• *Paride ed Elena* (Gluck)
• lyric voices

Ma, chi sei? (Erasto • Paride)
  (Paride, originally written for soprano
  castrato, is sung by either tenor or soprano.)
• *Paride ed Elena* (Gluck)
• lyric voices

Morta al mondo
  (Elisabetta [Queen] • Maria Stuarda)
• *Maria Stuarda* (Donizetti)
• lyric or dramatic voices

Pensa che sol per poco sospendo l'ira mia
  (Matilda • Elisabetta [Queen])
• *Elisabetta* (Rossini)
• lyric voices

Poca voglia di far bene (Curtio • Martio)
  (Both roles may have been sung originally by castrati.)

• *Sant'Alessio* (Landi)
• light voices

Ravisa qual alma (Armando • Palmide)
  (Armando, a pants role, was
  originally sung by a castrato.)
• *Il crociato in Egitto* (Meyerbeer)
• lyric or dramatic voices

Sorgi, o padre, e la figlia rimira
  (Eloisa • Bianca)
• *Bianca e Fernando* (Bellini)
• lyric voices

Sull'aria/Che soave zefiretto [Letter Duet]
  (La Contessa di Almaviva [Rosina] • Susanna)
• *Le nozze di Figaro* (Mozart)
• lyric voices

soprano • mezzo-soprano

ENGLISH

Fear no danger (Belinda • Second Woman)
• *Dido and Aeneas* (Purcell)
• light voices

Joys of freedom (Iöle • Dejanira)
• *Hercules* (Handel)
• light or lyric voices

You love him, seek to set him right
  (Anne Trulove • Baba)
• *The Rake's Progress* (Stravinsky)
• lyric voices

FRENCH

C'était bien gentil autrefois
  (Fanny [Sapho] • Irène)
• *Sapho* (Massenet)
• lyric voices

Dans ce séjour (La Comtesse Adèle
  di Formouters [Countess] • Ragonde)
• *Le comte Ory* (Rossini)
• light or lyric voices

Nuit paisible et sereine!
  [Nocturne Duet] (Héro • Ursula)
• *Béatrice et Bénédict* (Berlioz)
• light voices

Sous le dôme épais (Lakmé • Mallika)
• *Lakmé* (Delibes)
• light or lyric voices

GERMAN

Abends will ich schlafen gehn
  [Prayer] (Gretel • Hänsel)
• *Hänsel und Gretel* (Humperdinck)
• light or lyric voices

Ach! du bist wieder da (Die Feldmarschallin
  Fürstin Werdenberg [Marie Thérèse] [Marschallin] •
  Octavian, genannt Quinquin [Count Rofrano])
  (Octavian is sung by either
  soprano or mezzo-soprano.)

- *Der Rosenkavalier* (Strauss)
- lyric or dramatic voices

Ach, mich zieht's zu dir [Kissing Duet]
(Galathee • Ganymede)
- *Die schöne Galathee* (Suppé)
- light or lyric voices

Ein Augenblick ist wenig (Zerbinetta •
Der Komponist [The Composer])
(Der Komponist is sung by either
soprano or mezzo-soprano.)
- *Ariadne auf Naxos* (Strauss)
- lyric voices

Ein Männlein steht im Walde (Gretel • Hänsel)
- *Hänsel und Gretel* (Humperdinck)
- light or lyric voices

Er geht/Ja, eine Welt voll Leiden
(Irene • Adriano)
- *Rienzi* (Wagner)
- dramatic voices

Florenz hat schöne Frauen
(Fiametta • Boccaccio)
- *Boccaccio* (Suppé)
- light voices

Ich kenn' Ihn schon recht wohl
(Sophie • Octavian, genannt Quinquin
[Count Rofrano])
(Octavian is sung by either
soprano or mezzo-soprano.)
- *Der Rosenkavalier* (Strauss)
- lyric voices

Ist ein Traum, kann nicht wirklich?
(Sophie • Octavian, genannt Quinquin
[Count Rofrano])
(Octavian is sung by either
soprano or mezzo-soprano.)
- *Der Rosenkavalier* (Strauss)
- lyric voices

Lachst du mich aus? (Die Feldmarschallin
Fürstin Werdenberg [Marie Thérèse] [Marschallin]•
Octavian, genannt Quinquin [Count Rofrano])
(Octavian is sung by either
soprano or mezzo-soprano.)
- *Der Rosenkavalier* (Strauss)
- lyric or dramatic voices

**Mir ist die Ehre widerfahren/Mit Ihren Augen
voll Tränen** [Presentation of the Rose] (Sophie •
Octavian, genannt Quinquin [Count Rofrano])
(Octavian is sung by either soprano
or mezzo-soprano.)
- *Der Rosenkavalier* (Strauss)
- lyric voices

Nun ist die Hexe tot
[Gingerbread Waltz] (Gretel • Hänsel)
- *Hänsel und Gretel* (Humperdinck)
- light or lyric voices

Schelm, halt' fest! (Agathe • Ännchen)
(Ännchen is sung by either a
mezzo-soprano or a soprano.)
- *Der Freischütz* (Weber)
- lyric voices

**Suse, liebe Suse/Brüderchen
komm tanz mit mir** (Gretel • Hänsel)
- *Hänsel und Gretel* (Humperdinck)
- light or lyric voices

Von den edlen Kavalieren
(Lady Harriet Durham • Nancy)
- *Martha* (Flotow)
- lyric voices

Weit über Glanz und Erdenschimmer
(Florinda • Maragond)
- *Fierrabras* (Schubert)
- light or lyric voices

ITALIAN

Ah perdona al primo affetto (Servilia • Annio)
(Annio [a pants role] can be sung by
either soprano or mezzo-soprano.)
- *La clemenza di Tito* (Mozart)
- light or lyric voices

Ah! sì, fa core e abbracciami (Norma • Adalgisa)
(Adalgisa is sung by either
soprano or mezzo-soprano.)
- *Norma* (Bellini)
- lyric voices

Al fato dan legge (Fiordiligi • Dorabella)
(Dorabella is sung by either
soprano or mezzo-soprano.)
- *Così fan tutte* (Mozart)
- lyric voices

Aprite, presto aprite [Escape Duet]
(Susanna • Cherubino)
(Cherubino is sung by either
soprano or mezzo-soprano.)
- *Le nozze di Figaro* (Mozart)
- lyric voices

D'Eliso in sen m'attendi (Giunia • Cecilio)
(Cecilio, originally soprano castrato,
is for soprano or mezzo-soprano.)
- *Lucio Silla* (Mozart)
- lyric voices

Dio, che mi vedi in core/Va, infelice
(Anna Bolena • Giovanna Seymour)
- *Anna Bolena* (Donizetti)
- lyric or dramatic voices

Farewell Duet [commonly known title]
(Ermione • Oreste)
(Oreste was originally written
for mezzo-soprano castrato.)
- *Oreste* (Handel)
- lyric voices

Idolo del cor mio (Poppea • Nerone)
(Nerone, originally written for soprano castrato,
is soprano or mezzo-soprano today.)
• *L'incoronazione di Poppea* (Monteverdi)
• lyric or dramatic voices

Io son sua per l'amor
(Adriana Lecouvreur • La Principessa
di Bouillon [The Princess of Bouillon])
• *Adriana Lecouvreur* (Cilea)
• lyric voices

Mira, o Norma/Sì, fino all'ore estreme
(Norma • Adalgisa)
(Adalgisa is sung by either
soprano or mezzo-soprano.)
• *Norma* (Bellini)
• lyric voices

Ne più s'interporà (Poppea • Nerone)
(Nerone, originally written for soprano castrato,
is soprano or mezzo-soprano today.)
• *L'incoronazione di Poppea* (Monteverdi)
• lyric or dramatic voices

O guarda sorella (Fiordiligi • Dorabella)
(Dorabella can be sung by either
mezzo-soprano or soprano.)
• *Così fan tutte* (Mozart)
• lyric voices

Per le porte (Rosmene • Tirinto)
• *Imeneo* (Handel)
• light or lyric voices

**Pietà ti prenda del mio dolore/Alla
pompa che s'appresta** (Aïda • Amneris)
• *Aïda* (Verdi)
• dramatic voices

Prenderò quel brunettino (Fiordiligi • Dorabella)
(Dorabella can be sung by either
soprano or mezzo-soprano.)
• *Così fan tutte* (Mozart)
• lyric voices

Pur ti miro (Poppea • Nerone)
(Nerone, originally soprano castrato,
is soprano or mezzo-soprano today.)
• *L'incoronazione di Poppea* (Monteverdi)
• lyric or dramatic voices

**Scuoti quella fronda di ciliegio/
Tutti i fior** [Flower Duet]
(Cio-Cio-San [Madama Butterfly] • Suzuki)
• *Madama Butterfly* (Puccini)
• lyric voices

**Sì, fuggire: a noi non resta/
Ah! crudel d'onor ragioni** (Giulietta • Romeo)
• *I Capuleti e i Montecchi* (Bellini)
• lyric voices

**Soccorso, sostegno accordate/
Non si pianga** (Giulietta • Romeo)
• *I Capuleti e i Montecchi* (Bellini)
• lyric voices

Via resti servita (Susanna • Marcellina)
(Marcellina is sung by either
soprano or mezzo-soprano.)
• *Le nozze di Figaro* (Mozart)
• light or lyric voices

Vivere io non potrò (Elena • Malcolm)
• *La donna del lago* (Rossini)
• lyric or dramatic voices

soprano • contralto

ENGLISH

O Black Swan (Monica • Baba [Madame Flora])
• *The Medium* (Menotti)
• lyric voices

GERMAN

Ich will nichts hören/Träumst du Mutter?
(Elektra • Klytemnästra)
(Klytemnästra is soprano,
mezzo-soprano, or contralto.)
• *Elektra* (Strauss)
• dramatic voices

Nein, das ist wirklich doch zu keck!
(Frau Fluth [Mrs. Ford] • Frau Reich [Mrs. Page])
• *Die lustigen Weiber von Windsor* (Nicolai)
• lyric voices

ITALIAN

Al bel destin che attendevi (Linda • Pierotto)
• *Linda di Chamounix* (Donizetti)
• light or lyric voices

Avvezza al contento [Je goûtais les charmes]
(Euridice [Eurydice] • Orfeo [Orphée])
(Orfeo's role was originally written for alto castrato,
and is tenor in the French version. Orfeo is often
sung by a mezzo-soprano.)
• *Orfeo ed Euridice* [*Orphée et Eurydice*] (Gluck)
• lyric voices

Dite, che fà, dov'è (Seleuce • Tolomeo)
(The role of Tolomeo was originally
sung by an alto castrato.)
• *Tolomeo* (Handel)
• light or lyric voices

E ben, per mia memoria (Ninetta • Pippo)
• *La gazza ladra* (Rossini)
• light voices

Giorno d'orrore (Semiramide • Arsace)
• *Semiramide* (Rossini)
• lyric voices

Io t'abbraccio: è più che morte
(Rodelinda • Bertarido)
(The role of Bertarido was originally
sung by an alto castrato.)
• *Rodelinda* (Handel)
• light or lyric voices

Per le porte del tormento (Elmira • Sosarme)
(The role of Sosarme was originally
sung by an alto castrato.)
• *Sosarme* (Handel)
• light or lyric voices

Se la vita ancor t'è cara (Semiramide • Arsace)
• *Semiramide* (Rossini)
• lyric voices

**Serbami ognor sì fido/Alle più calde
immagini** (Semiramide • Arsace)
• *Semiramide* (Rossini)
• lyric voices

Tu caro sei il dolce mio tesoro
(Elmira • Sosarme)
(The role of Sosarme was originally
sung by an alto castrato.)
• *Sosarme* (Handel)
• light or lyric voices

Vieni, appaga il tuo consorte [Viens, suis un
époux] (Euridice [Eurydice] • Orfeo [Orphée])
(Orfeo's role was originally written for alto castrato,
and is tenor in the French version. Orfeo is often
sung by a mezzo-soprano.)
• *Orfeo ed Euridice* [*Orphée et Eurydice*] (Gluck)
• lyric voices

Slikhalil' vï...vdokhnulil' vï [Have you not
heard...not sighed) (Tat'yana • Ol'ga)
• *Yevgeny Onegin* [*Eugene Onegin*] (Tchaikovsky)
• lyric or dramatic voices

Uzh vecher, oblakov pomerknuli kraya
(Liza • Milovzor [Daphnis] [Pauline])
• *Pikovaya dama* [*Pique Dame*]
[*The Queen of Spades*] (Tchaikovsky)
• lyric or dramatic voices

soprano • countertenor

Je vous revois (Amélite • Zoroastre)
(Zoroastre's role was originally
written for haute-contre.)
• *Zoroastre* (Rameau)
• light or lyric voices

Présent des cieux, divine flamme
(Amélite • Zoroastre)
(Zoroastre's role was originally
written for haute-contre.)
• *Zoroastre* (Rameau)
• light or lyric voices

soprano • tenor

Jako matka [Like a mother] (Mařenka • Jeník)
• *Prodaná Nevěsta* [*The Bartered Bride*] (Smetana)
• lyric voices

Milostné zvířátko uděláme z vás [We'll make a
nice little animal] (Esmeralda • Circus Master)
• *Prodaná Nevěsta* [*The Bartered Bride*] (Smetana)
• light voices

O nevýslovné štěstí lásky [O the unu
tterable happiness] (Milada • Dalibor)
• *Dalibor* (Smetana)
• dramatic voices

Ten staví se svatou skem [This man
becomes a saint] (Esmeralda • Circus Master)
• *Prodaná Nevěsta* [*The Bartered Bride*] (Smetana)
• light voices

Známt' já jednu dívčinu [I know a girl
who burns for you] (Mařenka • Vašek)
• *Prodaná Nevěsta* [*The Bartered Bride*] (Smetana)
• light or lyric voices

Anne! Here! (Anne Trulove • Tom Rakewell)
• *The Rake's Progress* (Stravinsky)
• lyric voices

Do you remember (Rose • Sam)
• *Street Scene* (Weill)
• light or lyric voices

Farewell for now (Anne Trulove • Tom Rakewell)
• *The Rake's Progress* (Stravinsky)
• lyric voices

Happy we (Galatea • Acis)
• *Acis and Galatea* (Handel)
• light voices

Happy were we (Elizabeth I •
Earl of Essex [Robert Devereux])
• *Gloriana* (Britten)
• lyric or dramatic voices

In a foolish dream/What should I forgive?
(Anne Trulove • Tom Rakewell)
• *The Rake's Progress* (Stravinsky)
• lyric voices

Jenifer, Jenifer, my darling (Jenifer • Mark)
• *The Midsummer Marriage* (Tippett)
• lyric voices

Love has a bitter core, Vanessa
(Vanessa • Anatol)
• *Vanessa* (Barber)
• lyric or dramatic voices

One Hand, One Heart (Maria • Tony)
• *West Side Story* (Bernstein)
• light or lyric voices

Remember that I care (Rose • Sam)
• *Street Scene* (Weill)
• light or lyric voices

Sirius rising as the sun's wheel (Jenifer • Mark)
• *The Midsummer Marriage* (Tippett)
• lyric voices

**The flocks shall leave
the mountains** (Galatea • Acis)
• *Acis and Galatea* (Handel)
• light voices

The woods are green
(Anne Trulove • Tom Rakewell)
• *The Rake's Progress* (Stravinsky)
• lyric voices

Well met, pretty maid (Sally • The Squire)
• *Thomas and Sally* (Arne)
• light voices

FRENCH

A l'autel j'allais rayonnant (Rozenn • Mylio)
• *Le roi d'Ys* (Lalo)
• lyric voices

Adieu, mes tendres soeurs (Julia • Licinius)
• *La vestale* (Spontini)
• lyric or dramatic voices

Adieu, mon bien-aimé (Hélène • Gaston)
• *Jérusalem* (Verdi)
• lyric or dramatic voices

Ah! ne fuis pas encore (Juliette • Roméo)
• *Roméo et Juliette* (Gounod)
• lyric voices

Ah! quel respect, Madame (La Comtesse Adèle
di Formouters [Countess] • Le Comte Ory [Count])
• *Le comte Ory* (Rossini)
• light or lyric voices

Ange adorable (Juliette • Roméo)
• *Roméo et Juliette* (Gounod)
• lyric voices

Aux cris de la douleur [Cari figli]
(Alceste • Admète)
• *Alceste* (Gluck)
• lyric or dramatic voices

Avance un pas (Babet • Blaise)
• *Blaise et Babet* (Dezède)
• light voices

Avec bonté voyez ma peine
(Isabelle • Robert le Diable)
• *Robert le Diable* (Meyerbeer)
• lyric voices

Ce domaine est celui des contes d'Avenel
(Anna • Georges Brown/Julien Avanel)
• *La dame blanche* (Boieldieu)
• light or lyric voices

Ce que je veux (Salomé • Jean [John the Baptist])
• *Hérodiade* (Massenet)
• dramatic voices

C'est le dieu de la jeunesse (Lakmé • Gérald)
• *Lakmé* (Delibes)
• light or lyric voices

**Comment, dans ma reconnaissance/Près du
tombeau, peut-être** [Quale o prode/ Presso alla
tomba] (Hélène [Elena] • Henri [Arrigo])

Les vêpres siciliennes [*I vespri siciliani*] (Verdi)
• lyric or dramatic voices

De cet aveu si tendre [A voti così ardente]
(Marie [Maria] • Tonio)
• *La fille du régiment* [*La figlia del reggimento*]
(Donizetti)
• light or lyric voices

**De courroux d'effroi/Ami! le coeur/
Pour moi rayonne** [O sdegni miei/E dolce raggio]
(Hélène [Elena] • Henri [Arrigo])
• *Les vêpres siciliennes* [*I vespri siciliani*] (Verdi)
• lyric or dramatic voices

Depuis longtemps (Louise • Julien)
• *Louise* (Charpentier)
• lyric voices

D'où viens-tu? (Pénélope • Ulysse)
• *Pénélope* (Fauré)
• lyric or dramatic voices

Et je sais votre nom
(Manon • Des Grieux [Le Chevalier])
• *Manon* (Massenet)
• light or lyric voices

Grâce au hazard (Madeleine • Chapelou)
• *Le postillon de Lonjumeau* (Adam)
• light or lyric voices

Irritons notre barbarie (Arcabonne • Arcalaus)
(The role of Arcalaus was originally
written for haute-contre.)
• *Amadis* (Lully)
• light or lyric voices

**J'avais fait un beau rêve/Oui, voilà
l'héroisme /Au revoir**
[Sogno dorato io feci!/Ma lassù] (Elisabeth
[Elisabetta] • Don Carlos [Don Carlo])
• *Don Carlos* [*Don Carlo*] (Verdi)
• lyric or dramatic voices

Je crois entendre les doux compliments
(Philine • Wilhelm Meister)
• *Mignon* (Thomas)
• light or lyric voices

Je goûtais les charmes [Avvezza al contento]
(Eurydice [Euridice] • Orphée [Orfeo])
(Orphée's role was originally written for alto castrato
in the Italian version.)
• *Orphée et Eurydice* [*Orfeo ed Euridice*] (Gluck)
• lyric voices

Je ne souffre plus (Manon • Des Grieux)
• *Manon Lescaut* (Auber)
• light or lyric voices

**Je viens solliciter/O bien perdu/Que sous
mes pieds** [Io vengo a domandar] (Elisabeth
[Elisabetta] • Don Carlos [Don Carlo])
• *Don Carlos* [*Don Carlo*] (Verdi)
• lyric or dramatic voices

La brise est douce et parfumée
[Chanson de Magali] (Mireille • Vincent)

- *Mireille* (Gounod)
- lyric voices

Laisse-moi contempler ton visage/O nuit/Partez, partez (Marguerite • Faust, Dr.)
- *Faust* (Gounod)
- lyric voices

Lakmé, c'est toi (Lakmé • Gérald)
- *Lakmé* (Delibes)
- light or lyric voices

L'amour qui brûle dans notre âme (Julia • Licinius)
- *La vestale* (Spontini)
- lyric or dramatic voices

Les rendez-vous de noble compagnie (Nicette • Girot)
- *Le Pré aux Clercs* (Hérold)
- light voices

L'espoir fuit de mon coeur (Echo • Cynire)
- *Echo et Narcisse* (Gluck)
- lyric voices

L'heure fatale est sonnée! [L'ora fatale è suonata!] (Elisabeth [Elisabetta] • Don Carlos [Don Carlo])
- *Don Carlos* [*Don Carlo*] (Verdi)
- lyric or dramatic voices

Malheureux et non coupable (Hélène • Henri)
- *Les vêpres siciliennes* [I vespri siciliani] (Verdi)
- lyric or dramatic voices

N'espérez pas me fuir/Écoutez-moi (Elvire • Alphonse)
- *La muette de Portici* (Auber)
- light or lyric voices

O dieu Brahma! (Leïla • Nadir)
- *Les pêcheurs de perles* (Bizet)
- lyric voices

O fatale Toison (Médée • Jason)
- *Médée* (Chérubini)
- dramatic voices

O lumière sainte (Leïla • Nadir)
- *Les pêcheurs de perles* (Bizet)
- lyric voices

O nuit divine (Juliette • Roméo)
- *Roméo et Juliette* (Gounod)
- lyric voices

O Teresa, vous que j'aime plus que ma vie (Teresa • Benvenuto Cellini)
- *Benvenuto Cellini* (Berlioz)
- lyric or dramatic voices

O transports, ô douce extase (Sélika • Vasco da Gama)
- *L'africaine* (Meyerbeer)
- lyric or dramatic voices

On l'appelle Manon (Manon • Des Grieux [Le Chevalier])
- *Manon* (Massenet)
- light or lyric voices

Oui, c'est toi je t'aime (Marguerite • Faust, Dr.)
- *Faust* (Gounod)
- lyric voices

Oui, vous l'arrachez à mon âme (Mathilde • Arnold)
- *Guillaume Tell* (Rossini)
- lyric voices

Parle-moi de ma mère (Micaëla • Don José)
- *Carmen* (Bizet)
- lyric voices

Perfides ennemis [Nemici senza cor] (Médée • Jason)
- *Médée* (Chérubini)
- dramatic voices

Pour notre amour plus d'espérance/Sur la rive étrangère (Mathilde • Arnold)
- *Guillaume Tell* (Rossini)
- lyric voices

Quand des sommets de la montagne (Teresa • Benvenuto Cellini)
- *Benvenuto Cellini* (Berlioz)
- lyric or dramatic voices

Quand nos jours s'éteindront (Salomé • Jean [John the Baptist])
- *Hérodiade* (Massenet)
- dramatic voices

Que ces moments sont doux (Alphise • Abaris) (Abaris was originally written for haute-contre.)
- *Les Boréades* (Rameau)
- lyric voices

Que faites-vous donc?/De quels transports/Toujours unis [Che mai fate voi?/Di qual amor] (Elisabeth [Elisabetta] • Don Carlos [Don Carlo])
- *Don Carlos* [*Don Carlo*] (Verdi)
- lyric or dramatic voices

Que le tendre amour nous engage (Scylla • Glaucus) (Glaucus was written originally written for haute-contre.)
- *Scylla et Glaucus* (Leclair)
- light or lyric voices

Quoi, tous les deux (Madeleine • Chapelou)
- *Le postillon de Lonjumeau* (Adam)
- light or lyric voices

Si vous le permettiez, princes/Ulysse! (Pénélope • Ulysse)
- *Pénélope* (Fauré)
- lyric or dramatic voices

Sur cet autel sacré (Julia • Licinius)
- *La vestale* (Spontini)
- lyric or dramatic voices

Toi! Vous! (Manon • Des Grieux [Le Chevalier])
- *Manon* (Massenet)
- light or lyric voices

Ton coeur n'a pas compris le mien
(Leïla • Nadir)
• *Les pêcheurs de perles* (Bizet)
• lyric voices

Tous les deux, amoureux (Fleurette • Saphir)
• *Barbe-bleue* (Offenbach)
• light or lyric voices

Tu pleures? Oui, de honte sur moi
(Manon • Des Grieux [Le Chevalier])
• *Manon* (Massenet)
• light or lyric voices

**Va! je t'ai pardonné/Nuit d'hyménée!/
Il faut partir** (Juliette • Roméo)
• *Roméo et Juliette* (Gounod)
• lyric voices

Viens! fuyons au bout au monde
(Juliette • Roméo)
• *Roméo et Juliette* (Gounod)
• lyric voices

Viens, nous quitterons cette ville
(Cendrillon • Prince)
(The Prince was composed for a soprano,
   but today is always sung by a tenor.)
• *Cendrillon* (Massenet)
• lyric voices

Viens, suis un époux [Vieni, appaga il tuo
consorte] (Eurydice [Euridice] • Orphée [Orfeo])
(The role of Orphée was originally written for
   alto castrato in the Italian.)
• *Orphée et Eurydice* [*Orfeo ed Euridice*] (Gluck)
• lyric voices

Viens, viens, je cède éperdu [Vieni, ah! vieni]
(Léonor [Leonora] • Fernand [Fernando])
• *La favorite* [*La favorita*] (Donizetti)
• lyric or dramatic voices

Vincenette a votre âge (Mireille • Vincent)
• *Mireille* (Gounod)
• lyric voices

GERMAN

Blickt sein Auge doch so ehrlich
(Lady Harriet Durham • Lyonel)
• *Martha* (Flotow)
• lyric voices

Brüderlein fein (Youth • Fortunatus Wurzel)
• *Das Mädchen aus der Feenwelt* (Drechsler)
• light or lyric voices

Darf eine nied're Magd es wagen
(Marie • Ivanov)
• *Zar und Zimmermann* (Lortzing)
• lyric voices

Das Essen ist da (Marta • Pedro)
• *Tiefland* (Albert)
• dramatic voices

Das Tor ist zu, Wir sind allein (Marta • Pedro)
• *Tiefland* (Albert)
• dramatic voices

Der Lenz ist gekommen
(Lady Harriet Durham • Lyonel)
• *Martha* (Flotow)
• lyric voices

Die Kinder sind's (Marietta • Paul)
• *Die tote Stadt* (Korngold)
• lyric or dramatic voices

Diese Liebe, plötzlich geboren
(Die Gräfin [Countess Madeleine] • Flamand)
• *Capriccio* (Strauss)
• lyric or dramatic voices

Dieser Anstand, so manierlich
[Watch Duet] (Rosalinde • Eisenstein)
• *Die Fledermaus* (J. Strauss)
• lyric voices

Geh'! geh'! geh'! Herz von Flandern!
(Bastienne • Bastien)
• *Bastien und Bastienne* (Mozart)
• light voices

Geh' hin! (Bastienne • Bastien)
• *Bastien und Bastienne* (Mozart)
• light voices

Glück, das mir verlieb (Marietta • Paul)
• *Die tote Stadt* (Korngold)
• lyric or dramatic voices

Hier in stillen Schatten gründen
(Lady Harriet Durham • Lyonel)
• *Martha* (Flotow)
• lyric voices

Ich grüsse dich, du Bote
(Prima Donna/Ariadne • Bacchus)
• *Ariadne auf Naxos* (Strauss)
• dramatic voices

Ich setz den Fall (Laura • Symon Rymanovicz)
• *Der Bettelstudent* (Millöcker)
• light or lyric voices

Jetzt, Schätzchen, jetzt sind wir allein
(Marzelline • Jaquino)
• *Fidelio* (Beethoven)
• light voices

Kannst du zweifeln
(Anna Reich [Anne Page] • Fenton)
• *Die lustigen Weiber von Windsor* (Nicolai)
• light or lyric voices

Machen wir's den Schwalben nach
(Komtesse Stasi [Countess Stasi] • Edwin)
(Komtesse Stasi is a soubrette.)
• *Die Csárdásfürstin* (Kálmán)
• light or lyric voices

Meine Seele hüpft von Freuden
(Zaïde • Gomatz)
• *Zaïde* (Mozart)
• light or lyric voices

Meinetwegen sollst du sterben
(Konstanze • Belmonte)
• *Die Entführung aus dem Serail* (Mozart)
• lyric voices

Niemand liebt dich so wie ich
(Anna Elisa • Paganini)
• *Paganini* (Lehár)
• light or lyric voices

O, du lieber, o du g'scheiter (Hélène • Niki)
• *Ein Walzertraum* (Straus)
• light or lyric voices

O ew'ge Nacht (Isolde • Tristan)
• *Tristan und Isolde* (Wagner)
• dramatic voices

O namenlose Freude! (Leonore • Florestan)
• *Fidelio* (Beethoven)
• dramatic voices

O sink' hernieder, Nacht der Liebe
(Isolde • Tristan)
• *Tristan und Isolde* (Wagner)
• dramatic voices

O süsseste Wonne! seligstes Weib!
(Sieglinde • Siegmund)
• *Die Walküre* (Wagner)
• dramatic voices

O Tanz, o Rausch (Marietta • Paul)
• *Die tote Stadt* (Korngold)
• lyric or dramatic voices

Schenkt man sich Rosen in Tirol
(Electress Marie • Adam)
• *Der Vogelhändler* (Zeller)
• light or lyric voices

Schön wie die blaue Sommernacht
(Giuditta • Octavio)
• *Giuditta* (Lehár)
• lyric voices

Siegmund! Sieh' auf mich
(Brünnhilde • Siegmund)
• *Die Walküre* (Wagner)
• dramatic voices

Tausend kleine Engel singen (Sylva • Edwin)
• *Die Csárdásfürstin* (Kálmán)
• light or lyric voices

Thränen, Thränen (Fatime • Abu Hassan)
• *Abu Hassan* (Weber)
• lyric voices

Unheilvolle Daphne (Daphne • Apollo)
• *Daphne* (Strauss)
• dramatic voices

Verlässt die Kirche mich/
  Wohl liebst auch ich (Irene • Rienzi)
• *Rienzi* (Wagner)
• dramatic voices

Warum hat jeder Frühling, ach, nur einen
  Mai? (Sonja • Der Zarewitsch [Tsarevich])
• *Der Zarewitsch* (Lehár)
• light or lyric voices

Was musst' ich hören, Gott (Senta • Erik)
• *Der fliegende Holländer* (Wagner)
• dramatic voices

Was seh ich?/Nicht wollen die Götter
(Daphne • Apollo)
• *Daphne* (Strauss)
• dramatic voices

Welch ein Geschick!/Ha! du solltest
  für mich sterben (Konstanze • Belmonte)
• *Die Entführung aus dem Serail* (Mozart)
• lyric voices

Wunderbar! Ja, wunderbar (Marietta • Paul)
• *Die tote Stadt* (Korngold)
• lyric or dramatic voices

Zwei, die sich lieben, vergessen
die Welt (Anita • Pierrino)
• *Giuditta* (Lehár)
• light voices

ITALIAN

A voti così ardente [De cet aveu
si tendre] (Maria [Marie] • Tonio)
• *La figlia del reggimento*
  [*La fille du régiment*] (Donizetti)
• light or lyric voices

Ah! d'immenso, estremo affetto
(Beatrice • Orombello)
• *Beatrice di Tenda* (Bellini)
• lyric voices

Ah! dimmi...dimmi io t'amo (Linda • Carlo)
• *Linda di Chamounix* (Donizetti)
• light or lyric voices

Ah ferma!...Ah senti! (Paride • Elena)
(Paride, originally written for soprano
castrato, is sung by tenor or soprano.)
• *Paride ed Elena* (Gluck)
• lyric voices

Ah, per sempre/Pronti destrieri/
  Seguirti (Leonora • Don Alvaro)
• *La forza del destino* (Verdi)
• dramatic voices

Ah perchè (Alceste • Admeto)
• *Alceste* (Gluck)
• lyric or dramatic voices

Ah! se tu vuoi fuggir
(Alaide [La Straniera] • Arturo)
• *La Straniera* (Bellini)
• lyric voices

Ah sì, voliamo al tempio (Lina • Stiffelio)
• *Stiffelio* (Verdi)
• lyric or dramatic voices

Amaro sol per te (Fidelia • Edgar)
• *Edgar* (Puccini)
• lyric voices

Anima mia!/Risorge ne' tuoi lumi
(Alzira • Zamoro)
• *Alzira* (Verdi)
• lyric or dramatic voices

Bagnato dalle lagrime (Imogene • Gualtiero)
• *Il pirata* (Bellini)
• lyric or dramatic voices

Bimba dagli occhi pieni di malià
(Cio-Cio-San [Madama Butterfly] • Pinkerton)
• *Madama Butterfly* (Puccini)
• lyric or dramatic voices

Cara non dubitar/Io ti lascio
(Carolina • Paolino)
• *Il matrimonio segreto* (Cimarosa)
• light voices

Cara, sarò fedele (Armida • Rinaldo)
• *Armida* (Haydn)
• light or lyric voices

Cara sei tu il mio bene
(Rosina • Il Conte di Almaviva/Lindoro)
• *Il barbiere di Siviglia* (Paisiello)
• light voices

Cari figli [Aux cris de la douleur] (Alceste • Admeto)
• *Alceste* (Gluck)
• lyric or dramatic voices

Che mai fate voi?/De qual amor
[Que faites-vous donc?] (Elisabetta [Elisabeth] •
Don Carlo [Don Carlos [Don Carlo]])
• *Don Carlo* [*Don Carlos*] (Verdi)
• lyric or dramatic voices

Chiedi all'aura lusinghiera (Adina • Nemorino)
• *L'elisir d'amore* (Donizetti)
• light voices

Come il foco allo splendore (Euridice • Orfeo)
• *L'anima del filosofo* (Haydn)
• light voices

Da tutti abbandonata (Maria Stuarda • Leicester)
• *Maria Stuarda* (Donizetti)
• lyric or dramatic voices

Di pescatore ignobile (Lucrezia • Gennaro)
• *Lucrezia Borgia* (Donizetti)
• lyric or dramatic voices

Di tue pene sparve il sogno (Linda • Carlo)
• *Linda di Chamounix* (Donizetti)
• light or lyric voices

Dio ti giocondi, o sposo (Desdemona • Otello)
• *Otello* (Verdi)
• lyric or dramatic voices

Dolce mia vita sei (Melanto • Eurimaco)
• *Il ritorno d'Ulisse in patria* (Monteverdi)
• light or lyric voices

**Dunque, o cruda, e gloria e trono/
Vieni al tempio** (Giovanna • Carlo VII)
• *Giovanna d'Arco* (Verdi)
• lyric or dramatic voices

E ben altro il mio sogno (Giorgetta • Luigi)
• *Il Tabarro* (Puccini)
• lyric or dramatic voices

E deciso: tu parti (Zazà • Dufresne)
• *Zazà* (Leoncavallo)
• lyric voices

**E il sol dell'anima/Addio, addio speranza ed
anima** (Gilda • Il Duca di Mantua
[The Duke of Mantua])
• *Rigoletto* (Verdi)
• lyric voices

E ver?...sei d'altri? (Lida • Arrigo)
• *La battaglia di Legnano* (Verdi)
• lyric or dramatic voices

Ecco l'altare (Maddalena • Andrea Chénier)
• *Andrea Chénier* (Giordano)
• lyric or dramatic voices

Era d'amor l'immagine/Sul crin la rivale
(Elisabetta [Queen] • Leicester)
• *Maria Stuarda* (Donizetti)
• lyric or dramatic voices

**Forma ideal purissima/Amore, misterio
celeste** (Elèna [Helen of Troy] • Faust)
• *Mefistofele* (Boito)
• lyric or dramatic voices

Forse un dì conoscerete (Ninetta • Giannetto)
• *La gazza ladra* (Rossini)
• light voices

Fra gli amplessi (Fiordiligi • Ferrando)
• *Così fan tutte* (Mozart)
• lyric voices

Fra le tue braccia amore
(Manon Lescaut • Chevalier Des Grieux)
• *Manon Lescaut* (Puccini)
• lyric or dramatic voices

Fuggi, crudele, fuggi!
(Donna Anna • Don Ottavio)
(Don Ottavio is a light lyric tenor,
but Donna Anna is a dramatic soprano.)
• *Don Giovanni* (Mozart)
• lyric or dramatic voices

Già nella notte densa (Desdemona • Otello)
• *Otello* (Verdi)
• lyric or dramatic voices

Il suon dell'arpe angeliche
[Conversion Duet] (Paolina • Poliuto)
• *Poliuto* (Donizetti)
• lyric or dramatic voices

In mia man alfin tu sei (Norma • Pollione)
• *Norma* (Bellini)
• lyric or dramatic voices

Incauta, che festi! (Matilda • Leicester)
• *Elisabetta* (Rossini)
• lyric voices

Io non son che una povera fanciulla
(Minnie • Dick Johnson [Ramerrez])
• *La fanciulla del West* (Puccini)
• lyric or dramatic voices

Io ti rivedo/Ah! se un giorno
(Maria Stuarda • Leicester)
• *Maria Stuarda* (Donizetti)
• lyric or dramatic voices

**Io vengo a domandar/Perduto ben/
Sotto al mio piè** [Je viens solliciter]
(Elisabetta [Elisabeth] • Don Carlo [Don Carlos])
• *Don Carlo [Don Carlos]* (Verdi)
• lyric or dramatic voices

Labbra di foco (Nannetta • Fenton)
• *Falstaff* (Verdi)
• light or lyric voices

L'amo! L'adoro! (Elena • Paride)
(Paride, originally written for soprano castrato,
is sung by either tenor or soprano.)
• *Paride ed Elena* (Gluck)
• lyric voices

Lascia che pianga io solo (La Principessa
Fedora Romazoff [Princess Fedora] • Il Conte
Loris Ipanoff [Count Loris])
• *Fedora* (Giordano)
• dramatic voices

Libiamo ne' lieti calici [Brindisi]
(Violetta Valéry • Alfredo Germont)
• *La traviata* (Verdi)
• lyric voices

Lontano, lontano (Margherita • Faust)
• *Mefistofele* (Boito)
• lyric or dramatic voices

L'ora fatale è suonata! [L'heure fatale est sonnée!]
(Elisabetta [Elisabeth] • Don Carlo [Don Carlos])
• *Don Carlo [Don Carlos]* (Verdi)
• lyric or dramatic voices

Ma, chi sei? (Erasto • Paride)
(Paride, originally written for soprano
castrato, is sung by either tenor or soprano.)
• *Paride ed Elena* (Gluck)
• lyric voices

Ma come puoi lasciarmi (Magda • Ruggero)
• *La rondine* (Puccini)
• lyric voices

Mio caro ben non sospirar (Sidonia • Nino)
(Originally written for castrati.)
• *Astarto* (Bononcini)
• light voices

**Miserere d'un alma/Tu vedrai che
amore in terra** (Leonora • Manrico)
• *Il trovatore* (Verdi)
• lyric or dramatic voices

**Nel mirarti/Da quel dì/Vieni fra
queste braccia** (Elvira • Arturo)
• *I Puritani* (Bellini)
• lyric voices

No, no Turiddu, rimani (Santuzza • Turiddu)
• *Cavalleria rusticana* (Mascagni)
• dramatic voices

No, tu non sai/Tornerai, ma forse spenta
(Medora • Corrado)
• *Il corsaro* (Verdi)
• lyric or dramatic voices

Noi torneremo alla romita valle
(Aldona • Walter)
• *I Lituani* [*The Little Sweep*] (Ponchielli)
• dramatic voices

**Non, non morrai, chè i perfidi/Ah! speranza
dolce ancora** (Lucrezia Contarini • Jacopo Foscari)
• *I due Foscari* (Verdi)
• lyric or dramatic voices

**Non sai tu che se l'anima mia/
Oh qual soave brivido** (Amelia • Riccardo)
• *Un ballo in maschera* (Verdi)
• lyric or dramatic voices

O cara, o cara (Damigella • Valletto)
(Valletto was originally sung by a castrato.)
• *L'incoronazione di Poppea* (Monteverdi)
• light voices

O mia vita! O mia core (Ennone • Paride)
• *Il pomo d'oro* (Cesti)
• light or lyric voices

**O sdegni miei/Arrigo! ah parli a un core/E
dolce raggio** [De courroux/Pour moi rayonne]
(Elena [Hélène] • Arrigo [Henri])
• *I vespri siciliani* [*Les vêpres siciliennes*] (Verdi)
• lyric or dramatic voices

O soave fanciulla (Mimì • Rodolfo)
• *La Bohème* (Puccini)
• lyric voices

Ogni virtù più bella (Ismene • Evandro)
• *Alceste* (Gluck)
• light voices

**Oh belle, a questa misera/
Ah, vieni, sol morte** (Giselda • Oronte)
• *I Lombardi* (Verdi)
• lyric or dramatic voices

Oh Luigi! Luigi! Bada a te! (Giorgetta • Luigi)
• *Il Tabarro* (Puccini)
• lyric or dramatic voices

Or dammi il braccio tuo (Iris • Osaka)
• *Iris* (Mascagni)
• lyric or dramatic voices

Ora soave (Maddalena • Andrea Chénier)
• *Andrea Chénier* (Giordano)
• lyric or dramatic voices

Parigi, o cara/Ah, gran Dio! morir sì giovane
(Violetta Valéry • Alfredo Germont)
• *La traviata* (Verdi)
• lyric voices

Parla, in tuo cor virgineo (Amelia [Maria
Boccanegra] • Gabriele Adorno)
• *Simon Boccanegra* (Verdi)
• lyric or dramatic voices

Perchè mai cercate (Magda • Ruggero)
• *La rondine* (Puccini)
• lyric voices

Perchè mai, destin crudel
  (Elisabetta [Queen] • Norfolk)
• *Elisabetta* (Rossini)
• lyric voices

Perdona! perdona/No, più nobile sei
  (Adriana Lecouvreur • Maurizio)
• *Adriana Lecouvreur* (Cilea)
• lyric or dramatic voices

**Piangi, piangi, il tuo dolore/Maledetto
il dì ch'io nacqui** (Luisa • Rodolfo)
• *Luisa Miller* (Verdi)
• lyric or dramatic voices

**Plauso! Voce di gioia!/Sin la tomba
è a me negata** (Antonina • Eutopio)
• *Belisario* (Donizetti)
• lyric or dramatic voices

Prendi, l'anel ti dono (Amina • Elvino)
• *La sonnambula* (Bellini)
• lyric voices

Principessa di morte/Mio fiore!
  (Turandot • Calaf)
• *Turandot* (Puccini)
• dramatic voices

Qual contento (Angelica • Medoro)
• *Orlando Paladino* (Haydn)
• light voices

Qual cor tradisti (Norma • Pollione)
• *Norma* (Bellini)
• lyric or dramatic voices

Quale, o prode/Presso alla tomba
  [Comment/Près du tombeau]
  (Elena [Hélène] • Arrigo [Henri])
• *I vespri siciliani* [*Les vêpres siciliennes*] (Verdi)
• lyric or dramatic voices

**Quando narravi l'esule tua vita/
E tu m'amavi** (Desdemona • Otello)
• *Otello* (Verdi)
• lyric or dramatic voices

Qui il padre ancor respira (Lucia • Arturo)
• *Lucia di Lammermoor* (Donizetti)
• lyric voices

Rosina vezzosina (Rosina • Errico)
• *La vera Costanza* (Haydn)
• light or lyric voices

Se viver non degg'io (Aspasia • Sifare)
  (Sifare was sung by either
  soprano (pants role) or tenor.)
• *Mitridate* (Mozart)
• lyric voices

Seid la vuole/La terra, il ciel m'abborrino
  (Gulnara • Corrado)
• *Il corsaro* (Verdi)
• lyric or dramatic voices

Sento un certo/Dolce Amor!
  (Aminta • Henry Morosus)
• *Die schweigsame Frau* (Strauss)
• lyric or dramatic voices

Serba, serba i tuoi segreti
  (Alaide [La Straniera] • Arturo)
• *La Straniera* (Bellini)
• lyric voices

**Sì, quello io son, ravvisami/Oh t'innebria
nell'amplesso** (Odabello • Foresto)
• *Attila* (Verdi)
• dramatic voices

S'io non moro (Ilia • Idamante)
  (Idamante, originally castrato, is sung
  by tenor, soprano, or mezzo-soprano.)
• *Idomeneo* (Mozart)
• light or lyric voices

**Sogno dorato io feci!/Sì l'eroismo è
questo/Ma lassù** [J'avais fait un beau rêve]
  (Elisabetta [Elisabeth] • Don Carlo [Don Carlos])
• *Don Carlo* [*Don Carlos*] (Verdi)
• lyric or dramatic voices

Son geloso del zefiro errante (Amina • Elvino)
• *La sonnambula* (Bellini)
• lyric voices

Son quest'occhi un stral d'Amore (Rezia • Ali)
• *L'incontro improvviso* (Haydn)
• light voices

Spiegarti non poss'io (Ilia • Idamante)
  (Idamante, originally castrato, is sung
  by tenor, soprano, or mezzo-soprano.)
• *Idomeneo* (Mozart)
• light or lyric voices

**Sulla tomba che rinserra/Verranno
a te sull'aure** (Lucia • Edgardo)
• *Lucia di Lammermoor* (Donizetti)
• lyric voices

**Suzel, buon dì/Han della porpora
vivo il colore** (Suzel • Fritz Kobus)
• *L'amico Fritz* (Mascagni)
• lyric voices

**T'abbraccio/Qual mare, qual terra/
Lassù resplendere** (Amalia • Carlo)
• *I Masnadieri* (Verdi)
• lyric or dramatic voices

Tornami a dir che m'ami (Norina • Ernesto)
• *Don Pasquale* (Donizetti)
• light voices

Tu dall'infanzia mia (Anna • Roberto)
• *Le villi* (Puccini)
• lyric voices

Tu mi lasci? (Sandrina • Belfiore)
• *La finta Giardiniera* (Mozart)
• light or lyric voices

Tu sciagurato! ah! fuggi (Imogene • Gualtiero)
• *Il pirata* (Bellini)
• lyric or dramatic voices

Tu sei la mia vittoria
(Adriana Lecouvreur • Maurizio)
• *Adriana Lecouvreur* (Cilea)
• lyric or dramatic voices

Tu, tu, amore?/E fascino d'amor
(Manon Lescaut • Chevalier Des Grieux)
• *Manon Lescaut* (Puccini)
• lyric or dramatic voices

Un certo ruscelletto (Clarice • Ecclitico)
• *Il mondo della luna* (Haydn)
• light or lyric voices

**Un dì felice, eterea/De quell'amor ch'è
palpito** (Violetta Valéry • Alfredo Germont)
• *La traviata* (Verdi)
• lyric voices

Ve' come gli astri stessi (Elvira • Ernani)
• *Ernani* (Verdi)
• lyric or dramatic voices

Vedete? io son fedele
(Manon Lescaut • Chevalier Des Grieux)
• *Manon Lescaut* (Puccini)
• lyric or dramatic voices

**Vedi?...di morte l'angelo/
O terra addio** (Aïda • Radames)
• *Aïda* (Verdi)
• lyric or dramatic voices

Vendetta d'un momento (Lida • Arrigo)
• *La battaglia di Legnano* (Verdi)
• lyric or dramatic voices

Vicino a te s'acqueta/La nostra morte
(Maddalena • Andrea Chénier)
• *Andrea Chénier* (Giordano)
• lyric or dramatic voices

Viene la sera (Cio-Cio-San
[Madama Butterfly] • Pinkerton)
• *Madama Butterfly* (Puccini)
• lyric or dramatic voices

**Vieni a mirar la cerula/
Sì, sì, dell'ara il giubilo**
(Amelia [Maria Boccanegra] • Gabriele Adorno)
• *Simon Boccanegra* (Verdi)
• lyric or dramatic voices

Vieni, ah! vieni [Viens, viens, je cède éperdu]
(Leonora [Léonor] • Fernando [Fernand])
• *La favorita* [*La favorite*] (Donizetti)
• lyric or dramatic voices

**Vieni, cerchiam pe' mari/Taci, taci:
rimorsi amari** (Imogene • Gualtiero)
• *Il pirata* (Bellini)
• lyric or dramatic voices

RUSSIAN

Swan Lake Duet [commonly known title]
(Undina • Hulbrand)
• *Undina* (Tchaikovsky)
• lyric voices

SPANISH

Coloquio en la reja (Rosario • Fernando)
• *Goyescas* (Granados)
• lyric voices

soprano • baritone

ENGLISH

Ah Minette, at last we meet in death
(Minette • Tom [Cat])
• *The English Cat* (Henze)
• lyric voices

Hello? Hello? Where are you, my darling?
(Lucy • Ben)
• *The Telephone* (Menotti)
• light or lyric voices

I have a song to sing, O!
(Elsie Maynard • Jack Point)
• *The Yeomen of the Guard* (Sullivan)
• light voices

Pretty Polly, say (Polly Peachum • Macheath)
• *The Beggar's Opera* (Pepusch)
• light voices

Prithee, pretty maiden (Patience • Grosvenor)
• *Patience* (Sullivan)
• light voices

Promise Duet [commonly known title]
(Minette • Tom [Cat])
• *The English Cat* (Henze)
• lyric voices

Why does beauty bring desire?
(Minette • Tom [Cat])
• *The English Cat* (Henze)
• lyric voices

FRENCH

Au bruit de la guerre [Apparvi alla luce]
(Marie [Maria] • Sulpice [Sulpizio])
• *La fille du régiment* [*La figlia
del reggimento*] (Donizetti)
• light or lyric voices

Baigne d'eau mes mains (Thaïs • Athanaël)
• *Thaïs* (Massenet)
• lyric or dramatic voices

C'est sur ce banc (Pénélope • Eumée)
• *Pénélope* (Fauré)
• lyric or dramatic voices

Doute de la lumière (Ophélie • Hamlet)
• *Hamlet* (Thomas)
• lyric voices

Esprits de haine et de rage (Armide • Hidraot)
• *Armide* (Gluck)
• dramatic voices

Esprits de haine et de rage (Armide • Hidraot)
• *Armide* (Lully)
• dramatic voices

Oui, je vous hais (Alexina • Henri de Valois)
• *Le roi malgré lui* (Chabrier)
• lyric voices

Pour moi, je ne crains rien (Leïla • Zurga)
• *Les pêcheurs de perles* (Bizet)
• lyric voices

Quand j'ai quitté le château de mon père/O mon amour [Quando le soglie paterne vareai/Ah! l'alto ardor] (Leonora [Léonor] • Alfonso [Alphonse])
• *La favorita* [*La favorite*] (Donizetti)
• lyric or dramatic voices

Te souvient-il du lumineux voyage [Méditation] (Thaïs • Athanaël)
• *Thaïs* (Massenet)
• lyric or dramatic voices

GERMAN

Bei jedem Walzerschritt (Hanna Glawari • Graf Danilo Danilowitsch [Count Danilo])
• *Die lustige Witwe* (Lehár)
• light or lyric voices

Bei Männern, welche Liebe fühlen (Pamina • Papageno)
• *Die Zauberflöte* (Mozart)
• light or lyric voices

Das süsse Lied verhallt (Elsa • Lohengrin)
• *Lohengrin* (Wagner)
• dramatic voices

Gut'n Abend, Meister! (Eva • Hans Sachs)
• *Die Meistersinger von Nürnberg* (Wagner)
• lyric or dramatic voices

Marta!...Tu mit mir, was du willst (Marta • Sebastiano)
• *Tiefland* (Albert)
• dramatic voices

Orest! Orest! Orest! (Elektra • Orest)
• *Elektra* (Strauss)
• dramatic voices

Pa-pa-pa- (Papagena • Papageno)
• *Die Zauberflöte* (Mozart)
• light voices

Sie woll'n mich heiraten (Arabella • Mandryka)
• *Arabella* (Strauss)
• lyric or dramatic voices

So jetzt hätt' ich ihn gefangen (Frau Fluth [Mrs. Ford] • Herr Fluth [Mr. Ford])
• *Die lustigen Weiber von Windsor* (Nicolai)
• lyric voices

Und du wirst mein Gebieter sein [Submission Duet] (Arabella • Mandryka)
• *Arabella* (Strauss)
• lyric or dramatic voices

Was willst du, fremder Mensch? (Elektra • Orest)
• *Elektra* (Strauss)
• dramatic voices

Wie aus der Ferne längst vergang'n Zeiten (Senta • Der Holländer [The Dutchman])
• *Der fliegende Holländer* (Wagner)
• dramatic voices

ITALIAN

Amai, ma un solo istante/Or del padre benedetta (Giovanna • Giacomo)
• *Giovanna d'Arco* (Verdi)
• lyric or dramatic voices

Apparvi alla luce [Au bruit de la guerre] (Maria [Marie] • Sulpizio [Sulpice])
• *La figlia del reggimento* [*La fille du régiment*] (Donizetti)
• light or lyric voices

Bambina, non ti crucciar (Adriana Lecouvreur • Michonnet)
• *Adriana Lecouvreur* (Cilea)
• lyric or dramatic voices

Caro! bella! più amabile beltà (Cleopatra • Giulio Cesare) (Giulio Cesare was originally written for soprano castrato.)
• *Giulio Cesare in Egitto* (Handel)
• lyric or dramatic voices

Colei Sofronia (Eleonora • Tasso)
• *Torquato Tasso* (Donizetti)
• lyric or dramatic voices

Colma di gioia ho l'anima (Alzira • Gusmano)
• *Alzira* (Verdi)
• lyric or dramatic voices

Crudel! perchè finora (Susanna • Il Conte di Almaviva [Count])
• *Le nozze di Figaro* (Mozart)
• lyric voices

Da qual dì che t'ho veduta (Elvira • Don Carlo)
• *Ernani* (Verdi)
• lyric or dramatic voices

Den non parlare al misero/ Ah! veglia, o donna (Gilda • Rigoletto)
• *Rigoletto* (Verdi)
• lyric or dramatic voices

Digli ch'è sangue italico (Lida • Rolando)
• *La battaglia di Legnano* (Verdi)
• lyric or dramatic voices

Dinnè, perchè in quest'eremo/Figlia! a tal nome io palpito (Amelia [Maria Boccanegra] • Simon Boccanegra [The Doge of Genoa])
• *Simon Boccanegra* (Verdi)
• lyric or dramatic voices

Donna? chi sei?/Oh di qual'onta aggravasi/Deh perdona (Abigaille • Nabucco)
• *Nabucco* (Verdi)
• dramatic voices

Ed io pure in faccia agl'uomini/ Or meco venite (Lina • Stankar)
• *Stiffelio* (Verdi)
• lyric or dramatic voices

**Fatal mia donna!/Allor questa voce/
Vieni altrove!** (Lady Macbeth • Macbeth)
• *Macbeth* (Verdi)
• dramatic voices

**Fuggiam gli ardori inospiti/Sì: fuggiam
da queste mura** (Aïda • Amonasro)
• *Aïda* (Verdi)
• dramatic voices

**Il pallor funesto, orrendo/Soffriva nel
pianto languia** (Lucia • Enrico Ashton)
• *Lucia di Lammermoor* (Donizetti)
• lyric voices

Io t'amo, Amalia/Ti scosta, o malnato
(Amalia • Francesco)
• *I Masnadieri* (Verdi)
• lyric or dramatic voices

**La tomba è un letto/Di rughe/Andrem,
raminghi e poveri** (Luisa • Miller)
• *Luisa Miller* (Verdi)
• lyric or dramatic voices

**Mira, di acerbe lagrime/Vivrà!...Contende il
giubilo** (Leonora • Il Conte di Luna [Count])
• *Il trovatore* (Verdi)
• lyric or dramatic voices

Odio e livore!—ingrato!
(Beatrice • Filippo Maria Visconti)
• *Beatrice di Tenda* (Bellini)
• lyric voices

Ora a noi (Cio-Cio-San
[Madama Butterfly] • Sharpless)
• *Madama Butterfly* (Puccini)
• lyric or dramatic voices

Ora di morte e di vendetta
(Lady Macbeth • Macbeth)
• *Macbeth* (Verdi)
• dramatic voices

**Perchè, perchè non m'ami più?/
Resta vicino a me** (Giorgetta • Michele)
• *Il Tabarro* (Puccini)
• lyric or dramatic voices

Piangi, fanciulla, piangi! (Gilda • Rigoletto)
• *Rigoletto* (Verdi)
• lyric or dramatic voices

Pronta io son (Norina • Dr. Malatesta)
• *Don Pasquale* (Donizetti)
• light voices

**Pura siccome un angelo/
Dite alla giovine/Morro!**
(Violetta Valéry • Giorgio Germont)
• *La traviata* (Verdi)
• lyric voices

**Quando le soglie paterne vareai/Ah! l'alto
ardor** [Quand j'ai quitté/O mon amour] (Leonora
[Léonor [Leonora]] • Alfonso [Alphonse])
• *La favorita* [*La favorite*] (Donizetti)
• lyric or dramatic voices

Quel tuo visetto amabile (Eurilla • Pasquale)
• *Orlando Paladino* (Haydn)
• light voices

**Rivedrai le foreste imbalsamate/
Padre!...a costoro** (Aïda • Amonasro)
• *Aïda* (Verdi)
• dramatic voices

Sei splendida e lucente
(Manon Lescaut • Lescaut)
• *Manon Lescaut* (Puccini)
• lyric or dramatic voices

**Silvio! a quest'ora/E allor perchè, dì, tu
m'hai stregato** (Nedda • Silvio
[Campagnuolo] [A Villager])
• *Pagliacci* (Leoncavallo)
• lyric voices

Speravo di trovarvi qui (Mimì • Marcello)
• *La Bohème* (Puccini)
• lyric voices

Tu por lo sai, che giudice (Lucrezia
Contarini • Francesco Foscari [Doge])
• *I due Foscari* (Verdi)
• lyric or dramatic voices

**Tutte le feste al tempio/Sì, vendetta,
tremenda vendetta** (Gilda • Rigoletto)
• *Rigoletto* (Verdi)
• lyric or dramatic voices

V'ho ingannato!/Lassù, in cielo
(Gilda • Rigoletto)
• *Rigoletto* (Verdi)
• lyric or dramatic voices

Vieni, Gulnara!/Sia l'istante maledetto
(Gulnara • Seid)
• *Il corsaro* (Verdi)
• lyric or dramatic voices

RUSSIAN

My heart is worn with fear [commonly known
title] (Tat'yana • Yevgeny Onegin [Eugene Onegin])
• *Yevgeny Onegin* [*Eugene Onegin*] (Tchaikovsky)
• lyric or dramatic voices

Onegin, I was then far younger
[commonly known title]
(Tat'yana • Yevgeny Onegin [Eugene Onegin])
• *Yevgeny Onegin* [*Eugene Onegin*] (Tchaikovsky)
• lyric or dramatic voices

On—moy sokol yasnïy!
[It is he, my bright falcon] (Yaroslavna • Igor')
• *Knyaz' Igor'* [*Prince Igor*] (Borodin)
• lyric or dramatic voices

soprano • bass-baritone

ENGLISH

Bess, you is my woman (Bess • Porgy)
• *Porgy and Bess* (Gershwin)
• dramatic voices

Oh take, oh take those lips away
(Cleopatra • Antony)
• *Antony and Cleopatra* (Barber)
• dramatic voices

GERMAN

Als junger Liebe Lust mir verblich
(Brünnhilde • Wotan)
• *Die Walküre* (Wagner)
• dramatic voices

Jochanaan, ich bin verliebt (Salome • Jochanaan)
• *Salome* (Strauss)
• dramatic voices

Mir anvertraut (Sein Weib [Wife of Barak] • Barak)
• *Die Frau ohne Schatten* (Strauss)
• dramatic voices

ITALIAN

Come frenar il pianto!
(Ninetta • Fernando Villabella)
• *La gazza ladra* (Rossini)
• light voices

So ben che difforme (Nedda • Tonio)
• *Pagliacci* (Leoncavallo)
• lyric or dramatic voices

Un buon servo del visconte (Linda • Antonio)
• *Linda di Chamounix* (Donizetti)
• light or lyric voices

RUSSIAN

Vsyo na zemle dlyz schast' ya roditsya
[Everything is born for love] (Virineya • Pavel)
• *Virineya* (Slonimsky)
• dramatic voices

soprano • bass

ENGLISH

**Every wearied body/God is merciful
and just** (Anne Trulove • Trulove)
• *The Rake's Progress* (Stravinsky)
• lyric voices

FRENCH

Ah! du moins à Médée (Médée • Créon)
• *Médée* (Chérubini)
• dramatic voices

**Quand j'ai quitté le château de mon père/
O mon amour** [Quando le soglie paterne vareai]
(Léonor [Leonora] • Alphonse [Alfonso])
• *La favorite* [*La favorita*] (Donizetti)
• lyric or dramatic voices

Sortez de l'esclavage (Telaïre • Pollux)
• *Castor et Pollux* (Rameau)
• lyric voices

GERMAN

Ich gehe, doch rate ich dir (Blonde • Osmin)
• *Die Entführung aus dem Serail* (Mozart)
• light or lyric voices

Lass Er doch hören (Gretchen • Baculus)
• *Der Wildschütz* (Lortzing)
• lyric or dramatic voices

Nein, nein! I' trink' kein Wein
(Octavian, genannt Quinquin [Count
Rofrano] • Baron Ochs auf Lerchenau)
• *Der Rosenkavalier* (Strauss)
• lyric or dramatic voices

Nur hurtig fort, nur frisch gegraben
(Leonore • Rocco)
• *Fidelio* (Beethoven)
• lyric or dramatic voices

Piccolo, piccolo (Franzi • Count Lothar)
• *Ein Walzertraum* (Straus)
• light voices

Wo ist mein Bruder?/Morgen mittag um elf
(Die Gräfin [Countess Madeleine] • Major-Domo)
• *Capriccio* (Strauss)
• lyric or dramatic voices

ITALIAN

Carlo! io muoio
(Amalia • Massimiliano [Count Moor])
• *I Masnadieri* (Verdi)
• lyric or dramatic voices

Cinque, dieci, venti (Susanna • Figaro)
• *Le nozze di Figaro* (Mozart)
• lyric voices

Contento tu sarai [Reconciliation Duet]
(Serpina • Uberto)
• *Serva padrona, La* (Pergolesi)
• light voices

Credete alla femmine (Fiorilla • Selim)
• *Il turco in Italia* (Rossini)
• light voices

Il mio garzone il piffaro sonava
(Rachelina • Pistofolo [Notaio])
• *La molinara* (Paisiello)
• light or lyric voices

**Infelice, delusa/Chi può legger nel
futuro/Sull'alba** (Leonora • Guardiano [Padre])
• *La forza del destino* (Verdi)
• lyric or dramatic voices

Io son ricco e tu sei bella
(Adina • Dr. Dulcamara)
• *L'elisir d'amore* (Donizetti)
• light voices

Lo conosco a quegl'occhieti
[Conflict Duet] (Serpina • Uberto)
• *Serva padrona, La* (Pergolesi)
• light voices

Nel veder quel tuo sembiante
(Beatrice • Il Conte Caramella [Count])
• *I due supposti Conti* (Cimarosa)
• light or lyric voices

O felice Mustafà/O Girello in povertà
(Mustafà • Girello)
(Mustafà is a pants role for soprano.)
• *Girello* (Stradella)
• light voices

Pace, caro mio sposo (Lilla • Lubino)
• *Una cosa rara* (Martín y Soler)
• light voices

Per piacere alla Signora (Fiorilla • Geronio)
• *Il turco in Italia* (Rossini)
• light voices

Per te ho io nel core (Checca • Vastiano)
• *Flaminio* (Pergolesi)
• light voices

Per te ho io nel core (Serpina • Uberto)
• *Serva padrona, La* (Pergolesi)
• light voices

Quando di luce rosea (Maria Stuarda • Talbot)
• *Maria Stuarda* (Donizetti)
• lyric or dramatic voices

Quanto amore (Adina • Dr. Dulcamara)
• *L'elisir d'amore* (Donizetti)
• light voices

Quella ricordati (Semiramide • Assur)
• *Semiramide* (Rossini)
• lyric voices

**Sai com'arde in petto mio/Piangi,
o figlia/A quel nome** (Elvira • Giorgio)
• *I Puritani* (Bellini)
• lyric voices

Se a caso Madama (Susanna • Figaro)
• *Le nozze di Figaro* (Mozart)
• lyric voices

Son disperato (Vespina • Nanni)
• *L'infedeltà delusa* (Haydn)
• light voices

Tu m'apristi in cor ferita (Imogene • Ernesto)
• *Il pirata* (Bellini)
• lyric or dramatic voices

RUSSIAN

Quarrel Duet [commonly known title]
(Odarka • Karas [Zaparozhets])
• *Zaparozhets za Dunayem* [*A Cossack
beyond the Danube*] (Gulak-Artemovsky)
• lyric or dramatic voices

---

mezzo-soprano

---

mezzo-soprano • soprano

ENGLISH

Fear no danger (Second Woman • Belinda)
• *Dido and Aeneas* (Purcell)
• light voices

Joys of freedom (Dejanira • Iöle)
• *Hercules* (Handel)
• light or lyric voices

You love him, seek to set him right
(Baba • Anne Trulove)
• *The Rake's Progress* (Stravinsky)
• lyric voices

FRENCH

C'était bien gentil autrefois
(Irène • Fanny [Sapho])
• *Sapho* (Massenet)
• lyric voices

Dans ce séjour (Ragonde • La Comtesse
Adèle di Formouters [Countess])
• *Le comte Ory* (Rossini)
• light or lyric voices

Nuit paisible et sereine!
[Nocturne Duet] (Ursula • Héro)
• *Béatrice et Bénédict* (Berlioz)
• light voices

Sous le dôme épais (Mallika • Lakmé)
• *Lakmé* (Delibes)
• light or lyric voices

GERMAN

Abends will ich schlafen gehn
[Prayer] (Hänsel • Gretel)
• *Hänsel und Gretel* (Humperdinck)
• light or lyric voices

Ach! du bist wieder da (Octavian, genannt
Quinquin [Count Rofrano] • Die Feldmarchallin
Fürstin Werdenberg [Marie Thérèse] [Marschallin])
(Octavian is sung by either soprano
or mezzo-soprano.)
• *Der Rosenkavalier* (Strauss)
• lyric or dramatic voices

Ach, mich zieht's zu dir [Kissing Duet]
(Ganymede • Galathee)
• *Die schöne Galathee* (Suppé)
• light or lyric voices

Ein Augenblick ist wenig (Der Komponist
[The Composer] • Zerbinetta)
(Der Komponist is sung by either
soprano or mezzo-soprano.)
• *Ariadne auf Naxos* (Strauss)
• lyric voices

Ein Männlein steht im Walde (Hänsel • Gretel)
• *Hänsel und Gretel* (Humperdinck)
• light or lyric voices

Er geht/Ja, eine Welt voll Leiden
(Adriano • Irene)
• *Rienzi* (Wagner)
• dramatic voices

Florenz hat schöne Frauen
(Boccaccio • Fiametta)
• *Boccaccio* (Suppé)
• light voices

Ich kenn' Ihn schon recht wohl (Octavian, genannt Quinquin [Count Rofrano] • Sophie)
(Octavian is sung by either soprano or mezzo-soprano.)
• *Der Rosenkavalier* (Strauss)
• lyric voices

Ist ein Traum, kann nicht wirklich? (Octavian, genannt Quinquin [Count Rofrano] • Sophie)
(Octavian is sung by either soprano or mezzo-soprano.)
• *Der Rosenkavalier* (Strauss)
• lyric voices

Lachst du mich aus? (Octavian, genannt Quinquin [Count Rofrano] • Die Feldmarchallin Fürstin Werdenberg [Marie Thérèse] [Marschallin])
(Octavian is sung by either soprano or mezzo-soprano.)
• *Der Rosenkavalier* (Strauss)
• lyric or dramatic voices

Mir ist die Ehre widerfahren/Mit Ihren Augen voll Tränen [Presentation of the Rose] (Octavian, genannt Quinquin [Count Rofrano] • Sophie)
(Octavian is sung by either soprano or mezzo-soprano.)
• *Der Rosenkavalier* (Strauss)
• lyric voices

Nun ist die Hexe tot [Gingerbread Waltz] (Hänsel • Gretel)
• *Hänsel und Gretel* (Humperdinck)
• light or lyric voices

Schelm, halt' fest! (Ännchen • Agathe)
(Ännchen is sung by either a mezzo-soprano or a soprano.)
• *Der Freischütz* (Weber)
• lyric voices

Suse, liebe Suse/Brüderchen komm tanz mit mir (Hänsel • Gretel)
• *Hänsel und Gretel* (Humperdinck)
• light or lyric voices

Von den edlen Kavalieren (Nancy • Lady Harriet Durham)
• *Martha* (Flotow)
• lyric voices

Weit über Glanz und Erdenschimmer (Maragond • Florinda)
• *Fierrabras* (Schubert)
• light or lyric voices

ITALIAN

Ah perdona al primo affetto (Annio • Servilia)
(Annio [a pants role] can be sung by either soprano or mezzo-soprano.)
• *La clemenza di Tito* (Mozart)
• light or lyric voices

Ah! sì, fa core e abbracciami (Adalgisa • Norma)
(Adalgisa is sung by either soprano or mezzo-soprano.)
• *Norma* (Bellini)
• lyric voices

Al fato dan legge (Dorabella • Fiordiligi)
(Dorabella is sung by either soprano or mezzo-soprano.)
• *Così fan tutte* (Mozart)
• lyric voices

Aprite, presto aprite [Escape Duet] (Cherubino • Susanna)
(Cherubino is sung by either soprano or mezzo-soprano.)
• *Le nozze di Figaro* (Mozart)
• lyric voices

D'Eliso in sen m'attendi (Cecilio • Giunia)
(Cecilio, originally soprano castrato, is for soprano or mezzo-soprano.)
• *Lucio Silla* (Mozart)
• lyric voices

Dio, che mi vedi in core/Va, infelice (Giovanna Seymour • Anna Bolena)
• *Anna Bolena* (Donizetti)
• lyric or dramatic voices

Farewell Duet [commonly known title] (Oreste • Ermione)
(Oreste was originally written for mezzo-soprano castrato.)
• *Oreste* (Handel)
• lyric voices

Idolo del cor mio (Nerone • Poppea)
(Nerone, originally written for soprano castrato, is soprano or mezzo-soprano today.)
• *L'incoronazione di Poppea* (Monteverdi)
• lyric or dramatic voices

Io son sua per l'amor (La Principessa di Bouillon [The Princess of Bouillon • Adriana Lecouvreur)
• *Adriana Lecouvreur* (Cilea)
• lyric voices

Mira, o Norma/Sì, fino all'ore estreme (Adalgisa • Norma)
(Adalgisa is sung by either soprano or mezzo-soprano.)
• *Norma* (Bellini)
• lyric voices

Ne più s'interporà (Nerone • Poppea)
(Nerone, originally written for soprano castrato, is soprano or mezzo-soprano today.)
• *L'incoronazione di Poppea* (Monteverdi)
• lyric or dramatic voices

O guarda sorella (Dorabella • Fiordiligi)
(Dorabella can be sung by either mezzo-soprano or soprano.)
• *Così fan tutte* (Mozart)
• lyric voices

Per le porte (Tirinto • Rosmene)
• *Imeneo* (Handel)
• light or lyric voices

**Pietà ti prenda del mio dolore/Alla pompa
che s'appresta** (Amneris • Aïda)
• *Aïda* (Verdi)
• dramatic voices

Prenderò quel brunettino (Dorabella • Fiordiligi)
(Dorabella can be sung by either
soprano or mezzo-soprano.)
• *Così fan tutte* (Mozart)
• lyric voices

Pur ti miro (Nerone • Poppea)
(Nerone, originally soprano castrato,
is soprano or mezzo-soprano today.)
• *L'incoronazione di Poppea* (Monteverdi)
• lyric or dramatic voices

**Scuoti quella fronda di ciliegio/
Tutti i fior** [Flower Duet]
(Suzuki • Cio-Cio-San [Madama Butterfly])
• *Madama Butterfly* (Puccini)
• lyric voices

**Sì, fuggire: a noi non resta/Ah!
crudel d'onor ragioni** (Romeo • Giulietta)
• *I Capuleti e i Montecchi* (Bellini)
• lyric voices

**Soccorso, sostegno accordate/
Non si pianga** (Romeo • Giulietta)
• *I Capuleti e i Montecchi* (Bellini)
• lyric voices

Via resti servita (Marcellina • Susanna)
(Marcellina is sung by either
soprano or mezzo-soprano.)
• *Le nozze di Figaro* (Mozart)
• light or lyric voices

Vivere io non potrò (Malcolm • Elena)
• *La donna del lago* (Rossini)
• lyric or dramatic voices

mezzo-soprano • mezzo-soprano
FRENCH

Belle nuit, ô nuit d'amour [Barcarolle]
(Nicklausse • Giulietta)
(Both roles can be sung by either
soprano or mezzo-soprano.)
• *Les contes d'Hoffmann* (Offenbach)
• lyric voices

GERMAN

Unter ist mein Stern gegangen
(Euryanthe • Eglantine)
(Either role can be sung by either a
mezzo-soprano or a soprano.)
• *Euryanthe* (Weber)
• dramatic voices

ITALIAN

Come ti piace, imponi (Sesto • Vitellia)
(Sesto was written for castrato; each role
can be sung by soprano or mezzo-soprano.)
• *La clemenza di Tito* (Mozart)
• lyric or dramatic voices

Deh prendi un dolce amplesso (Sesto • Annio)
(Annio [pants role] and Sesto [castrato] both
can be sung by soprano or mezzo-soprano.)
• *La clemenza di Tito* (Mozart)
• lyric voices

L'amo come il fulgor del creato
(Laura • La Gioconda)
(The role of La Gioconda is sung by
either soprano or mezzo-soprano.)
• *La Gioconda* (Ponchielli)
• lyric or dramatic voices

mezzo-soprano • contralto
FRENCH

Sa voix fait naître dans mon sein
(Didon • Anna)
(Didon is sung by either a
soprano or a mezzo-soprano.)
• *Les Troyens* (Berlioz)
• dramatic voices

ITALIAN

Son nata a lagrimar (Sesto • Cornelia)
(Sesto, originally a castrato, can be
sung by soprano or mezzo-soprano.)
• *Giulio Cesare in Egitto* (Handel)
• lyric voices

mezzo-soprano • tenor
ENGLISH

If one last doubt (Cressida • Troilus [Prince])
• *Troilus and Cressida* (Walton)
• dramatic voices

Now close your arms (Cressida • Troilus [Prince])
• *Troilus and Cressida* (Walton)
• dramatic voices

FRENCH

A cette heure suprême (Charlotte • Werther)
• *Werther* (Massenet)
• lyric voices

Ai-je dit vrai/Ah! qu'il est loin
(Charlotte • Werther)
• *Werther* (Massenet)
• lyric voices

Comment le dédain pourrait-il mourir?
(Béatrice • Bénédict)
• *Béatrice et Bénédict* (Berlioz)
• light or lyric voices

Errante sur tes pas (Didon • Énée)
• *Les Troyens* (Berlioz)
• dramatic voices

Grand Dieu! sa misère est si grande!
(Zayda • Sébastien)
• *Dom Sébastien* (Donizetti)
• lyric or dramatic voices

Il faut nous séparer (Charlotte • Werther)
• *Werther* (Massenet)
• lyric voices

Il grandira, car il est espagnol (La
Périchole • Piquillo)
• *La Périchole* (Offenbach)
• light voices

Je suis heureuse! l'air m'enivre
(Mignon • Wilhelm Meister)
• *Mignon* (Thomas)
• lyric voices

Je vais revoir (Isolier [Page]
• Le Comte Ory [Count])
• *Le comte Ory* (Rossini)
• light or lyric voices

L'amour est un flambeau (Béatrice • Bénédict)
• *Béatrice et Bénédict* (Berlioz)
• light or lyric voices

Mes longs cheveux descendant
(Mélisande • Pelléas)
• *Pelléas et Mélisande* (Debussy)
• lyric voices

O ciel! où courez-vous?/Tu l'as dit
[O ciel! dove vai tu?] (Valentine • Raoul)
• *Les Huguenots* (Meyerbeer)
• lyric or dramatic voices

O Dieu! de quelle ivresse (Giulietta • Hoffmann)
• *Les contes d'Hoffmann* (Offenbach)
• lyric or dramatic voices

**Oui, c'est moi/N'achevez pas/Ah!
ce premier baiser** (Charlotte • Werther)
• *Werther* (Massenet)
• lyric voices

Toi qui m'es apparue (Cendrillon • Prince)
(The Prince was composed for a soprano,
but today is always sung by a tenor.)
• *Cendrillon* (Massenet)
• lyric voices

<h2 style="text-align:center">GERMAN</h2>

Bleib und wache bis sie dich ruft (Die Amme
[The Nurse] • Der Kaiser [The Emperor])
• *Die Frau ohne Schatten* (Strauss)
• dramatic voices

Hier weilest du/Wie liebt' ich dich
(Euryanthe • Adolar)
• *Euryanthe* (Weber)
• dramatic voices

Hin nimm die Seele mein (Euryanthe • Adolar)
• *Euryanthe* (Weber)
• dramatic voices

Wenn zum Gebet (Bostana • Nureddin)
• *Der Barbier von Bagdad* (Cornelius)
• lyric voices

<h2 style="text-align:center">ITALIAN</h2>

Ah! tu dei vivere/Che ti salva
(Amneris • Radames)
• *Aïda* (Verdi)
• dramatic voices

Bocca, bocca (Nerone • Lucano)
(Nerone, originally written for soprano castrato,
is soprano or mezzo-soprano today.)
• *L'incoronazione di Poppea* (Monteverdi)
• lyric voices

Deh, non turbare (Laura • Enzo)
• *La Gioconda* (Ponchielli)
• lyric or dramatic voices

**Eccomi giunto inosservato e solo/
A te sarà** (Desdemona • Otello)
• *Otello* (Rossini)
• lyric voices

Ella è morta, o sciagurato (Romeo • Tebaldo)
• *I Capuleti e i Montecchi* (Bellini)
• lyric voices

Oh, il Signore vi manda (Santuzza • Alfio)
• *Cavalleria rusticana* (Mascagni)
• dramatic voices

Perigliarti ancor languente (Azucena • Manrico)
• *Il trovatore* (Verdi)
• lyric or dramatic voices

Quale inchiesta! (Amneris • Radames)
• *Aïda* (Verdi)
• dramatic voices

Sì, la stanchezza/Ai nostri monti
(Azucena • Manrico)
• *Il trovatore* (Verdi)
• lyric or dramatic voices

Stolto! a un sol mio grido (Romeo • Tebaldo)
• *I Capuleti e i Montecchi* (Bellini)
• lyric voices

Tu qui, Santuzza? (Santuzza • Turiddu)
• *Cavalleria rusticana* (Mascagni)
• dramatic voices

Un soave non so che
(Cenerentola [Angelica] • Don Ramiro)
• *La Cenerentola* (Rossini)
• light voices

**Va, crudele, al dio spietato/
Vieni in Roma** (Adalgisa • Pollione)
• *Norma* (Bellini)
• lyric voices

<h2 style="text-align:center">RUSSIAN</h2>

Chudnïy pervenets tvoren'ya [Wondrous
firstling of creation] (Iolanta • Vaudémont)
• *Iolanta* (Tchaikovsky)
• lyric or dramatic voices

Dmitry! Tsarevich! (Marina • Dmitry)
• *Boris Godunov* (Musorgsky)
• lyric or dramatic voices

mezzo-soprano • baritone

ENGLISH

On the banks of the sweet Garonne
(Fatima • Sherasmin)
• *Oberon* (Weber)
• lyric voices

FRENCH

Ah! ah! tout va bien (Mélisande • Golaud)
• *Pelléas et Mélisande* (Debussy)
• lyric or dramatic voices

Cat Duet [commonly known title]
(Female Cat • Tom Cat)
• *l'Enfant et les sortilèges* (Ravel)
• light or lyric voices

Je ne pourrai plus sortir (Mélisande • Golaud)
• *Pelléas et Mélisande* (Debussy)
• lyric or dramatic voices

Reviens à toi, vierge adorée
(Cassandre • Chorèbe)
• *Les Troyens* (Berlioz)
• dramatic voices

GERMAN

Musik ist eine heilige Kunst
(Der Komponist [The Composer] •
Ein Musiklehrer [A Music Master])
• *Ariadne auf Naxos* (Strauss)
• lyric voices

ITALIAN

Ad essi non perdono (Santuzza • Alfio)
• *Cavalleria rusticana* (Mascagni)
• dramatic voices

Ah! se potessi piangere (Irene • Belisario)
• *Belisario* (Donizetti)
• lyric or dramatic voices

Per queste tue manine (Zerlina • Leporello)
• *Don Giovanni* (Mozart)
• light voices

Sì, il parto mantengo (La Gioconda • Barnaba)
• *La Gioconda* (Ponchielli)
• dramatic voices

Turiddu mi tolse (Santuzza • Alfio)
• *Cavalleria rusticana* (Mascagni)
• dramatic voices

mezzo-soprano • bass-baritone

GERMAN

Komm denn (Eglantine • Lysiart)
• *Euryanthe* (Weber)
• dramatic voices

ITALIAN

Là ci darem la mano/Andiam mio bene
(Zerlina • Don Giovanni)
• *Don Giovanni* (Mozart)
• light or lyric voices

mezzo-soprano • bass

FRENCH

As-tu souffert?/As-tu pleuré?
(Mignon • Lothario)
• *Mignon* (Thomas)
• lyric voices

Dans la nuit où seul je veille
(Valentine • Marcel)
• *Les Huguenots* (Meyerbeer)
• lyric voices

Derrière ce pilier (Valentine • Marcel)
• *Les Huguenots* (Meyerbeer)
• lyric voices

Légères hirondelles (Mignon • Lothario)
• *Mignon* (Thomas)
• lyric voices

Mais Alice, qu'as-tu donc? (Alice • Bertram)
• *Robert le Diable* (Meyerbeer)
• lyric or dramatic voices

Oui, je souffre votre tendresse
(Dulcinée • Don Quichotte)
• *Don Quichotte* (Massenet)
• lyric voices

Printemps revient (Cendrillon • Pandolphe)
• *Cendrillon* (Massenet)
• lyric voices

GERMAN

Lasst mich hier (Euryanthe • Louis VI)
• *Euryanthe* (Weber)
• dramatic voices

ITALIAN

Fama! sì: l'avrete
(Giovanna Seymour • Enrico [Henry VIII])
• *Anna Bolena* (Donizetti)
• lyric or dramatic voices

Il core vi dono (Dorabella • Guglielmo)
• *Così fan tutte* (Mozart)
• lyric voices

Oh qual parlar (Giovanna
Seymour • Enrico [Henry VIII])
• *Anna Bolena* (Donizetti)
• lyric or dramatic voices

Quarrel Duet [commonly known title]
(Vespetta • Pimpinone)
• *Pimpinone* (Albinoni)
• light voices

Qui chiamata m'avete? (Laura • Alvise)
• *La Gioconda* (Ponchielli)
• lyric or dramatic voices

RUSSIAN

Farewell my son, I am dying [commonly
known title] (Fyodor • Boris Godunov)
• *Boris Godunov* (Musorgsky)
• lyric or dramatic voices

---

contralto

---

contralto • soprano

ENGLISH

O Black Swan (Baba [Madame Flora] • Monica)
• *The Medium* (Menotti)
• lyric voices

GERMAN

Ich will nichts hören/Träumst du Mutter?
(Klytemnästra • Elektra)
(Klytemnästra is soprano,
mezzo-soprano, or contralto.)
• *Elektra* (Strauss)
• dramatic voices

Nein, das ist wirklich doch zu keck! (Frau
Reich [Mrs. Page] • Frau Fluth [Mrs. Ford])
• *Die lustigen Weiber von Windsor* (Nicolai)
• lyric voices

ITALIAN

Al bel destin che attendevi (Pierotto • Linda)
• *Linda di Chamounix* (Donizetti)
• light or lyric voices

Avvezza al contento [Je goûtais les charmes]
(Orfeo [Orphée] • Euridice [Eurydice])
(Orfeo's role was originally written for alto castrato,
and is tenor in the French version. Orfeo is often
sung by a mezzo-soprano.)
• *Orfeo ed Euridice* [*Orphée et Eurydice*] (Gluck)
• lyric voices

Dite, che fà, dov'è (Tolomeo • Seleuce)
(The role of Tolomeo was originally
sung by an alto castrato.)
• *Tolomeo* (Handel)
• light or lyric voices

E ben, per mia memoria (Pippo • Ninetta)
• *La gazza ladra* (Rossini)
• light voices

Giorno d'orrore (Arsace • Semiramide)
• *Semiramide* (Rossini)
• lyric voices

Io t'abbraccio: è più che morte
(Bertarido • Rodelinda)
(The role of Bertarido was originally
sung by an alto castrato.)
• *Rodelinda* (Handel)
• light or lyric voices

Per le porte del tormento (Sosarme • Elmira)
(The role of Sosarme was originally
sung by an alto castrato.)
• *Sosarme* (Handel)
• light or lyric voices

Se la vita ancor t'è cara (Arsace • Semiramide)
• *Semiramide* (Rossini)
• lyric voices

**Serbami ognor sì fido/Alle più calde
immagini** (Arsace • Semiramide)
• *Semiramide* (Rossini)
• lyric voices

Tu caro sei il dolce mio tesoro
(Sosarme • Elmira)
(The role of Sosarme was originally
sung by an alto castrato.)
• *Sosarme* (Handel)
• light or lyric voices

Vieni, appaga il tuo consorte [Viens, suis un
époux] (Orfeo [Orphée] • Euridice [Eurydice])
(Orfeo's role was originally written for alto castrato,
and is tenor in the French version. Orfeo is often
sung by a mezzo-soprano.)
• *Orfeo ed Euridice* [*Orphée et Eurydice*] (Gluck)
• lyric voices

RUSSIAN

Slikhalil' vï...vdokhnulil' vï [Have you not
heard...not sighed] (Ol'ga • Tat'yana)
• *Yevgeny Onegin* [*Eugene Onegin*] (Tchaikovsky)
• lyric or dramatic voices

Uzh vecher, oblakov pomerknuli kraya
(Milovzor [Daphnis] [Pauline] • Liza)
• *Pikovaya dama* [*Pique Dame*]
[*The Queen of Spades*] (Tchaikovsky)
• lyric or dramatic voices

contralto • mezzo-soprano

FRENCH

Sa voix fait naître dans mon sein
(Anna • Didon)
(Didon is sung by either a
soprano or a mezzo-soprano.)
• *Les Troyens* (Berlioz)
• dramatic voices

ITALIAN

Son nata a lagrimar (Cornelia • Sesto)
(Sesto, originally a castrato, can be
sung by soprano or mezzo-soprano.)
• *Giulio Cesare in Egitto* (Handel)
• lyric voices

contralto • tenor

FRENCH

C'est toi! c'est moi! (Carmen • Don José)
• *Carmen* (Bizet)
• lyric or dramatic voices

En ces lieux/Samson, ô toi, mon bien-aimé
(Dalila • Samson)
• *Samson et Dalila* (Saint-Saëns)
• dramatic voices

**Non, tu ne m'aimes pas/Là-bas, là-bas
dans la montagne** (Carmen • Don José)
• *Carmen* (Bizet)
• lyric or dramatic voices

ITALIAN

Dall'aule raggianti/Deh! la parola amara (Federica • Rodolfo)
• *Luisa Miller* (Verdi)
• lyric or dramatic voices

RUSSIAN

Ti li Vladimir moy? [Is it you, Vladimir mine?] (Konchakovna • Vladimir)
• *Knyaz' Igor'* [*Prince Igor*] (Borodin)
• lyric or dramatic voices

contralto • baritone

FRENCH

J'ai gravi la montagne/La victoire facile (Dalila • Le Grand Prêtre du Dagon [The High Priest of Dagon])
• *Samson et Dalila* (Saint-Saëns)
• dramatic voices

GERMAN

Kein Andres, das mir so im Herzen loht (Clairon • Count)
• *Capriccio* (Strauss)
• lyric or dramatic voices

ITALIAN

Dunque io son? (Rosina • Figaro)
• *Il barbiere di Siviglia* (Rossini)
• light voices

contralto • bass

ENGLISH

Obey my will (Juno • Somnus)
• *Semele* (Handel)
• lyric voices

FRENCH

Si tu m'aimes, Carmen (Carmen • Escamillo)
• *Carmen* (Bizet)
• lyric or dramatic voices

GERMAN

Da lieg' ich! Was einem Kavalier (Annina • Baron Ochs auf Lerchenau)
• *Der Rosenkavalier* (Strauss)
• lyric or dramatic voices

ITALIAN

Ai capricci della sorte (Isabella • Taddeo)
• *L'italiana in Algeri* (Rossini)
• light or lyric voices

D'un tenero amore (Arsace • Assur)
• *Semiramide* (Rossini)
• lyric voices

O che muso, che figura! (Isabella • Mustafà)
• *L'italiana in Algeri* (Rossini)
• light or lyric voices

countertenor

countertenor • soprano

FRENCH

Je vous revois (Zoroastre • Amélite) (Zoroastre's role was originally written for haute-contre.)
• *Zoroastre* (Rameau)
• light or lyric voices

Présent des cieux, divine flamme (Zoroastre • Amélite) (Zoroastre's role was originally written for haute-contre.)
• *Zoroastre* (Rameau)
• light or lyric voices

tenor

tenor • soprano

CZECH

Jako matka [Like a mother] (Jeník • Mařenka)
• *Prodaná Nevěsta* [*The Bartered Bride*] (Smetana)
• lyric voices

Milostné zvířátko uděláme z vás [We'll make a nice little animal] (Circus Master • Esmeralda)
• *Prodaná Nevěsta* [*The Bartered Bride*] (Smetana)
• light voices

O nevýslovné štěstí lásky [O the unutterable happiness] (Dalibor • Milada)
• *Dalibor* (Smetana)
• dramatic voices

Ten staví se svatou skem [This man becomes a saint] (Circus Master • Esmeralda)
• *Prodaná Nevěsta* [*The Bartered Bride*] (Smetana)
• light voices

Známt' já jednu dívčinu [I know a girl who burns for you] (Vašek • Mařenka)
• *Prodaná Nevěsta* [*The Bartered Bride*] (Smetana)
• light or lyric voices

ENGLISH

Anne! Here! (Tom Rakewell • Anne Trulove)
• *The Rake's Progress* (Stravinsky)
• lyric voices

Do you remember (Sam • Rose)
• *Street Scene* (Weill)
• light or lyric voices

Farewell for now (Tom Rakewell • Anne Trulove)
• *The Rake's Progress* (Stravinsky)
• lyric voices

Happy we (Acis • Galatea)
• *Acis and Galatea* (Handel)
• light voices

Happy were we (Earl of Essex
[Robert Devereux] • Elizabeth I)
• *Gloriana* (Britten)
• lyric or dramatic voices

In a foolish dream/What should I forgive?
(Tom Rakewell • Anne Trulove)
• *The Rake's Progress* (Stravinsky)
• lyric voices

Jenifer, Jenifer, my darling (Mark • Jenifer)
• *The Midsummer Marriage* (Tippett)
• lyric voices

Love has a bitter core, Vanessa
(Anatol • Vanessa)
• *Vanessa* (Barber)
• lyric or dramatic voices

One Hand, One Heart (Tony • Maria)
• *West Side Story* (Bernstein)
• light or lyric voices

Remember that I care (Sam • Rose)
• *Street Scene* (Weill)
• light or lyric voices

Sirius rising as the sun's wheel (Mark • Jenifer)
• *The Midsummer Marriage* (Tippett)
• lyric voices

The flocks shall leave the mountains
(Acis • Galatea)
• *Acis and Galatea* (Handel)
• light voices

The woods are green
(Tom Rakewell • Anne Trulove)
• *The Rake's Progress* (Stravinsky)
• lyric voices

Well met, pretty maid (The Squire • Sally)
• *Thomas and Sally* (Arne)
• light voices

FRENCH

A l'autel j'allais rayonnant (Mylio • Rozenn)
• *Le roi d'Ys* (Lalo)
• lyric voices

Adieu, mes tendres soeurs (Licinius • Julia)
• *La vestale* (Spontini)
• lyric or dramatic voices

Adieu, mon bien-aimé (Gaston • Hélène)
• *Jérusalem* (Verdi)
• lyric or dramatic voices

Ah! ne fuis pas encore (Roméo • Juliette)
• *Roméo et Juliette* (Gounod)
• lyric voices

Ah! quel respect, Madame
(Le Comte Ory [Count] • La Comtesse
Adèle di Formouters [Countess])
• *Le comte Ory* (Rossini)
• light or lyric voices

Ange adorable (Roméo • Juliette)
• *Roméo et Juliette* (Gounod)
• lyric voices

Aux cris de la douleur [Cari figli]
(Admète • Alceste)
• *Alceste* (Gluck)
• lyric or dramatic voices

Avance un pas (Blaise • Babet)
• *Blaise et Babet* (Dezède)
• light voices

Avec bonté voyez ma peine
(Robert le Diable • Isabelle)
• *Robert le Diable* (Meyerbeer)
• lyric voices

Ce domaine est celui des contes d'Avenel
(Georges Brown/Julien Avanel • Anna)
• *La dame blanche* (Boieldieu)
• light or lyric voices

Ce que je veux (Jean [John the Baptist] • Salomé)
• *Hérodiade* (Massenet)
• dramatic voices

C'est le dieu de la jeunesse (Gérald • Lakmé)
• *Lakmé* (Delibes)
• light or lyric voices

**Comment, dans ma reconnaissance/Près du
tombeau, peut-être** [Quale o prode/ Presso alla
tomba] (Henri [Arrigo] • Hélène [Elena])
• *Les vêpres siciliennes* [*I vespri siciliani*] (Verdi)
• lyric or dramatic voices

De cet aveu si tendre [A voti
così ardente] (Tonio • Marie [Maria])
• *La fille du régiment* [*La figlia
del reggimento*] (Donizetti)
• light or lyric voices

**De courroux d'effroi/Ami! le coeur/Pour moi
rayonne** [O sdegni miei/E dolce raggio]
(Henri [Arrigo] • Hélène [Elena])
• *Les vêpres siciliennes* [*I vespri siciliani*] (Verdi)
• lyric or dramatic voices

Depuis longtemps (Julien • Louise)
• *Louise* (Charpentier)
• lyric voices

D'où viens-tu? (Ulysse • Pénélope)
• *Pénélope* (Fauré)
• lyric or dramatic voices

Et je sais votre nom
(Des Grieux [Le Chevalier] • Manon)
• *Manon* (Massenet)
• light or lyric voices

Grâce au hazard (Chapelou • Madeleine)
• *Le postillon de Lonjumeau* (Adam)
• light or lyric voices

Irritons notre barbarie (Arcalaus • Arcabonne)
(The role of Arcalaus was originally
written for haute-contre.)
• *Amadis* (Lully)
• light or lyric voices

**J'avais fait un beau rêve/
Oui, voilà l'héroisme /Au revoir**
[Sogno dorato io feci!/Ma lassù]
(Don Carlos [Don Carlo] • Elisabeth [Elisabetta])
• *Don Carlos [Don Carlo]* (Verdi)
• lyric or dramatic voices

Je crois entendre les doux compliments
(Wilhelm Meister • Philine)
• *Mignon* (Thomas)
• light or lyric voices

Je goûtais les charmes [Avvezza al contento]
(Orphée [Orfeo] • Eurydice [Euridice])
(Orphée's role was originally written for
alto castrato in the Italian version.)
• *Orphée et Eurydice [Orfeo ed Euridice]* (Gluck)
• lyric voices

Je ne souffre plus (Des Grieux • Manon)
• *Manon Lescaut* (Auber)
• light or lyric voices

**Je viens solliciter/Ô bien perdu/Que sous
mes pieds** [Io vengo a domandar] (Don Carlos
[Don Carlo] • Elisabeth [Elisabetta])
• *Don Carlos [Don Carlo]* (Verdi)
• lyric or dramatic voices

La brise est douce et parfumée
[Chanson de Magali] (Vincent • Mireille)
• *Mireille* (Gounod)
• lyric voices

**Laisse-moi contempler ton visage/O nuit/
Partez, partez** (Faust, Dr. • Marguerite)
• *Faust* (Gounod)
• lyric voices

Lakmé, c'est toi (Gérald • Lakmé)
• *Lakmé* (Delibes)
• light or lyric voices

**L'amour qui brûle dans
notre âme** (Licinius • Julia)
• *La vestale* (Spontini)
• lyric or dramatic voices

**Les rendez-vous de noble
compagnie** (Girot • Nicette)
• *Le Pré aux Clercs* (Hérold)
• light voices

L'espoir fuit de mon coeur (Cynire • Echo)
• *Echo et Narcisse* (Gluck)
• lyric voices

L'heure fatale est sonnée! [L'ora fatale è suonata!]
(Don Carlos [Don Carlo] • Elisabeth [Elisabetta])
• *Don Carlos [Don Carlo]* (Verdi)
• lyric or dramatic voices

Malheureux et non coupable (Henri • Hélène)
• *Les vêpres siciliennes* (Verdi)
• lyric or dramatic voices

**N'espérez pas me fuir/
Écoutez-moi** (Alphonse • Elvire)
• *La muette de Portici* (Auber)
• light or lyric voices

O dieu Brahma! (Nadir • Leïla)
• *Les pêcheurs de perles* (Bizet)
• lyric voices

O fatale Toison (Jason • Médée)
• *Médée* (Chérubini)
• dramatic voices

O lumière sainte (Nadir • Leïla)
• *Les pêcheurs de perles* (Bizet)
• lyric voices

O nuit divine (Roméo • Juliette)
• *Roméo et Juliette* (Gounod)
• lyric voices

**O Teresa, vous que j'aime plus
que ma vie** (Benvenuto Cellini • Teresa)
• *Benvenuto Cellini* (Berlioz)
• lyric or dramatic voices

O transports, ô douce extase
(Vasco da Gama • Sélika)
• *L'africaine* (Meyerbeer)
• lyric or dramatic voices

On l'appelle Manon
(Des Grieux [Le Chevalier] • Manon)
• *Manon* (Massenet)
• light or lyric voices

Oui, c'est toi je t'aime
(Faust, Dr. • Marguerite)
• *Faust* (Gounod)
• lyric voices

Oui, vous l'arrachez à mon âme
(Arnold • Mathilde)
• *Guillaume Tell* (Rossini)
• lyric voices

Parle-moi de ma mère (Don José • Micaëla)
• *Carmen* (Bizet)
• lyric voices

Perfides ennemis [Nemici senza cor]
(Jason • Médée)
• *Médée* (Chérubini)
• dramatic voices

**Pour notre amour plus d'espérance/
Sur la rive étrangère** (Arnold • Mathilde)
• *Guillaume Tell* (Rossini)
• lyric voices

Quand des sommets de la montagne
(Benvenuto Cellini • Teresa)
• *Benvenuto Cellini* (Berlioz)
• lyric or dramatic voices

Quand nos jours s'éteindront
(Jean [John the Baptist] • Salomé)
• *Hérodiade* (Massenet)
• dramatic voices

Que ces moments sont doux (Abaris • Alphise)
(Abaris was originally written for haute-contre.)
• *Les Boréades* (Rameau)
• lyric voices

Que faites-vous donc?/De quels transports/Toujours unis [
Che mai fate voi?/Di qual amor]
(Don Carlos [Don Carlo] • Elisabeth [Elisabetta])
• *Don Carlos* [*Don Carlo*] (Verdi)
• lyric or dramatic voices

Que le tendre amour nous engage
(Glaucus • Scylla)
(Glaucus was written originally
written for haute-contre.)
• *Scylla et Glaucus* (Leclair)
• light or lyric voices

Quoi, tous les deux (Chapelou • Madeleine)
• *Le postillon de Lonjumeau* (Adam)
• light or lyric voices

Si vous le permettiez, princes/Ulysse!
(Ulysse • Pénélope)
• *Pénélope* (Fauré)
• lyric or dramatic voices

Sur cet autel sacré (Licinius • Julia)
• *La vestale* (Spontini)
• lyric or dramatic voices

Toi! Vous! (Des Grieux [Le Chevalier] • Manon)
• *Manon* (Massenet)
• light or lyric voices

Ton coeur n'a pas compris le mien
(Nadir • Leïla)
• *Les pêcheurs de perles* (Bizet)
• lyric voices

Tous les deux, amoureux (Saphir • Fleurette)
• *Barbe-bleue* (Offenbach)
• light or lyric voices

Tu pleures? Oui, de honte sur moi
(Des Grieux [Le Chevalier] • Manon)
• *Manon* (Massenet)
• light or lyric voices

**Va! je t'ai pardonné/Nuit d'hyménée!
/Il faut partir** (Roméo • Juliette)
• *Roméo et Juliette* (Gounod)
• lyric voices

**Viens! fuyons au bout
au monde** (Roméo • Juliette)
• *Roméo et Juliette* (Gounod)
• lyric voices

**Viens, nous quitterons
cette ville** (Prince • Cendrillon)
(The Prince was composed for a soprano,
but today is always sung by a tenor.)

• *Cendrillon* (Massenet)
• lyric voices

Viens, suis un époux [Vieni, appaga il tuo
consorte] (Orphée [Orfeo] • Eurydice [Euridice])
(The role of Orphée was originally written for alto
castrato in the Italian.)
• *Orphée et Eurydice* [*Orfeo ed Euridice*] (Gluck)
• lyric voices

Viens, viens, je cède éperdu [Vieni, ah! vieni]
(Fernand [Fernando] • Léonor [Leonora])
• *La favorite* [*La favorita*] (Donizetti)
• lyric or dramatic voices

Vincenette a votre âge (Vincent • Mireille)
• *Mireille* (Gounod)
• lyric voices

GERMAN

Blickt sein Auge doch so ehrlich
(Lyonel • Lady Harriet Durham)
• *Martha* (Flotow)
• lyric voices

Brüderlein fein (Fortunatus Wurzel • Youth)
• *Das Mädchen aus der Feenwelt* (Drechsler)
• light or lyric voices

Darf eine nied're Magd es wagen
(Ivanov • Marie)
• *Zar und Zimmermann* (Lortzing)
• lyric voices

Das Essen ist da (Pedro • Marta)
• *Tiefland* (Albert)
• dramatic voices

Das Tor ist zu, Wir sind allein (Pedro • Marta)
• *Tiefland* (Albert)
• dramatic voices

Der Lenz ist gekommen
(Lyonel • Lady Harriet Durham)
• *Martha* (Flotow)
• lyric voices

Die Kinder sind's (Paul • Marietta)
• *Die tote Stadt* (Korngold)
• lyric or dramatic voices

Diese Liebe, plötzlich geboren
(Flamand • Die Gräfin [Countess Madeleine])
• *Capriccio* (Strauss)
• lyric or dramatic voices

Dieser Anstand, so manierlich [Watch Duet]
(Eisenstein • Rosalinde)
• *Die Fledermaus* (J. Strauss)
• lyric voices

Geh'! geh'! geh'! Herz von Flandern!
(Bastien • Bastienne)
• *Bastien und Bastienne* (Mozart)
• light voices

Geh' hin! (Bastien • Bastienne)
• *Bastien und Bastienne* (Mozart)
• light voices

Glück, das mir verlieb (Paul • Marietta)
• *Die tote Stadt* (Korngold)
• lyric or dramatic voices

Hier in stillen Schatten gründen
(Lyonel • Lady Harriet Durham)
• *Martha* (Flotow)
• lyric voices

Ich grüsse dich, du Bote
(Bacchus • Prima Donna/Ariadne)
• *Ariadne auf Naxos* (Strauss)
• dramatic voices

Ich setz den Fall (Symon Rymanovicz • Laura)
• *Der Bettelstudent* (Millöcker)
• light or lyric voices

Jetzt, Schätzchen, jetzt sind wir allein
(Jaquino • Marzelline)
• *Fidelio* (Beethoven)
• light voices

Kannst du zweifeln
(Fenton • Anna Reich [Anne Page])
• *Die lustigen Weiber von Windsor* (Nicolai)
• light or lyric voices

Machen wir's den Schwalben nach
(Edwin • Komtesse Stasi [Countess Stasi])
(Komtesse Stasi is a soubrette.)
• *Die Csárdásfürstin* (Kálmán)
• light or lyric voices

Meine Seele hüpft von Freuden
(Gomatz • Zaïde)
• *Zaïde* (Mozart)
• light or lyric voices

Meinetwegen sollst du sterben
(Belmonte • Konstanze)
• *Die Entführung aus dem Serail* (Mozart)
• lyric voices

Niemand liebt dich so wie ich
(Paganini • Anna Elisa)
• *Paganini* (Lehár)
• light or lyric voices

O, du lieber, o du g'scheiter (Niki • Hélène)
• *Ein Walzertraum* (Straus)
• light or lyric voices

O ew'ge Nacht (Tristan • Isolde)
• *Tristan und Isolde* (Wagner)
• dramatic voices

O namenlose Freude! (Florestan • Leonore)
• *Fidelio* (Beethoven)
• dramatic voices

**O sink' hernieder, Nacht
der Liebe** (Tristan • Isolde)
• *Tristan und Isolde* (Wagner)
• dramatic voices

O süsseste Wonne! seligstes Weib!
(Siegmund • Sieglinde)
• *Die Walküre* (Wagner)
• dramatic voices

O Tanz, o Rausch (Paul • Marietta)
• *Die tote Stadt* (Korngold)
• lyric or dramatic voices

Schenkt man sich Rosen in Tirol
(Adam • Electress Marie)
• *Der Vogelhändler* (Zeller)
• light or lyric voices

Schön wie die blaue Sommernacht
(Octavio • Giuditta)
• *Giuditta* (Lehár)
• lyric voices

Siegmund! Sieh' auf mich
(Siegmund • Brünnhilde)
• *Die Walküre* (Wagner)
• dramatic voices

Tausend kleine Engel singen (Edwin • Sylva)
• *Die Csárdásfürstin* (Kálmán)
• light or lyric voices

Thränen, Thränen (Abu Hassan • Fatime)
• *Abu Hassan* (Weber)
• lyric voices

Unheilvolle Daphne (Apollo • Daphne)
• *Daphne* (Strauss)
• dramatic voices

**Verlässt die Kirche mich/Wohl
liebst auch ich** (Rienzi • Irene)
• *Rienzi* (Wagner)
• dramatic voices

**Warum hat jeder Frühling, ach, nur einen
Mai?** (Der Zarewitsch [Tsarevich] • Sonja)
• *Der Zarewitsch* (Lehár)
• light or lyric voices

Was musst' ich hören, Gott (Erik • Senta)
• *Der fliegende Holländer* (Wagner)
• dramatic voices

Was seh ich?/Nicht wollen die Götter
(Apollo • Daphne)
• *Daphne* (Strauss)
• dramatic voices

**Welch ein Geschick!/Ha! du solltest
für mich sterben** (Belmonte • Konstanze)
• *Die Entführung aus dem Serail* (Mozart)
• lyric voices

Wunderbar! Ja, wunderbar (Paul • Marietta)
• *Die tote Stadt* (Korngold)
• lyric or dramatic voices

**Zwei, die sich lieben, vergessen
die Welt** (Pierrino • Anita)
• *Giuditta* (Lehár)
• light voices

ITALIAN

A voti così ardente [De cet aveu si tendre]
(Tonio • Maria [Marie])
• *La figlia del reggimento* [*La fille du régiment*]
(Donizetti)
• light or lyric voices

Ah! d'immenso, estremo affetto
(Orombello • Beatrice)
• *Beatrice di Tenda* (Bellini)
• lyric voices

Ah! dimmi...dimmi io t'amo (Carlo • Linda)
• *Linda di Chamounix* (Donizetti)
• light or lyric voices

Ah ferma!...Ah senti! (Paride • Elena)
(Paride, originally written for soprano
castrato, is sung by tenor or soprano.)
• *Paride ed Elena* (Gluck)
• lyric voices

**Ah, per sempre/Pronti destrieri/
Seguirti** (Don Alvaro • Leonora)
• *La forza del destino* (Verdi)
• dramatic voices

Ah perchè (Admeto • Alceste)
• *Alceste* (Gluck)
• lyric or dramatic voices

Ah! se tu vuoi fuggir
(Arturo • Alaide [La Straniera])
• *La Straniera* (Bellini)
• lyric voices

Ah sì, voliamo al tempio (Stiffelio • Lina)
• *Stiffelio* (Verdi)
• lyric or dramatic voices

Amaro sol per te (Edgar • Fidelia)
• *Edgar* (Puccini)
• lyric voices

Anima mia!/Risorge ne' tuoi lumi
(Zamoro • Alzira)
• *Alzira* (Verdi)
• lyric or dramatic voices

Bagnato dalle lagrime (Gualtiero • Imogene)
• *Il pirata* (Bellini)
• lyric or dramatic voices

Bimba dagli occhi pieni di malià
(Pinkerton • Cio-Cio-San [Madama Butterfly])
• *Madama Butterfly* (Puccini)
• lyric or dramatic voices

Cara non dubitar/Io ti lascio
(Paolino • Carolina)
• *Il matrimonio segreto* (Cimarosa)
• light voices

Cara, sarò fedele (Rinaldo • Armida)
• *Armida* (Haydn)
• light or lyric voices

Cara sei tu il mio bene (Il Conte di
Almaviva/Lindoro • Rosina)
• *Il barbiere di Siviglia* (Paisiello)
• light voices

Cari figli [Aux cris de la douleur] (Admeto • Alceste)
• *Alceste* (Gluck)
• lyric or dramatic voices

**Che mai fate voi?/De qual
amor** [Que faites-vous donc?]
(Don Carlo [Don Carlos] • Elisabetta [Elisabeth])
• *Don Carlo [Don Carlos]* (Verdi)
• lyric or dramatic voices

Chiedi all'aura lusinghiera (Nemorino • Adina)
• *L'elisir d'amore* (Donizetti)
• light voices

Come il foco allo splendore (Orfeo • Euridice)
• *L'anima del filosofo* (Haydn)
• light voices

Da tutti abbandonata (Leicester • Maria Stuarda)
• *Maria Stuarda* (Donizetti)
• lyric or dramatic voices

Di pescatore ignobile (Gennaro • Lucrezia)
• *Lucrezia Borgia* (Donizetti)
• lyric or dramatic voices

Di tue pene sparve il sogno (Carlo • Linda)
• *Linda di Chamounix* (Donizetti)
• light or lyric voices

Dio ti giocondi, o sposo (Otello • Desdemona)
• *Otello* (Verdi)
• lyric or dramatic voices

Dolce mia vita sei (Eurimaco • Melanto)
• *Il ritorno d'Ulisse in patria* (Monteverdi)
• light or lyric voices

**Dunque, o cruda, e gloria e trono/
Vieni al tempio** (Carlo VII • Giovanna)
• *Giovanna d'Arco* (Verdi)
• lyric or dramatic voices

E ben altro il mio sogno (Luigi • Giorgetta)
• *Il Tabarro* (Puccini)
• lyric or dramatic voices

E deciso: tu parti (Dufresne • Zazà)
• *Zazà* (Leoncavallo)
• lyric voices

**E il sol dell'anima/Addio, addio speranza
ed anima** (Il Duca di Mantua
[The Duke of Mantua] • Gilda)
• *Rigoletto* (Verdi)
• lyric voices

E ver?...sei d'altri? (Arrigo • Lida)
• *La battaglia di Legnano* (Verdi)
• lyric or dramatic voices

Ecco l'altare (Andrea Chénier • Maddalena)
• *Andrea Chénier* (Giordano)
• lyric or dramatic voices

Era d'amor l'immagine/Sul crin la rivale
(Leicester • Elisabetta [Queen])
• *Maria Stuarda* (Donizetti)
• lyric or dramatic voices

**Forma ideal purissima/Amore, misterio
celeste** (Faust • Elèna [Helen of Troy])
• *Mefistofele* (Boito)
• lyric or dramatic voices

Forse un dì conoscerete (Giannetto • Ninetta)
• *La gazza ladra* (Rossini)
• light voices

Fra gli amplessi (Ferrando • Fiordiligi)
• *Così fan tutte* (Mozart)
• lyric voices

Fra le tue braccia amore
(Chevalier Des Grieux • Manon Lescaut)
• *Manon Lescaut* (Puccini)
• lyric or dramatic voices

Fuggi, crudele, fuggi!
(Don Ottavio • Donna Anna)
(Don Ottavio is a light lyric tenor,
but Donna Anna is a dramatic soprano.)
• *Don Giovanni* (Mozart)
• lyric or dramatic voices

Già nella notte densa (Otello • Desdemona)
• *Otello* (Verdi)
• lyric or dramatic voices

Il suon dell'arpe angeliche
[Conversion Duet] (Poliuto • Paolina)
• *Poliuto* (Donizetti)
• lyric or dramatic voices

In mia man alfin tu sei (Pollione • Norma)
• *Norma* (Bellini)
• lyric or dramatic voices

Incauta, che festi! (Leicester • Matilda)
• *Elisabetta* (Rossini)
• lyric voices

Io non son che una povera fanciulla
(Dick Johnson [Ramerrez] • Minnie)
• *La fanciulla del West* (Puccini)
• lyric or dramatic voices

Io ti rivedo/Ah! se un giorno
(Leicester • Maria Stuarda)
• *Maria Stuarda* (Donizetti)
• lyric or dramatic voices

**Io vengo a domandar/Perduto ben/
Sotto al mio piè** [Je viens solliciter]
(Don Carlo [Don Carlos] • Elisabetta [Elisabeth])
• *Don Carlo* [*Don Carlos*] (Verdi)
• lyric or dramatic voices

Labbra di foco (Fenton • Nannetta)
• *Falstaff* (Verdi)
• light or lyric voices

L'amo! L'adoro! (Paride • Elena)
(Paride, originally written for soprano castrato,
is sung by either tenor or soprano.)
• *Paride ed Elena* (Gluck)
• lyric voices

Lascia che pianga io solo (Il Conte
Loris Ipanoff [Count Loris] • La Principessa
Fedora Romazoff [Princess Fedora])
• *Fedora* (Giordano)
• dramatic voices

Libiamo ne' lieti calici [Brindisi]
(Alfredo Germont • Violetta Valéry)
• *La traviata* (Verdi)
• lyric voices

Lontano, lontano (Faust • Margherita)
• *Mefistofele* (Boito)
• lyric or dramatic voices

L'ora fatale è suonata! [L'heure fatale est sonnée!]
(Don Carlo [Don Carlos] • Elisabetta [Elisabeth])
• *Don Carlo* [*Don Carlos*] (Verdi)
• lyric or dramatic voices

Ma, chi sei? (Paride • Erasto)
(Paride, originally written for soprano castrato,
is sung by either tenor or soprano.)
• *Paride ed Elena* (Gluck)
• lyric voices

Ma come puoi lasciarmi (Ruggero • Magda)
• *La rondine* (Puccini)
• lyric voices

Mio caro ben non sospirar (Nino • Sidonia)
(Originally written for castrati.)
• *Astarto* (Bononcini)
• light voices

**Miserere d'un alma/Tu vedrai che
amore in terra** (Manrico • Leonora)
• *Il trovatore* (Verdi)
• lyric or dramatic voices

**Nel mirarti/Da quel dì/Vieni fra
queste braccia** (Arturo • Elvira)
• *I Puritani* (Bellini)
• lyric voices

No, no Turiddu, rimani (Turiddu • Santuzza)
• *Cavalleria rusticana* (Mascagni)
• dramatic voices

**No, tu non sai/Tornerai, ma
forse spenta** (Corrado • Medora)
• *Il corsaro* (Verdi)
• lyric or dramatic voices

Noi torneremo alla romita valle
(Walter • Aldona)
• *I Lituani* [*The Little Sweep*] (Ponchielli)
• dramatic voices

**Non, non morrai, chè i perfidi/Ah! speranza
dolce ancora** (Jacopo Foscari • Lucrezia Contarini)
• *I due Foscari* (Verdi)
• lyric or dramatic voices

**Non sai tu che se l'anima mia/Oh
qual soave brivido** (Riccardo • Amelia)
• *Un ballo in maschera* (Verdi)
• lyric or dramatic voices

O cara, o cara (Valletto • Damigella)
(Valletto was originally sung by a castrato.)
• *L'incoronazione di Poppea* (Monteverdi)
• light voices

O mia vita! O mia core (Paride • Ennone)
• *Il pomo d'oro* (Cesti)
• light or lyric voices

**O sdegni miei/Arrigo! ah parli a un core/E
dolce raggio** [De courroux/Pour moi rayonne]
(Arrigo [Henri] • Elena [Hélène])
• *I vespri siciliani* [*Les vêpres siciliennes*] (Verdi)
• lyric or dramatic voices

O soave fanciulla (Rodolfo • Mimì)
• *La Bohème* (Puccini)
• lyric voices

Ogni virtù più bella (Evandro • Ismene)
• *Alceste* (Gluck)
• light voices

**Oh belle, a questa misera/Ah,
vieni, sol morte** (Oronte • Giselda)
• *I Lombardi* (Verdi)
• lyric or dramatic voices

Oh Luigi! Luigi! Bada a te! (Luigi • Giorgetta)
• *Il Tabarro* (Puccini)
• lyric or dramatic voices

Or dammi il braccio tuo (Osaka • Iris)
• *Iris* (Mascagni)
• lyric or dramatic voices

Ora soave (Andrea Chénier • Maddalena)
• *Andrea Chénier* (Giordano)
• lyric or dramatic voices

Parigi, o cara/Ah, gran Dio! morir sì giovane
(Alfredo Germont • Violetta Valéry)
• *La traviata* (Verdi)
• lyric voices

Parla, in tuo cor virgineo
(Gabriele Adorno • Amelia [Maria Boccanegra])
• *Simon Boccanegra* (Verdi)
• lyric or dramatic voices

Perchè mai cercate (Ruggero • Magda)
• *La rondine* (Puccini)
• lyric voices

Perchè mai, destin crudel
(Norfolk • Elisabetta [Queen])
• *Elisabetta* (Rossini)
• lyric voices

Perdona! perdona/No, più nobile sei
(Maurizio • Adriana Lecouvreur)
• *Adriana Lecouvreur* (Cilea)
• lyric or dramatic voices

**Piangi, piangi, il tuo dolore/Maledetto
il dì ch'io nacqui** (Rodolfo • Luisa)
• *Luisa Miller* (Verdi)
• lyric or dramatic voices

**Plauso! Voce di gioia!/Sin la tomba
è a me negata** (Eutopio • Antonina)
• *Belisario* (Donizetti)
• lyric or dramatic voices

Prendi, l'anel ti dono (Elvino • Amina)
• *La sonnambula* (Bellini)
• lyric voices

Principessa di morte/Mio fiore!
(Calaf • Turandot)
• *Turandot* (Puccini)
• dramatic voices

Qual contento (Medoro • Angelica)
• *Orlando Paladino* (Haydn)
• light voices

Qual cor tradisti (Pollione • Norma)
• *Norma* (Bellini)
• lyric or dramatic voices

Quale, o prode/Presso alla tomba
[Comment/Près du tombeau]
(Arrigo [Henri] • Elena [Hélène])
• *I vespri siciliani* [*Les vêpres siciliennes*] (Verdi)
• lyric or dramatic voices

**Quando narravi l'esule tua vita/
E tu m'amavi** (Otello • Desdemona)
• *Otello* (Verdi)
• lyric or dramatic voices

Qui il padre ancor respira (Arturo • Lucia)
• *Lucia di Lammermoor* (Donizetti)
• lyric voices

Rosina vezzosina (Errico • Rosina)
• *La vera Costanza* (Haydn)
• light or lyric voices

Se viver non degg'io (Sifare • Aspasia)
(Sifare was sung by either soprano
(pants role) or tenor.)
• *Mitridate* (Mozart)
• lyric voices

Seid la vuole/La terra, il ciel m'abborrino
(Corrado • Gulnara)
• *Il corsaro* (Verdi)
• lyric or dramatic voices

Sento un certo/Dolce Amor!
(Henry Morosus • Aminta)
• *Die schweigsame Frau* (Strauss)
• lyric or dramatic voices

Serba, serba i tuoi segreti
(Arturo • Alaide [La Straniera])
• *La Straniera* (Bellini)
• lyric voices

**Sì, quello io son, ravvisami/Oh t'innebria
nell'amplesso** (Foresto • Odabello)
• *Attila* (Verdi)
• dramatic voices

S'io non moro (Idamante • Ilia)
(Idamante, originally castrato, is
sung by tenor, soprano, or mezzo-soprano.)
• *Idomeneo* (Mozart)
• light or lyric voices

**Sogno dorato io feci!/Sì l'eroismo è
questo/Ma lassù** [J'avais fait un beau rêve]

(Don Carlo [Don Carlos] • Elisabetta [Elisabeth])
• *Don Carlo [Don Carlos]* (Verdi)
• lyric or dramatic voices

Son geloso del zefiro errante (Elvino • Amina)
• *La sonnambula* (Bellini)
• lyric voices

Son quest'occhi un stral d'Amore (Ali • Rezia)
• *L'incontro improvviso* (Haydn)
• light voices

Spiegarti non poss'io (Idamante • Ilia)
 (Idamante, originally castrato, is sung
  by tenor, soprano, or mezzo-soprano.)
• *Idomeneo* (Mozart)
• light or lyric voices

**Sulla tomba che rinserra/Verranno
a te sull'aure** (Edgardo • Lucia)
• *Lucia di Lammermoor* (Donizetti)
• lyric voices

**Suzel, buon dì/Han della porpora
vivo il colore** (Fritz Kobus • Suzel)
• *L'amico Fritz* (Mascagni)
• lyric voices

**T'abbraccio/Qual mare, qual terra/
Lassù resplendere** (Carlo • Amalia)
• *I Masnadieri* (Verdi)
• lyric or dramatic voices

Tornami a dir che m'ami (Ernesto • Norina)
• *Don Pasquale* (Donizetti)
• light voices

Tu dall'infanzia mia (Roberto • Anna)
• *Le villi* (Puccini)
• lyric voices

Tu mi lasci? (Belfiore • Sandrina)
• *La finta Giardiniera* (Mozart)
• light or lyric voices

Tu sciagurato! ah! fuggi (Gualtiero • Imogene)
• *Il pirata* (Bellini)
• lyric or dramatic voices

Tu sei la mia vittoria
 (Maurizio • Adriana Lecouvreur)
• *Adriana Lecouvreur* (Cilea)
• lyric or dramatic voices

Tu, tu, amore?/E fascino d'amor
 (Chevalier Des Grieux • Manon Lescaut)
• *Manon Lescaut* (Puccini)
• lyric or dramatic voices

Un certo ruscelletto (Ecclitico • Clarice)
• *Il mondo della luna* (Haydn)
• light or lyric voices

**Un dì felice, eterea/De quell'amor ch'è
palpito** (Alfredo Germont • Violetta Valéry)
• *La traviata* (Verdi)
• lyric voices

Ve' come gli astri stessi (Ernani • Elvira)
• *Ernani* (Verdi)
• lyric or dramatic voices

Vedete? io son fedele
 (Chevalier Des Grieux • Manon Lescaut)
• *Manon Lescaut* (Puccini)
• lyric or dramatic voices

**Vedi?...di morte l'angelo/
O terra addio** (Radames • Aïda)
• *Aïda* (Verdi)
• lyric or dramatic voices

Vendetta d'un momento (Arrigo • Lida)
• *La battaglia di Legnano* (Verdi)
• lyric or dramatic voices

Vicino a te s'acqueta/La nostra morte
 (Andrea Chénier • Maddalena)
• *Andrea Chénier* (Giordano)
• lyric or dramatic voices

Viene la sera (Pinkerton • Cio-Cio-San
[Madama Butterfly])
• *Madama Butterfly* (Puccini)
• lyric or dramatic voices

**Vieni a mirar la cerula/Sì, sì, dell'ara il
giubilo** (Gabriele Adorno • Amelia
[Maria Boccanegra])
• *Simon Boccanegra* (Verdi)
• lyric or dramatic voices

Vieni, ah! vieni [Viens, viens, je cède éperdu]
 (Fernando [Fernand] • Leonora [Léonor])
• *La favorita [La favorite]* (Donizetti)
• lyric or dramatic voices

**Vieni, cerchiam pe' mari/Taci, taci: rimorsi
amari** (Gualtiero • Imogene)
• *Il pirata* (Bellini)
• lyric or dramatic voices

RUSSIAN

Swan Lake Duet [commonly known title]
 (Hulbrand • Undina)
• *Undina* (Tchaikovsky)
• lyric voices

SPANISH

Coloquio en la reja (Fernando • Rosario)
• *Goyescas* (Granados)
• lyric voices

tenor • mezzo-soprano

ENGLISH

If one last doubt (Troilus [Prince] • Cressida)
• *Troilus and Cressida* (Walton)
• dramatic voices

Now close your arms (Troilus [Prince] • Cressida)
• *Troilus and Cressida* (Walton)
• dramatic voices

FRENCH

A cette heure suprême (Werther • Charlotte)
• *Werther* (Massenet)
• lyric voices

Ai-je dit vrai/Ah! qu'il est loin
(Werther • Charlotte)
• *Werther* (Massenet)
• lyric voices

Comment le dédain pourrait-il mourir?
(Bénédict • Béatrice)
• *Béatrice et Bénédict* (Berlioz)
• light or lyric voices

Errante sur tes pas (Énée • Didon)
• *Les Troyens* (Berlioz)
• dramatic voices

Grand Dieu! sa misère est si grande!
(Sébastien • Zayda)
• *Dom Sébastien* (Donizetti)
• lyric or dramatic voices

Il faut nous séparer (Werther • Charlotte)
• *Werther* (Massenet)
• lyric voices

Il grandira, car il est espagnol
(Piquillo • La Périchole)
• *La Périchole* (Offenbach)
• light voices

Je suis heureuse! l'air m'enivre
(Wilhelm Meister • Mignon)
• *Mignon* (Thomas)
• lyric voices

Je vais revoir (Le Comte
Ory [Count] • Isolier [Page])
• *Le comte Ory* (Rossini)
• light or lyric voices

L'amour est un flambeau (Bénédict • Béatrice)
• *Béatrice et Bénédict* (Berlioz)
• light or lyric voices

Mes longs cheveux descendant
(Pelléas • Mélisande)
• *Pelléas et Mélisande* (Debussy)
• lyric voices

O ciel! où courez-vous?/Tu l'as dit
[O ciel! dove vai tu?] (Raoul • Valentine)
• *Les Huguenots* (Meyerbeer)
• lyric or dramatic voices

O Dieu! de quelle ivresse (Hoffmann • Giulietta)
• *Les contes d'Hoffmann* (Offenbach)
• lyric or dramatic voices

**Oui, c'est moi/N'achevez pas/
Ah! ce premier baiser** (Werther • Charlotte)
• *Werther* (Massenet)
• lyric voices

Toi qui m'es apparue (Prince • Cendrillon)
(The Prince was composed for a soprano,
but today is always sung by a tenor.)
• *Cendrillon* (Massenet)
• lyric voices

GERMAN

Bleib und wache bis sie dich ruft (Der Kaiser
[The Emperor] • Die Amme [The Nurse])

• *Die Frau ohne Schatten* (Strauss)
• dramatic voices

Hier weilest du/Wie liebt' ich dich
(Adolar • Euryanthe)
• *Euryanthe* (Weber)
• dramatic voices

Hin nimm die Seele mein (Adolar • Euryanthe)
• *Euryanthe* (Weber)
• dramatic voices

Wenn zum Gebet (Nureddin • Bostana)
• *Der Barbier von Bagdad* (Cornelius)
• lyric voices

ITALIAN

Ah! tu dei vivere/Che ti salva
(Radames • Amneris)
• *Aïda* (Verdi)
• dramatic voices

Bocca, bocca (Lucano • Nerone)
(Nerone, originally written for soprano castrato,
is soprano or mezzo-soprano today.)
• *L'incoronazione di Poppea* (Monteverdi)
• lyric voices

Deh, non turbare (Enzo • Laura)
• *La Gioconda* (Ponchielli)
• lyric or dramatic voices

**Eccomi giunto inosservato e solo/
A te sarà** (Otello • Desdemona)
• *Otello* (Rossini)
• lyric voices

Ella è morta, o sciagurato (Tebaldo • Romeo)
La Bohème (Opera)
• *I Capuleti e i Montecchi* (Bellini)
• lyric voices

Oh, il Signore vi manda (Alfio • Santuzza)
• *Cavalleria rusticana* (Mascagni)
• dramatic voices

Perigliarti ancor languente (Manrico • Azucena)
• *Il trovatore* (Verdi)
• lyric or dramatic voices

Quale inchiesta! (Radames • Amneris)
• *Aïda* (Verdi)
• dramatic voices

Sì, la stanchezza/Ai nostri monti
(Manrico • Azucena)
• *Il trovatore* (Verdi)
• lyric or dramatic voices

Stolto! a un sol mio grido (Tebaldo • Romeo)
• *I Capuleti e i Montecchi* (Bellini)
• lyric voices

Tu qui, Santuzza? (Turiddu • Santuzza)
• *Cavalleria rusticana* (Mascagni)
• dramatic voices

Un soave non so che
(Don Ramiro • Cenerentola [Angelica])
• *La Cenerentola* (Rossini)
• light voices

Va, crudele, al dio spietato/
Vieni in Roma (Pollione • Adalgisa)
• *Norma* (Bellini)
• lyric voices

RUSSIAN

Chudnïy pervenets tvoren'ya [Wondrous
firstling of creation] (Vaudémont • Iolanta)
• *Iolanta* (Tchaikovsky)
• lyric or dramatic voices

Dmitry! Tsarevich! (Dmitry • Marina)
• *Boris Godunov* (Musorgsky)
• lyric or dramatic voices

tenor • contralto
FRENCH

C'est toi! c'est moi! (Don José • Carmen)
• *Carmen* (Bizet)
• lyric or dramatic voices

En ces lieux/Samson, ô toi,
mon bien-aimé (Samson • Dalila)
• *Samson et Dalila* (Saint-Saëns)
• dramatic voices

Non, tu ne m'aimes pas/Là-bas, là-bas dans
la montagne (Don José • Carmen)
• *Carmen* (Bizet)
• lyric or dramatic voices

ITALIAN

Dall'aule raggianti/Deh!
la parola amara (Rodolfo • Federica)
• *Luisa Miller* (Verdi)
• lyric or dramatic voices

RUSSIAN

Tï li Vladimir moy? [Is it you, Vladimir mine?]
(Vladimir • Konchakovna)
• *Knyaz' Igor'* [*Prince Igor*] (Borodin)
• lyric or dramatic voices

tenor • tenor
ITALIAN

Deh, scusa i trasporti (Norfolk • Leicester)
• *Elisabetta* (Rossini)
• lyric voices

Non m'inganno; al mio rivale (Rodrigo • Otello)
• *Otello* (Rossini)
• lyric voices

tenor • baritone
ENGLISH

We're called gondolieri (Marco • Giuseppe)
• *The Gondoliers* (Sullivan)
• light voices

FRENCH

Au bonheur dont mon âme est pleine
(Werther • Albert)
• *Werther* (Massenet)
• lyric or dramatic voices

Au fond du temple saint (Nadir • Zurga)
• *Les pêcheurs de perles* (Bizet)
• lyric voices

De votre audace téméraire
(Achille • Agamemnon)
• *Iphigénie en Aulide* (Gluck)
• lyric voices

Dieu tu semas dans nos âmes
[Dio, che nell'alma infondere] (Don Carlos
[Don Carlo] • Rodrigue [Le Marquis de Posa])
• *Don Carlos* [*Don Carlo*] (Verdi)
• lyric or dramatic voices

Fuyons les douceurs dangereuses
(Danish Knight • Ubalde)
• *Armide* (Gluck)
• lyric voices

Le voilà, c'est l'infant/Toi!
mon Rodrigue! c'est toi (Don Carlos
[Don Carlo] • Rodrigue [Le Marquis de Posa])
• *Don Carlos* (Verdi)
• lyric or dramatic voices

Quand ma bonté toujours nouvelle [Quando al
mio sen] (Henri [Arrigo] • Montfort [Montforte])
• *Les vêpres siciliennes* [*I vespri siciliani*] (Verdi)
• lyric or dramatic voices

GERMAN

Die Welt hat das genialste
(Symon Rymanovicz • Jan)
• *Der Bettelstudent* (Millöcker)
• light voices

Leise, ganz leise (Niki • Montschi)
• *Ein Walzertraum* (Straus)
• light or lyric voices

ITALIAN

Ah, Mimì, tu più non torni (Rodolfo • Marcello)
• *La Bohème* (Puccini)
• lyric voices

All'idea di quel metallo (Il Conte d'Almaviva
/Lindoro [Count Almaviva] • Figaro)
• *Il barbiere di Siviglia* (Rossini)
• light voices

Amore o grillo (Pinkerton • Sharpless)
• *Madama Butterfly* (Puccini)
• lyric or dramatic voices

Ben vi scorgo (Arrigo • Rolando)
• *La battaglia di Legnano* (Verdi)
• lyric or dramatic voices

Col sangue/Le minaccie/Ah, segnasti la tua
sorte (Don Alvaro • Don Carlo di Vargas)
• *La forza del destino* (Verdi)
• lyric or dramatic voices

Di': que' ribaldi tremano (Corrado • Seid)
• *Il corsaro* (Verdi)
• lyric or dramatic voices

Dio, che nell'alma infondere [Dieu tu semas
dans nos âmes] (Don Carlo [Don Carlos] • Rodrigo
[Marchese di Posa] [Rodrigue [Le Marquis de Posa])
• *Don Carlo [Don Carlos]* (Verdi)
• lyric or dramatic voices

**Enzo Grimaldi, Principe
di Santafiore** (Enzo • Barnaba)
• *La Gioconda* (Ponchielli)
• lyric or dramatic voices

**Nè gustare/Voi che si larghe cure/Sleale! Il
segreto** (Don Alvaro • Don Carlo di Vargas)
• *La forza del destino* (Verdi)
• lyric or dramatic voices

**No, d'un imene il vincolo/Morte! Ov'io non
cada** (Don Alvaro • Don Carlo di Vargas)
• *La forza del destino* (Verdi)
• lyric or dramatic voices

O grido di quest'anima (Enzo • Barnaba)
• *La Gioconda* (Ponchielli)
• lyric or dramatic voices

O padre sospirato, o figlio desiato
(Telemaco • Ulisse)
(Ulisse was sung by either tenor or baritone.)
• *Il ritorno d'Ulisse in patria* (Monteverdi)
• lyric voices

Quando al mio sen [Quand ma bonté toujours
nouvelle] (Arrigo [Henri] • Montforte [Montfort])
• *I vespri siciliani [Les vêpres siciliennes]* (Verdi)
• lyric or dramatic voices

Sì, dell'ardir, degl'empi (Gerardo • Lusignano)
• *Caterina Cornaro* (Donizetti)
• lyric or dramatic voices

Sì, pel ciel (Otello • Iago)
• *Otello* (Verdi)
• dramatic voices

Solenne in quest'ora
(Don Alvaro • Don Carlo di Vargas)
• *La forza del destino* (Verdi)
• lyric or dramatic voices

Venti scudi (Nemorino • Belcore)
• *L'elisir d'amore* (Donizetti)
• light voices

Verdi spiagge al lieto giorno (Eumete • Ulisse)
(Ulisse was sung by either tenor or baritone.)
• *Il ritorno d'Ulisse in patria* (Monteverdi)
• lyric voices

tenor • bass-baritone

ENGLISH

**And do you prefer the storm to Auntie's
parlour?** (Peter Grimes • Captain Balstrode)
• *Peter Grimes* (Britten)
• dramatic voices

How dark and dreadful is this place
(Tom Rakewell • Nick Shadow)
• *The Rake's Progress* (Stravinsky)
• lyric or dramatic voices

**My tale shall be told both by young
and by old** (Tom Rakewell • Nick Shadow)
• *The Rake's Progress* (Stravinsky)
• lyric or dramatic voices

Thanks to this excellent device
(Tom Rakewell • Nick Shadow)
• *The Rake's Progress* (Stravinsky)
• lyric or dramatic voices

GERMAN

Blühenden Lebens labendes Blut
(Siegfried • Gunther)
• *Götterdämmerung* (Wagner)
• dramatic voices

ITALIAN

**No, non temer/Se uniti
negli affanni** (Rodrigo • Iago)
(Iago was written for either tenor or bass-baritone.)
• *Otello* (Rossini)
• light or lyric voices

tenor • bass

CZECH

Nuže, milý chasníku [Now, dear
young fellow] (Jeník • Kecal)
• *Prodaná Nevěsta [The Bartered Bride]* (Smetana)
• lyric voices

FRENCH

Ah! l'honnête homme! (Raimbaut • Bertram)
• *Robert le Diable* (Meyerbeer)
• light voices

Ami, leur rage (Admète • Hercule)
• *Alceste* (Gluck)
• lyric or dramatic voices

C'est à toi de trembler
(Licinius • Pontifex Maximus)
• *La vestale* (Spontini)
• lyric or dramatic voices

Contente-toi d'une victime (Tisiphone • Thésée)
(Tisiphone, tenor, was originally
sung by haute-contre.)
• *Hippolyte et Aricie* (Rameau)
• lyric voices

Dans Venise la belle [Barcarolle]
(Baptiste • Cornarino Cornarini [Doge of Venice])
• *Le pont des soupirs* (Offenbach)
• light voices

Des chevaliers de ma patrie
(Robert le Diable • Bertram)
• *Robert le Diable* (Meyerbeer)
• lyric voices

Je me sens, hélas, tout chose (Ouf • Siroco)
• *L'étoile du Nord* (Chabrier)
• light voices

Me voici (Faust, Dr. • Méphistophélès)
• *Faust* (Gounod)
• lyric voices

**Mieux vaut mourir que rester
miserable!** (Masniello • Pietro)
• *La muette de Portici* (Auber)
• lyric voices

**Où vas-tu/Ah! Mathilde, idole
de mon âme** (Arnold • Guillaume Tell)
• *Guillaume Tell* (Rossini)
• lyric voices

Sais-tu que devant la tiare [Non sai tu che un
giusto] (Fernand [Fernando] • Balthazar [Badassare])
• *La favorite* [*La favorita*] (Donizetti)
• lyric or dramatic voices

GERMAN

Darf ich wohl den Worten trauen
(Ivanov • Van Bett)
• *Zar und Zimmermann* (Lortzing)
• light or lyric voices

Ja, seit früher Kindheit Tagen
(Lyonel • Plumkett)
• *Martha* (Flotow)
• lyric voices

Mars und Merkur (Nureddin • Abul)
• *Der Barbier von Bagdad* (Cornelius)
• lyric or dramatic voices

So geht indes hinein (Fenton • Herr Reich [Mr.
Page])
• *Die lustigen Weiber von Windsor* (Nicolai)
• light or lyric voices

Trotze nicht (Adolar • Lysiart)
• *Euryanthe* (Weber)
• dramatic voices

Vivat Bacchus (Pedrillo • Osmin)
• *Die Entführung aus dem Serail* (Mozart)
• light or lyric voices

Wer ein Liebchen hat gefunden
(Belmonte • Osmin)
• *Die Entführung aus dem Serail* (Mozart)
• light or lyric voices

**Wie dünkt mich doch die Aue heut'
so schön** (Parsifal • Gurnemanz)
• *Parsifal* (Wagner)
• dramatic voices

ITALIAN

Come il bacio d'un padre amoroso
(Carlo • Massimiliano [Count Moor])
• *I Masnadieri* (Verdi)
• lyric or dramatic voices

Non sai tu che un giusto [Sais-tu que devant la
tiare] (Fernando [Fernand] • Badassare [Balthazar])
• *La favorita* [*La favorite*] (Donizetti)
• lyric or dramatic voices

O che umor (Il Conte di
Almaviva/Lindoro • Bartolo)
• *Il barbiere di Siviglia* (Paisiello)
• light voices

Obbligato, ah, sì! obbligato!
(Nemorino • Dr. Dulcamara)
• *L'elisir d'amore* (Donizetti)
• light voices

Pace e gioia sia con voi (Il Conte d'Almaviva
/Lindoro [Count Almaviva • Bartolo)
• *Il barbiere di Siviglia* (Rossini)
• light voices

Pappataci! (Lindoro • Taddeo)
• *L'italiana in Algeri* (Rossini)
• light or lyric voices

Prender moglie! (Ernesto • Don Pasquale)
• *Don Pasquale* (Donizetti)
• light voices

Se inclinassi a prender moglie
(Lindoro • Mustafà)
• *L'italiana in Algeri* (Rossini)
• light or lyric voices

Se tu mi doni un'ora (Faust • Mefistofele)
• *Mefistofele* (Boito)
• lyric or dramatic voices

Secondate, aurette amiche
(Ferrando • Guglielmo)
• *Così fan tutte* (Mozart)
• light or lyric voices

Sì...sulla salma del fratello
(Arturo • Baron Valdeburgo)
• *La Straniera* (Bellini)
• lyric voices

Zitto, zitto, piano, piano
(Don Ramiro • Dandini)
• *La Cenerentola* (Rossini)
• light voices

RUSSIAN

Just think, my son [commonly known title]
(Grigory • Pimen)
• *Boris Godunov* (Musorgsky)
• lyric or dramatic voices

---

baritone

baritone • soprano

ENGLISH

**Ah Minette, at last we meet
in death** (Tom [Cat] • Minette)
• *The English Cat* (Henze)
• lyric voices

Hello? Hello? Where are you, my darling? (Ben • Lucy)
• *The Telephone* (Menotti)
• light or lyric voices

I have a song to sing, O!
(Jack Point • Elsie Maynard)
• *The Yeomen of the Guard* (Sullivan)
• light voices

Pretty Polly, say (Macheath • Polly Peachum)
• *The Beggar's Opera* (Pepusch)
• light voices

Prithee, pretty maiden (Grosvenor • Patience)
• *Patience* (Sullivan)
• light voices

Promise Duet [commonly known title]
(Tom [Cat] • Minette)
• *The English Cat* (Henze)
• lyric voices

Why does beauty bring desire?
(Tom [Cat] • Minette)
• *The English Cat* (Henze)
• lyric voices

FRENCH

Au bruit de la guerre [Apparvi alla luce]
(Sulpice [Sulpizio] • Marie [Maria])
• *La fille du régiment* [*La figlia del reggimento*] (Donizetti)
• light or lyric voices

Baigne d'eau mes mains (Athanaël • Thaïs)
• *Thaïs* (Massenet)
• lyric or dramatic voices

C'est sur ce banc (Eumée • Pénélope)
• *Pénélope* (Fauré)
• lyric or dramatic voices

Doute de la lumière (Hamlet • Ophélie)
• *Hamlet* (Thomas)
• lyric voices

Esprits de haine et de rage (Hidraot • Armide)
• *Armide* (Gluck)
• dramatic voices

Esprits de haine et de rage (Hidraot • Armide)
• *Armide* (Lully)
• dramatic voices

Oui, je vous hais (Henri de Valois • Alexina)
• *Le roi malgré lui* (Chabrier)
• lyric voices

Pour moi, je ne crains rien (Zurga • Leïla)
• *Les pêcheurs de perles* (Bizet)
• lyric voices

Te souvient-il du lumineux voyage [Méditation]
(Athanaël • Thaïs)
• *Thaïs* (Massenet)
• lyric or dramatic voices

GERMAN

Bei jedem Walzerschritt (Graf Danilo Danilowitsch [Count Danilo]• Hanna Glawari)
• *Die lustige Witwe* (Lehár)
• light or lyric voices

Bei Männern, welche Liebe fühlen
(Papageno • Pamina)
• *Die Zauberflöte* (Mozart)
• light or lyric voices

Das süsse Lied verhallt (Lohengrin • Elsa)
• *Lohengrin* (Wagner)
• dramatic voices

Gut'n Abend, Meister! (Hans Sachs • Eva)
• *Die Meistersinger von Nürnberg* (Wagner)
• lyric or dramatic voices

Marta!...Tu mit mir, was du willst
(Sebastiano • Marta)
• *Tiefland* (Albert)
• dramatic voices

Orest! Orest! Orest! (Orest • Elektra)
• *Elektra* (Strauss)
• dramatic voices

Pa-pa-pa- (Papageno • Papagena)
• *Die Zauberflöte* (Mozart)
• light voices

Sie woll'n mich heiraten (Mandryka • Arabella)
• *Arabella* (Strauss)
• lyric or dramatic voices

So jetzt hätt' ich ihn gefangen
(Herr Fluth [Mr. Ford] • Frau Fluth [Mrs. Ford])
• *Die lustigen Weiber von Windsor* (Nicolai)
• lyric voices

Und du wirst mein Gebieter sein
[Submission Duet] (Mandryka • Arabella)
• *Arabella* (Strauss)
• lyric or dramatic voices

Was willst du, fremder Mensch?
(Orest • Elektra)
• *Elektra* (Strauss)
• dramatic voices

Wie aus der Ferne längst vergang'n Zeiten
(Der Holländer [The Dutchman] • Senta)
• *Der fliegende Holländer* (Wagner)
• dramatic voices

ITALIAN

Amai, ma un solo istante/Or del padre benedetta (Giacomo • Giovanna)
• *Giovanna d'Arco* (Verdi)
• lyric or dramatic voices

Apparvi alla luce [Au bruit de la guerre]
(Sulpizio [Sulpice] • Maria [Marie])
• *La figlia del reggimento* [*La fille du régiment*] (Donizetti)
• light or lyric voices

Bambina, non ti crucciar
(Michonnet • Adriana Lecouvreur)
• *Adriana Lecouvreur* (Cilea)
• lyric or dramatic voices

Caro! bella! più amabile
beltà (Giulio Cesare • Cleopatra)
(Giulio Cesare was originally
written for soprano castrato.)
• *Giulio Cesare in Egitto* (Handel)
• lyric or dramatic voices

Colei Sofronia (Tasso • Eleonora)
• *Torquato Tasso* (Donizetti)
• lyric or dramatic voices

Colma di gioia ho l'anima (Gusmano • Alzira)
• *Alzira* (Verdi)
• lyric or dramatic voices

Crudel! perchè finora
(Il Conte di Almaviva [Count] • Susanna)
• *Le nozze di Figaro* (Mozart)
• lyric voices

Da qual dì che t'ho veduta (Don Carlo • Elvira)
• *Ernani* (Verdi)
• lyric or dramatic voices

Den non parlare al misero/
Ah! veglia, o donna (Rigoletto • Gilda)
• *Rigoletto* (Verdi)
• lyric or dramatic voices

Digli ch'è sangue italico (Rolando • Lida)
• *La battaglia di Legnano* (Verdi)
• lyric or dramatic voices

Dinnè, perchè in quest'eremo/Figlia! a tal
nome io palpito (Simon Boccanegra [The Doge
of Genoa] • Amelia [Maria Boccanegra])
• *Simon Boccanegra* (Verdi)
• lyric or dramatic voices

Donna? chi sei?/Oh di qual'onta
aggravasi/Deh perdona (Nabucco • Abigaille)
• *Nabucco* (Verdi)
• dramatic voices

Ed io pure in faccia agl'uomini/
Or meco venite (Stankar • Lina)
• *Stiffelio* (Verdi)
• lyric or dramatic voices

Fatal mia donna!/Allor questa voce/
Vieni altrove! (Macbeth • Lady Macbeth)
• *Macbeth* (Verdi)
• dramatic voices

Fuggiam gli ardori inospiti/Sì: fuggiam
da queste mura (Amonasro • Aïda)
• *Aïda* (Verdi)
• dramatic voices

Il pallor funesto, orrendo/Soffriva nel
pianto languia (Enrico Ashton • Lucia)
• *Lucia di Lammermoor* (Donizetti)
• lyric voices

Io t'amo, Amalia/Ti scosta,
o malnato (Francesco • Amalia)
• *I Masnadieri* (Verdi)
• lyric or dramatic voices

La tomba è un letto/Di rughe/Andrem,
raminghi e poveri (Miller • Luisa)
• *Luisa Miller* (Verdi)
• lyric or dramatic voices

Mira, di acerbe lagrime/Vivrà!...Contende il
giubilo (Il Conte di Luna [Count] • Leonora)
• *Il trovatore* (Verdi)
• lyric or dramatic voices

Odio e livore!—ingrato!
(Filippo Maria Visconti • Beatrice)
• *Beatrice di Tenda* (Bellini)
• lyric voices

Ora a noi (Sharpless • Cio-Cio-San
[Madama Butterfly])
• *Madama Butterfly* (Puccini)
• lyric or dramatic voices

Ora di morte e di vendetta
(Macbeth • Lady Macbeth)
• *Macbeth* (Verdi)
• dramatic voices

Perchè, perchè non m'ami più?/
Resta vicino a me (Michele • Giorgetta)
• *Il Tabarro* (Puccini)
• lyric or dramatic voices

Piangi, fanciulla, piangi! (Rigoletto • Gilda)
• *Rigoletto* (Verdi)
• lyric or dramatic voices

Pronta io son (Dr. Malatesta • Norina)
• *Don Pasquale* (Donizetti)
• light voices

Pura siccome un angelo/
Dite alla giovine/Morro!
(Giorgio Germont • Violetta Valéry)
• *La traviata* (Verdi)
• lyric voices

Quando le soglie paterne vareai/
Ah! l'alto ardor [Quand j'ai quitté/O mon
amour] (Alfonso [Alphonse] • Leonora [Léonor])
• *La favorita* [*La favorite*] (Donizetti)
• lyric or dramatic voices

Quel tuo visetto amabile (Pasquale • Eurilla)
• *Orlando Paladino* (Haydn)
• light voices

Rivedrai le foreste imbalsamate/
Padre!...a costoro (Amonasro • Aïda)
• *Aïda* (Verdi)
• dramatic voices

Sei splendida e lucente
(Lescaut • Manon Lescaut)
• *Manon Lescaut* (Puccini)
• lyric or dramatic voices

Silvio! a quest'ora/E allor perchè, dì, tu m'hai stregato (Silvio [Campagnuolo] [A Villager] • Nedda)
• *Pagliacci* (Leoncavallo)
• lyric voices

Speravo di trovarvi qui (Marcello • Mimì)
• *La Bohème* (Puccini)
• lyric voices

Tu por lo sai, che giudice (Francesco Foscari [Doge] • Lucrezia Contarini)
• *I due Foscari* (Verdi)
• lyric or dramatic voices

Tutte le feste al tempio/Sì, vendetta, tremenda vendetta (Rigoletto • Gilda)
• *Rigoletto* (Verdi)
• lyric or dramatic voices

V'ho ingannato!/Lassù, in cielo (Rigoletto • Gilda)
• *Rigoletto* (Verdi)
• lyric or dramatic voices

Vieni, Gulnara!/Sia l'istante maledetto (Seid • Gulnara)
• *Il corsaro* (Verdi)
• lyric or dramatic voices

RUSSIAN

My heart is worn with fear [commonly known title] (Yevgeny Onegin [Eugene Onegin] • Tat'yana)
• *Yevgeny Onegin [Eugene Onegin]* (Tchaikovsky)
• lyric or dramatic voices

Onegin, I was then far younger [commonly known title] (Yevgeny Onegin [Eugene Onegin] • Tat'yana)
• *Yevgeny Onegin [Eugene Onegin]* (Tchaikovsky)
• lyric or dramatic voices

On—moy sokol yasnïy! [It is he, my bright falcon] (Igor' • Yaroslavna)
• *Knyaz' Igor' [Prince Igor]* (Borodin)
• lyric or dramatic voices

baritone • mezzo-soprano

ENGLISH

On the banks of the sweet Garonne (Sherasmin • Fatima)
• *Oberon* (Weber)
• lyric voices

FRENCH

Ah! ah! tout va bien (Golaud • Mélisande)
• *Pelléas et Mélisande* (Debussy)
• lyric or dramatic voices

Cat Duet [commonly known title] (Tom Cat • Female Cat)
• *l'Enfant et les sortilèges* (Ravel)
• light or lyric voices

Je ne pourrai plus sortir (Golaud • Mélisande)
• *Pelléas et Mélisande* (Debussy)
• lyric or dramatic voices

Reviens à toi, vierge adorée (Chorèbe • Cassandre)
• *Les Troyens* (Berlioz)
• dramatic voices

GERMAN

Musik ist eine heilige Kunst (Ein Musiklehrer [A Music Master] • Der Komponist [The Composer])
• *Ariadne auf Naxos* (Strauss)
• lyric voices

ITALIAN

Ad essi non perdono (Alfio • Santuzza)
• *Cavalleria rusticana* (Mascagni)
• dramatic voices

Ah! se potessi piangere (Belisario • Irene)
• *Belisario* (Donizetti)
• lyric or dramatic voices

Per queste tue manine (Leporello • Zerlina)
• *Don Giovanni* (Mozart)
• light voices

Sì, il parto mantengo (Barnaba • La Gioconda)
• *La Gioconda* (Ponchielli)
• dramatic voices

Turiddu mi tolse (Alfio • Santuzza)
• *Cavalleria rusticana* (Mascagni)
• dramatic voices

baritone • contralto

FRENCH

J'ai gravi la montagne/La victoire facile (Le Grand Prêtre du Dagon [The High Priest of Dagon] • Dalila)
• *Samson et Dalila* (Saint-Saëns)
• dramatic voices

GERMAN

Kein Andres, das mir so im Herzen loht (Count • Clairon)
• *Capriccio* (Strauss)
• lyric or dramatic voices

ITALIAN

Dunque io son? (Figaro • Rosina)
• *Il barbiere di Siviglia* (Rossini)
• light voices

baritone • tenor

ENGLISH

We're called gondolieri (Giuseppe • Marco)
• *The Gondoliers* (Sullivan)
• light voices

**Au bonheur dont mon âme
est pleine** (Albert • Werther)
• *Werther* (Massenet)
• lyric or dramatic voices

Au fond du temple saint (Zurga • Nadir)
• *Les pêcheurs de perles* (Bizet)
• lyric voices

De votre audace téméraire
(Agamemnon • Achille)
• *Iphigénie en Aulide* (Gluck)
• lyric voices

Dieu tu semas dans nos âmes
[Dio, che nell'alma infondere] (Rodrigue
[La Marquis de Posa] [Rodrigo [Marchese
di Posa]] • Don Carlos [Don Carlo])
• *Don Carlos* [*Don Carlo*] (Verdi)
• lyric or dramatic voices

Fuyons les douceurs dangereuses
(Ubalde • Danish Knight)
• *Armide* (Gluck)
• lyric voices

**Le voilà, c'est l'infant/Toi! mon
Rodrigue! c'est toi** (Rodrigue
[La Marquis de Posa] • Don Carlos)
• *Don Carlos* (Verdi)
• lyric or dramatic voices

Quand ma bonté toujours nouvelle [Quando al
mio sen] (Montfort [Montforte] • Henri [Arrigo])
• *Les vêpres siciliennes* [*I vespri siciliani*] (Verdi)
• lyric or dramatic voices

Die Welt hat das genialste
(Jan • Symon Rymanovicz)
• *Der Bettelstudent* (Millöcker)
• light voices

Leise, ganz leise (Montschi • Niki)
• *Ein Walzertraum* (Straus)
• light or lyric voices

Ah, Mimì, tu più non torni (Marcello • Rodolfo)
• *La Bohème* (Puccini)
• lyric voices

All'idea di quel metallo (Figaro • Il Conte
d'Almaviva/Lindoro [Count Almaviva])
• *Il barbiere di Siviglia* (Rossini)
• light voices

Amore o grillo (Sharpless • Pinkerton)
• *Madama Butterfly* (Puccini)
• lyric or dramatic voices

Ben vi scorgo (Rolando • Arrigo)
• *La battaglia di Legnano* (Verdi)
• lyric or dramatic voices

**Col sangue/Le minaccie/Ah, segnasti la tua
sorte** (Don Carlo di Vargas • Don Alvaro)
• *La forza del destino* (Verdi)
• lyric or dramatic voices

Di': que' ribaldi tremano (Seid • Corrado)
• *Il corsaro* (Verdi)
• lyric or dramatic voices

Dio, che nell'alma infondere
[Dieu tu semas dans nos âmes]
(Rodrigo [Marchese di Posa] [Rodrigue
[Le Marquis de Posa] • Don Carlo [Don Carlos])
• *Don Carlo* [*Don Carlos*] (Verdi)
• lyric or dramatic voices

**Enzo Grimaldi, Principe
di Santafiore** (Barnaba • Enzo)
• *La Gioconda* (Ponchielli)
• lyric or dramatic voices

**Nè gustare/Voi che si larghe cure/Sleale! Il
segreto** (Don Carlo di Vargas • Don Alvaro)
• *La forza del destino* (Verdi)
• lyric or dramatic voices

**No, d'un imene il vincolo/Morte! Ov'io non
cada** (Don Carlo di Vargas • Don Alvaro)
• *La forza del destino* (Verdi)
• lyric or dramatic voices

O grido di quest'anima (Barnaba • Enzo)
• *La Gioconda* (Ponchielli)
• lyric or dramatic voices

**O padre sospirato, o figlio
desiato** (Ulisse • Telemaco)
(Ulisse was sung by either tenor or baritone.)
• *Il ritorno d'Ulisse in patria* (Monteverdi)
• lyric voices

Quando al mio sen [Quand ma bonté toujours
nouvelle] (Montforte [Montfort] • Arrigo [Henri])
• *I vespri siciliani* [*Les vêpres siciliennes*] (Verdi)
• lyric or dramatic voices

Sì, dell'ardir, degl'empi (Lusignano • Gerardo)
• *Caterina Cornaro* (Donizetti)
• lyric or dramatic voices

Sì, pel ciel (Iago • Otello)
• *Otello* (Verdi)
• dramatic voices

Solenne in quest'ora
(Don Carlo di Vargas • Don Alvaro)
• *La forza del destino* (Verdi)
• lyric or dramatic voices

Venti scudi (Belcore • Nemorino)
• *L'elisir d'amore* (Donizetti)
• light voices

Verdi spiaggie al lieto giorno (Ulisse • Eumete)
(Ulisse was sung by either tenor or baritone.)
• *Il ritorno d'Ulisse in patria* (Monteverdi)
• lyric voices

baritone • baritone

ITALIAN

C'è a Windsor una dama (Falstaff • Ford)
• *Falstaff* (Verdi)
• lyric or dramatic voices

baritone • bass-baritone

GERMAN

Welko! das Bild? (Mandryka
• Graf Waldner [Count])
• *Arabella* (Strauss)
• lyric or dramatic voices

baritone • bass

FRENCH

**O Roi! j'arrive de Flandre/Est-ce
la paix que vous donnez?** [O signor,
di Fiandra arrivo] (Rodrigue [Le Marquis
de Posa] • King Philip II [Filippo II])
• *Don Carlos* [*Don Carlo*] (Verdi)
• lyric or dramatic voices

**Pour mon pays/Un souffle ardent/
Enfant! à mon coeur** (Rodrigue
[Le Marquis de Posa] • King Philip II)
• *Don Carlos* (Verdi)
• lyric or dramatic voices

GERMAN

O! Ihr beschämt mich
(Herr Fluth [Mr. Ford] • Falstaff)
• *Die lustigen Weiber von Windsor* (Nicolai)
• lyric voices

Wie freu' ich mich (Herr Fluth [Mr. Ford] •
Falstaff)
• *Die lustigen Weiber von Windsor* (Nicolai)
• lyric voices

ITALIAN

**Cheti, cheti, immantinente/Aspetta, aspetta,
cara sposina** (Dr. Malatesta • Don Pasquale)
• *Don Pasquale* (Donizetti)
• light voices

Coughing Duet [commonly known title]
(Giuliano • Petronio)
• *I filosofi immaginari* (Paisiello)
• light voices

Del mondo i disinganni
(Fra Melitone • Guardiano [Padre])
• *La forza del destino* (Verdi)
• lyric voices

**Delle faci festante al barlume/
Piango, perchè mi parla** (Simon
Boccanegra [The Doge of Genoa] • Fiesco)
• *Simon Boccanegra* (Verdi)
• lyric or dramatic voices

Due vaticini (Macbeth • Banco)
• *Macbeth* (Verdi)
• dramatic voices

**Il rival salvar tu dêi/Suoni la tromba
intrepida** (Riccardo • Giorgio)
• *I Puritani* (Bellini)
• lyric voices

O signor, di Fiandra arrivo [O Roi! j'arrive de
Flandre] (Rodrigo [Marchese di Posa] [Rodrigue
[Le Marquis de Posa] • Filippo II [King Philip II])
• *Don Carlo* [*Don Carlos*] (Verdi)
• lyric or dramatic voices

Qual cieco fato/Del mar sul lido (Simon
Boccanegra [The Doge of Genoa] • Fiesco)
• *Simon Boccanegra* (Verdi)
• lyric or dramatic voices

**Tardo per gli anni/Vanitosi! che
abbietti e dormenti** (Ezio • Attila)
• *Attila* (Verdi)
• dramatic voices

RUSSIAN

Dudu, rududu, rududu (Kum • Cherevik)
• *Sorochinskaya yarmarka* [*The Fair
at Sorochintzī*] (Musorgsky)
• dramatic voices

bass-baritone

bass-baritone • soprano

ENGLISH

Bess, you is my woman (Porgy • Bess)
• *Porgy and Bess* (Gershwin)
• dramatic voices

Oh take, oh take those lips away
(Antony • Cleopatra)
• *Antony and Cleopatra* (Barber)
• dramatic voices

GERMAN

Als junger Liebe Lust mir verblich
(Wotan • Brünnhilde)
• *Die Walküre* (Wagner)
• dramatic voices

Jochanaan, ich bin verliebt (Jochanaan • Salome)
• *Salome* (Strauss)
• dramatic voices

Mir anvertraut (Barak • Sein Weib [Wife of Barak])
• *Die Frau ohne Schatten* (Strauss)
• dramatic voices

ITALIAN

Come frenar il pianto!
(Fernando Villabella • Ninetta)
• *La gazza ladra* (Rossini)
• light voices

So ben che difforme (Tonio • Nedda)
• *Pagliacci* (Leoncavallo)
• lyric or dramatic voices

Un buon servo del visconte (Antonio • Linda)
• *Linda di Chamounix* (Donizetti)
• light or lyric voices

RUSSIAN

Vsyo na zemle dlyz schast' ya roditsya
[Everything is born for love] (Pavel • Virineya)
• *Virineya* (Slonimsky)
• dramatic voices

bass-baritone • mezzo-soprano

GERMAN

Komm denn (Lysiart • Eglantine)
• *Euryanthe* (Weber)
• dramatic voices

ITALIAN

Là ci darem la mano/Andiam mio bene
(Don Giovanni • Zerlina)
• *Don Giovanni* (Mozart)
• light or lyric voices

bass-baritone • tenor

ENGLISH

And do you prefer the storm to Auntie's parlour? (Captain Balstrode • Peter Grimes)
• *Peter Grimes* (Britten)
• dramatic voices

How dark and dreadful is this place
(Nick Shadow • Tom Rakewell)
• *The Rake's Progress* (Stravinsky)
• lyric or dramatic voices

My tale shall be told both by young and by old (Nick Shadow • Tom Rakewell)
• *The Rake's Progress* (Stravinsky)
• lyric or dramatic voices

Thanks to this excellent device
(Nick Shadow • Tom Rakewell)
• *The Rake's Progress* (Stravinsky)
• lyric or dramatic voices

GERMAN

Blühenden Lebens labendes Blut
(Gunther • Siegfried)
• *Götterdämmerung* (Wagner)
• dramatic voices

ITALIAN

No, non temer/Se uniti negli affanni (Iago • Rodrigo)
(Iago was written for either tenor or bass-baritone.)
• *Otello* (Rossini)
• light or lyric voices

bass-baritone • baritone

GERMAN

Welko! das Bild? (Graf Waldner [Count] • Mandryka)
• *Arabella* (Strauss)
• lyric or dramatic voices

bass-baritone • bass-baritone

ITALIAN

Eh, via buffone (Leporello • Don Giovanni)
(Mozart's delineation of baritone and bass voices is unclear.)
• *Don Giovanni* (Mozart)
• light or lyric voices

O statua gentilissima (Leporello • Don Giovanni)
(Mozart's delineation of baritone and bass voices is unclear.)
• *Don Giovanni* (Mozart)
• light or lyric voices

bass-baritone • bass

GERMAN

Jetzt, Alter, jetzt hat es Eile!
(Don Pizarro • Rocco)
• *Fidelio* (Beethoven)
• lyric or dramatic voices

Wie? Hört' ich recht? (Der Holländer [The Dutchman] • Daland)
• *Der fliegende Holländer* (Wagner)
• dramatic voices

bass

bass • soprano

ENGLISH

Every wearied body/God is merciful and just (Trulove • Anne Trulove)
• *The Rake's Progress* (Stravinsky)
• lyric voices

FRENCH

Ah! du moins à Médée (Créon • Médée)
• *Médée* (Chérubini)
• dramatic voices

Quand j'ai quitté le château de mon père /O mon amour [Quando le soglie paterne vareai] (Alphonse [Alfonso] • Léonor [Leonora])
• *La favorite* [*La favorita*] (Donizetti)
• lyric or dramatic voices

Sortez de l'esclavage (Pollux • Telaïre)
• *Castor et Pollux* (Rameau)
• lyric voices

GERMAN

Ich gehe, doch rate ich dir (Osmin • Blonde)
• *Die Entführung aus dem Serail* (Mozart)
• light or lyric voices

Lass Er doch hören (Baculus • Gretchen)
• *Der Wildschütz* (Lortzing)
• lyric or dramatic voices

Nein, nein! I' trink' kein Wein
(Baron Ochs auf Lerchenau • Octavian,
genannt Quinquin [Count Rofrano])
• *Der Rosenkavalier* (Strauss)
• lyric or dramatic voices

Nur hurtig fort, nur frisch gegraben
(Rocco • Leonore)
• *Fidelio* (Beethoven)
• lyric or dramatic voices

Piccolo, piccolo (Count Lothar • Franzi)
• *Ein Walzertraum* (Straus)
• light voices

Wo ist mein Bruder?/Morgen mittag um elf
(Major-Domo • Die Gräfin [Countess Madeleine])
• *Capriccio* (Strauss)
• lyric or dramatic voices

ITALIAN

Carlo! io muoio (Massimiliano
[Count Moor] • Amalia)
• *I Masnadieri* (Verdi)
• lyric or dramatic voices

Cinque, dieci, venti (Figaro • Susanna)
• *Le nozze di Figaro* (Mozart)
• lyric voices

Contento tu sarai [Reconciliation Duet]
(Uberto • Serpina)
• *Serva padrona, La* (Pergolesi)
• light voices

Credete alla femmine (Selim • Fiorilla)
• *Il turco in Italia* (Rossini)
• light voices

Il mio garzone il piffaro sonava
(Pistofolo [Notaio] • Rachelina)
• *La molinara* (Paisiello)
• light or lyric voices

**Infelice, delusa/Chi può legger nel
futuro/Sull'alba** (Guardiano [Padre] • Leonora)
• *La forza del destino* (Verdi)
• lyric or dramatic voices

Io son ricco e tu sei bella
(Dr. Dulcamara • Adina)
• *L'elisir d'amore* (Donizetti)
• light voices

Lo conosco a quegl'occhieti [Conflict Duet]
(Uberto • Serpina)
• *Serva padrona, La* (Pergolesi)
• light voices

Nel veder quel tuo sembiante
(Il Conte Caramella [Count] • Beatrice)
• *I due supposti Conti* (Cimarosa)
• light or lyric voices

**O felice Mustafà/O Girello
in povertà** (Girello • Mustafà)
(Mustafà is a pants role for soprano.)
• *Girello* (Stradella)
• light voices

Pace, caro mio sposo (Lubino • Lilla)
• *Una cosa rara* (Martín y Soler)
• light voices

Per piacere alla Signora (Don Geronio • Fiorilla)
• *Il turco in Italia* (Rossini)
• light voices

Per te ho io nel core (Vastiano • Checca)
• *Flaminio* (Pergolesi)
• light voices

Per te ho io nel core (Uberto • Serpina)
• *Serva padrona, La* (Pergolesi)
• light voices

Quando di luce rosea (Talbot • Maria Stuarda)
• *Maria Stuarda* (Donizetti)
• lyric or dramatic voices

Quanto amore (Dr. Dulcamara • Adina)
• *L'elisir d'amore* (Donizetti)
• light voices

Quella ricordati (Assur • Semiramide)
• *Semiramide* (Rossini)
• lyric voices

**Sai com'arde in petto mio/Piangi,
o figlia/A quel nome** (Giorgio • Elvira)
• *I Puritani* (Bellini)
• lyric voices

Se a caso Madama (Figaro • Susanna)
• *Le nozze di Figaro* (Mozart)
• lyric voices

Son disperato (Nanni • Vespina)
• *L'infedeltà delusa* (Haydn)
• light voices

Tu m'apristi in cor ferita (Ernesto • Imogene)
• *Il pirata* (Bellini)
• lyric or dramatic voices

RUSSIAN

Quarrel Duet [commonly known title]
(Karas [Zaparozhets] • Odarka)
• *Zaparozhets za Dunayem* [*A Cossack
beyond the Danube*] (Gulak-Artemovsky)
• lyric or dramatic voices

bass • mezzo-soprano

FRENCH

As-tu souffert?/As-tu pleuré?
(Lothario • Mignon)

• *Mignon* (Thomas)
• lyric voices

Dans la nuit où seul je veille
(Marcel • Valentine)
• *Les Huguenots* (Meyerbeer)
• lyric voices

Derrière ce pilier (Marcel • Valentine)
• *Les Huguenots* (Meyerbeer)
• lyric voices

Légères hirondelles (Lothario • Mignon)
• *Mignon* (Thomas)
• lyric voices

Mais Alice, qu'as-tu donc? (Bertram • Alice)
• *Robert le Diable* (Meyerbeer)
• lyric or dramatic voices

Oui, je souffre votre tendresse
(Don Quichotte • Dulcinée)
• *Don Quichotte* (Massenet)
• lyric voices

Printemps revient (Pandolphe • Cendrillon)
• *Cendrillon* (Massenet)
• lyric voices

GERMAN

Lasst mich hier (Louis VI • Euryanthe)
• *Euryanthe* (Weber)
• dramatic voices

ITALIAN

Fama! sì: l'avrete (Enrico [Henry VIII] •
Giovanna Seymour)
• *Anna Bolena* (Donizetti)
• lyric or dramatic voices

Il core vi dono (Guglielmo • Dorabella)
• *Così fan tutte* (Mozart)
• lyric voices

Oh qual parlar (Enrico
[Henry VIII] • Giovanna Seymour)
• *Anna Bolena* (Donizetti)
• lyric or dramatic voices

Quarrel Duet [commonly known title]
(Pimpinone • Vespetta)
• *Pimpinone* (Albinoni)
• light voices

Qui chiamata m'avete? (Alvise • Laura)
• *La Gioconda* (Ponchielli)
• lyric or dramatic voices

RUSSIAN

Farewell my son, I am dying [commonly
known title] (Boris Godunov • Fyodor)
• *Boris Godunov* (Musorgsky)
• lyric or dramatic voices

bass • contralto

ENGLISH

Obey my will (Somnus • Juno)
• *Semele* (Handel)
• lyric voices

FRENCH

Si tu m'aimes, Carmen (Escamillo • Carmen)
• *Carmen* (Bizet)
• lyric or dramatic voices

GERMAN

Da lieg' ich! Was einem Kavalier
(Baron Ochs auf Lerchenau • Annina)
• *Der Rosenkavalier* (Strauss)
• lyric or dramatic voices

ITALIAN

Ai capricci della sorte (Taddeo • Isabella)
• *L'italiana in Algeri* (Rossini)
• light or lyric voices

D'un tenero amore (Assur • Arsace)
• *Semiramide* (Rossini)
• lyric voices

O che muso, che figura! (Mustafà • Isabella)
• *L'italiana in Algeri* (Rossini)
• light or lyric voices

bass • tenor

CZECH

Nuže, milý chasníku [Now, dear
young fellow] (Kecal • Jeník)
• *Prodaná Nevěsta* [*The Bartered Bride*] (Smetana)
• lyric voices

FRENCH

Ah! l'honnête homme! (Bertram • Raimbaut)
• *Robert le Diable* (Meyerbeer)
• light voices

Ami, leur rage (Hercule • Admète)
• *Alceste* (Gluck)
• lyric or dramatic voices

C'est à toi de trembler
(Pontifex Maximus • Licinius)
• *La vestale* (Spontini)
• lyric or dramatic voices

Contente-toi d'une victime (Thésée • Tisiphone)
(Tisiphone, tenor, was originally
sung by haute-contre.)
• *Hippolyte et Aricie* (Rameau)
• lyric voices

Dans Venise la belle [Barcarolle] (Cornarino
Cornarini [Doge of Venice] • Baptiste)
• *Le pont des soupirs* (Offenbach)
• light voices

Des chevaliers de ma patrie
(Bertram • Robert le Diable)
• *Robert le Diable* (Meyerbeer)
• lyric voices

Je me sens, hélas, tout chose (Siroco • Ouf)
• *L'étoile du Nord* (Chabrier)
• light voices

Me voici (Méphistophélès • Faust, Dr.)
• *Faust* (Gounod)
• lyric voices

Mieux vaut mourir que rester miserable! (Pietro • Masniello)
• *La muette de Portici* (Auber)
• lyric voices

Où vas-tu/Ah! Mathilde, idole de mon âme (Guillaume Tell • Arnold)
• *Guillaume Tell* (Rossini)
• lyric voices

Sais-tu que devant la tiare [Non sai tu che un giusto] (Balthazar [Badassare] • Fernand [Fernando])
• *La favorite* [*La favorita*] (Donizetti)
• lyric or dramatic voices

GERMAN

Darf ich wohl den Worten trauen
(Van Bett • Ivanov)
• *Zar und Zimmermann* (Lortzing)
• light or lyric voices

Ja, seit früher Kindheit Tagen
(Plumkett • Lyonel)
• *Martha* (Flotow)
• lyric voices

Mars und Merkur (Abul • Nureddin)
• *Der Barbier von Bagdad* (Cornelius)
• lyric or dramatic voices

So geht indes hinein
(Herr Reich [Mr. Page] • Fenton)
• *Die lustigen Weiber von Windsor* (Nicolai)
• light or lyric voices

Trotze nicht (Lysiart • Adolar)
• *Euryanthe* (Weber)
• dramatic voices

Vivat Bacchus (Osmin • Pedrillo)
• *Die Entführung aus dem Serail* (Mozart)
• light or lyric voices

Wer ein Liebchen hat gefunden
(Osmin • Belmonte)
• *Die Entführung aus dem Serail* (Mozart)
• light or lyric voices

Wie dünkt mich doch die Aue heut' so schön (Gurnemanz • Parsifal)
• *Parsifal* (Wagner)
• dramatic voices

ITALIAN

Come il bacio d'un padre amoroso
(Massimiliano [Count Moor] • Carlo)

• *I Masnadieri* (Verdi)
• lyric or dramatic voices

Non sai tu che un giusto [Sais-tu que devant la tiare] (Badassare [Balthazar] • Fernando [Fernand])
• *La favorita* [*La favorite*] (Donizetti)
• lyric or dramatic voices

O che umor (Bartolo • Il Conte di Almaviva/Lindoro)
• *Il barbiere di Siviglia* (Paisiello)
• light voices

Obbligato, ah, sì! obbligato!
(Dr. Dulcamara • Nemorino)
• *L'elisir d'amore* (Donizetti)
• light voices

Pace e gioia sia con voi (Bartolo • Il Conte d'Almaviva/Lindoro [Count Almaviva])
• *Il barbiere di Siviglia* (Rossini)
• light voices

Pappataci! (Taddeo • Lindoro)
• *L'italiana in Algeri* (Rossini)
• light or lyric voices

Prender moglie! (Don Pasquale • Ernesto)
• *Don Pasquale* (Donizetti)
• light voices

Se inclinassi a prender moglie
(Mustafà • Lindoro)
• *L'italiana in Algeri* (Rossini)
• light or lyric voices

Se tu mi doni un'ora (Mefistofele • Faust)
• *Mefistofele* (Boito)
• lyric or dramatic voices

Secondate, aurette amiche
(Guglielmo • Ferrando)
• *Così fan tutte* (Mozart)
• light or lyric voices

Sì...sulla salma del fratello
(Baron Valdeburgo • Arturo)
• *La Straniera* (Bellini)
• lyric voices

Zitto, zitto, piano, piano
(Dandini • Don Ramiro)
• *La Cenerentola* (Rossini)
• light voices

RUSSIAN

Just think, my son [commonly known title] (Pimen • Grigory)
• *Boris Godunov* (Musorgsky)
• lyric or dramatic voices

bass • baritone

FRENCH

O Roi! j'arrive de Flandre/Est-ce la paix que vous donnez? [O signor, di Fiandra arrivo] (King Philip II [Filippo II] • Rodrigue [Le Marquis de Posa])

• *Don Carlos* [*Don Carlo*] (Verdi)
• lyric or dramatic voices

**Pour mon pays/Un souffle ardent/
Enfant!** à **mon coeur** (King Philip II •
Rodrigue [Le Marquis de Posa])
• *Don Carlos* (Verdi)
• lyric or dramatic voices

O! Ihr beschämt mich
(Falstaff • Herr Fluth [Mr. Ford])
• *Die lustigen Weiber von Windsor* (Nicolai)
• lyric voices

Wie freu' ich mich (Falstaff • Herr Fluth [Mr.
Ford])
• *Die lustigen Weiber von Windsor* (Nicolai)
• lyric voices

**Cheti, cheti, immantinente/Aspetta, aspetta,
cara sposina** (Don Pasquale • Dr. Malatesta)
• *Don Pasquale* (Donizetti)
• light voices

Coughing Duet [commonly known title]
(Petronio • Giuliano)
• *I filosofi immaginari* (Paisiello)
• light voices

Del mondo i disinganni
(Guardiano [Padre] • Fra Melitone)
• *La forza del destino* (Verdi)
• lyric voices

**Delle faci festante al barlume/
Piango, perchè mi parla**
(Fiesco • Simon Boccanegra [The Doge of Genoa])
• *Simon Boccanegra* (Verdi)
• lyric or dramatic voices

Due vaticini (Banco • Macbeth)
• *Macbeth* (Verdi)
• dramatic voices

**Il rival salvar tu dêi/Suoni la tromba
intrepida** (Giorgio • Riccardo)
• *I Puritani* (Bellini)
• lyric voices

O signor, di Fiandra arrivo [O Roi! j'arrive de
Flandre] (Filippo II [King Philip II] • Rodrigue
[Le Marquis de Posa])
• *Don Carlo* [*Don Carlos*] (Verdi)
• lyric or dramatic voices

Qual cieco fato/Del mar sul lido
(Fiesco • Simon Boccanegra [The Doge of Genoa])
• *Simon Boccanegra* (Verdi)
• lyric or dramatic voices

**Tardo per gli anni/Vanitosi! che
abbietti e dormenti** (Attila • Ezio)
• *Attila* (Verdi)
• dramatic voices

Dudu, rududu, rududu (Cherevik • Kum)
• *Sorochinskaya yarmarka* [*The Fair
at Sorochintzi*] (Musorgsky)
• dramatic voices

bass • bass-baritone

Jetzt, Alter, jetzt hat es Eile!
(Rocco • Don Pizarro)
• *Fidelio* (Beethoven)
• lyric or dramatic voices

Wie? Hört' ich recht?
(Daland • Der Holländer [The Dutchman])
• *Der fliegende Holländer* (Wagner)
• dramatic voices

bass • bass

Suis-je devant le roi?/Dans ce beau pays
[Son io dinanzi al rè?] (Il Grande Inquisitore
[The Grand Inquisitor] • King Philip II [Filippo II])
• *Don Carlos* [*Don Carlo*] (Verdi)
• lyric or dramatic voices

**L'alto retaggio non ho bramato/O meco
incolume** (Wurm • Il Conte di Walter [Count])
• *Luisa Miller* (Verdi)
• lyric or dramatic voices

Se fiato in corpo avete
(Geronimo • Count Robinson)
(Count Robinson can be sung by
either baritone or bass.)
• *Il matrimonio segreto* (Cimarosa)
• light voices

**Son io dinanzi al rè?/Nell'ispana suol mai
l'eresia dominò** [Suis-je devant le roi?]
(Il Grande Inquisitore [The Grand Inquisitor]
• Filippo II [King Philip II])
• *Don Carlo* [*Don Carlos*] (Verdi)
• lyric or dramatic voices

Un segreto d'importanza
(Don Magnifico • Dandini)
(Both roles can be sung by either baritone or bass.)
• *La Cenerentola* (Rossini)
• light voices

Opera
to
Roles

Abu Hassan (Weber)
Abu Hassan • tenor
Fatime • soprano

Acis and Galatea (Handel)
Acis • tenor
Galatea • soprano

Adriana Lecouvreur (Cilea)
Adriana Lecouvreur • soprano
Maurizio • tenor
Michonnet • baritone
Principessa di Bouillon, La [*The Princess
of Bouillon*] • mezzo-soprano

Africaine, L' (Meyerbeer)
Sélika • soprano
Vasco da Gama • tenor

Aïda (Verdi)
Aïda • soprano
Amneris • mezzo-soprano
Amonasro • baritone
Radames • tenor

Alceste (Gluck)
Admète • tenor
Hercule • bass

Alceste (Gluck)
Admeto • tenor
Alceste • soprano
Aspasia • soprano

Eumelo • soprano
Evandro • tenor
Ismene • soprano

Alzira (Verdi)
Alzira • soprano
Gusmano • baritone
Zamoro • tenor

Amadis (Lully)
Arcabonne • soprano
Arcalaus • tenor

Amahl and the Night Visitors (Menotti)
Amahl • treble
Mother • soprano

Amico Fritz, L' (Mascagni)
Fritz Kobus • tenor
Suzel • soprano

Andrea Chénier (Giordano)
Andrea Chénier • tenor
Maddalena • soprano

Anima del filosofo, L' (Haydn)
Euridice • soprano
Orfeo • tenor

Anna Bolena (Donizetti)
Anna Bolena • soprano
Enrico [*Henry VIII*] • bass
Giovanna Seymour • mezzo-soprano

Antony and Cleopatra (Barber)
Antony • bass-baritone
Cleopatra • soprano

Arabella (Strauss)
Arabella • soprano
Mandryka • baritone
Waldner, Graf [Count] • bass-baritone
Zdenka • soprano

Ariadne auf Naxos (Strauss)
Arabella • soprano
Bacchus • tenor
Komponist, Der [*The Composer*] • mezzo-soprano
Musiklehrer, Ein [*A Music Master*] • baritone
Prima Donna/Ariadne • soprano
Zerbinetta • soprano

Armida (Haydn)
Armida • soprano
Rinaldo • tenor

Armide (Gluck)
Armide • soprano
Danish Knight • tenor
Hidraot • baritone
Ubalde • baritone

Armide (Lully)
Armide • soprano
Hidraot • baritone

Astarto (Bononcini)
Nino • tenor
Sidonia • soprano

Attila (Verdi)
Attila • bass
Ezio • baritone
Foresto • tenor
Odabello • soprano

Ballo in maschera, Un (Verdi)
Amelia • soprano
Riccardo • tenor

Barbe-bleue (Offenbach)
Fleurette • soprano
Saphir • tenor

Barbier von Bagdad, Der (Cornelius)
Abul • bass
Bostana • mezzo-soprano
Nureddin • tenor

Barbiere di Siviglia, Il (Paisiello)
Almaviva, Il Conte di/Lindoro • tenor
Bartolo • bass
Rosina • soprano

Barbiere di Siviglia, Il (Rossini)
Almaviva, Il Conte d'/Lindoro
[Count Almaviva] • tenor
Bartolo • bass

Figaro • baritone
Rosina • contralto

Bartered Bride, The [Prodaná Nevěsta] (Smetana)
Circus Master • tenor
Esmeralda • soprano
Jeník • tenor
Kecal • bass
Mařenka • soprano
Vašek • tenor

Bastien und Bastienne (Mozart)
Bastien • tenor
Bastienne • soprano

Battaglia di Legnano, La (Verdi)
Arrigo • tenor
Lida • soprano
Rolando • baritone

Beatrice di Tenda (Bellini)
Beatrice • soprano
Filippo Maria Visconti • baritone
Orombello • tenor

Béatrice et Bénédict (Berlioz)
Béatrice • mezzo-soprano
Bénédict • tenor
Héro • soprano
Ursula • mezzo-soprano

Beggar's Opera, The (Pepusch)
Lucy Lockit • soprano
Macheath • baritone
Polly Peachum • soprano

Belisario (Donizetti)
Antonina • soprano
Belisario • baritone
Eutopio • tenor
Irene • mezzo-soprano

Benvenuto Cellini (Berlioz)
Benvenuto Cellini • tenor
Teresa • soprano

Bettelstudent, Der (Millöcker)
Jan • baritone
Laura • soprano
Symon Rymanovicz • tenor

Bianca e Fernando (Bellini)
Bianca • soprano
Eloisa • soprano

Blaise et Babet (Dezède)
Babet • soprano
Blaise • tenor

Boccaccio (Suppé)
Boccaccio • mezzo-soprano
Fiametta • soprano

Bohème, La (Puccini)
Marcello • baritone
Mimì • soprano
Rodolfo • tenor

Boréades, Les (Rameau)
Abaris • tenor
Alphise • soprano

Boris Godunov (Musorgsky)
Boris Godunov • bass
Dmitry • tenor
Fyodor • mezzo-soprano
Grigory • tenor
Marina • mezzo-soprano
Pimen • bass

Capriccio (Strauss)
Clairon • contralto
Count • baritone
Flamand • tenor
Gräfin, Die [*The Countess*]
    [*Countess Madeleine*] • soprano
Major-Domo • bass

Capuleti e i Montecchi, I (Bellini)
Giulietta • soprano
Romeo • mezzo-soprano
Tebaldo • tenor

Carmen (Bizet)
Carmen • contralto
Escamillo • bass
José, Don • tenor
Micaëla • soprano

Castor et Pollux (Rameau)
Pollux • bass
Telaïre • soprano

Caterina Cornaro (Donizetti)
Gerardo • tenor
Lusignano • baritone

Cavalleria rusticana (Mascagni)
Alfio • tenor
Santuzza • soprano
Turiddu • tenor

Cendrillon (Massenet)
Cendrillon • mezzo-soprano
Pandolphe • bass
Prince • tenor

Cenerentola, La (Rossini)
Cenerentola [*Angelica*] • mezzo-soprano
Dandini • bass
Magnifico, Don • bass
Ramiro, Don • tenor

Cid, Le (Massenet)
Chimène • soprano
Infante [*Princess*] • soprano

Clemenza di Tito, La (Mozart)
Annio • mezzo-soprano
Servilia • soprano
Sesto • mezzo-soprano
Vitellia • mezzo-soprano

Comte Ory, Le (Rossini)
Adèle di Formouters, La Comtesse [Countess] • soprano
Isolier [*Page*] • mezzo-soprano
Ory, Le Comte [Count] • tenor
Ragonde • mezzo-soprano

Contes d'Hoffmann, Les (Offenbach)
Giulietta • mezzo-soprano
Hoffmann • tenor
Nicklausse • mezzo-soprano

Corsaro, Il (Verdi)
Corrado • tenor
Gulnara • soprano
Medora • soprano
Seid • baritone

Cosa rara, Una (Martín y Soler)
Lilla • soprano
Lubino • bass

Così fan tutte (Mozart)
Dorabella • mezzo-soprano
Ferrando • tenor
Fiordiligi • soprano
Guglielmo • bass

Cossack beyond the Danube, A
[Zaparozhets za Dunayem] (Gulak-Artemovsky)
Karas [*Zaparozhets*] • bass
Odarka • soprano

Crociato in Egitto, Il (Meyerbeer)
Armando • soprano
Palmide • soprano

Csárdásfürstin, Die (Kálmán)
Edwin • tenor
Stasi, Komtesse [Countess Stasi] • soprano
Sylva • soprano

Dalibor (Smetana)
Dalibor • tenor
Milada • soprano

Dame blanche, La (Boieldieu)
Anna • soprano
Georges Brown/Julien Avanel • tenor

Daphne (Strauss)
Apollo • tenor
Daphne • soprano

Dido and Aeneas (Purcell)
Belinda • soprano
Second Woman • mezzo-soprano

Dom Sébastien (Donizetti)
Sébastien • tenor
Zayda • mezzo-soprano

Don Carlo [Don Carlos] (Verdi)
Carlo, Don [*Don Carlo*] • tenor
Elisabetta [*Elisabeth*] • soprano
Filippo II [*King Philip II*] • bass
Grande Inquisitore, Il [*The Grand Inquisitor*] • bass
Rodrigo[*Marchese di Posa*] [*Rodrigue* [*Le Marquis de Posa*]] • baritone

Don Carlos (Verdi)
Carlos, Don [*Don Carlo*] • tenor
Elisabeth [*Elisabetta*] • soprano
Grande Inquisitore, Il [*The Grand Inquisitor*] • bass
Philip II, King [*Filippo II*] • bass
Rodrigue [*Le Marquis de Posa*] [*Rodrigo* [*Marchese di Posa*] • baritone

Don Giovanni (Mozart)
Anna, Donna • soprano
Giovanni, Don • bass-baritone
Leporello • bass-baritone
Ottavio, Don • tenor
Zerlina • mezzo-soprano

Don Pasquale (Donizetti)
Ernesto • tenor
Malatesta, Dr. • baritone
Norina • soprano
Pasquale, Don • baritone

Don Quichotte (Massenet)
Dulcinée • mezzo-soprano
Quichotte, Don • bass

Donna del lago, La (Rossini)
Elena • soprano
Malcolm • mezzo-soprano

Due Foscari, I (Verdi)
Francesco Foscari [*Doge*] • baritone
Jacopo Foscari • tenor
Lucrezia Contarini • soprano

Due supposti conti, I (Cimarosa)
Beatrice • soprano
Caramella, Il Conte [Count] • bass

Echo et Narcisse (Gluck)
Cynire • tenor
Echo • soprano

Edgar (Puccini)
Edgar • tenor
Fidelia • soprano

Elektra (Strauss)
Chrysothemis • soprano
Elektra • soprano
Klytemnästra • contralto
Orest • baritone

Elisabetta (Rossini)
Elisabetta • soprano
Leicester • tenor
Matilda • soprano
Norfolk • tenor

Elisir d'amore, L' (Donizetti)
Adina • soprano
Belcore • baritone
Dulcamara, Dr. • bass
Nemorino • tenor

Enfant et les sortilèges, l' (Ravel)
Female Cat • mezzo-soprano
Tom Cat • baritone

English Cat, The (Henze)
Minette • soprano
Tom [*Cat*] • baritone

Entführung aus dem Serail, Die (Mozart)
Belmonte • tenor
Blonde • soprano
Konstanze • soprano
Osmin • bass
Pedrillo • tenor

Ernani (Verdi)
Carlo, Don • baritone
Elvira • soprano
Ernani • tenor

Etoile du Nord, L' (Chabrier)
Ouf • tenor
Siroco • bass

Eugene Onegin [Yevgeny Onegin] (Tchaikovsky)
Ol'ga • contralto
Onegin • baritone
Tat'yana • soprano

Euryanthe (Weber)
Adolar • tenor
Eglantine • mezzo-soprano
Euryanthe • mezzo-soprano
Louis VI • bass
Lysiart • bass

The Fair at Sorochintzï [Sorochinskaya yarmarka] (Musorgsky)
Cherevik • bass
Kum • baritone

Falstaff (Verdi)
Falstaff • baritone
Fenton • tenor
Ford • baritone
Nannetta • soprano

Fanciulla del West, La (Puccini)
Dick Johnson [Ramerrez] • tenor
Minnie • soprano

Faust (Gounod)
Faust, Dr. • tenor
Marguerite • soprano
Méphistophélès • bass

Favorita, La [La Favorite] (Donizetti)
Alfonso [Alphonse] • baritone
Badassare [Balthazar] • bass
Fernando [Fernand] • tenor
Leonora [Léonor] • soprano

Favorite, La [La Favorite] (Donizetti)
Alphonse [Alfonso] • bass
Balthazar [Badassare] • bass
Fernand [Fernando] • tenor
Léonor [Leonora] • soprano

Fedora (Giordano)
Fedora Romazoff, La Principessa
   [Princess Fedora] • soprano
Loris Ipanoff, Il Conte [Count Loris] • tenor

Fidelio (Beethoven)
Florestan • tenor
Jaquino • tenor
Leonore • soprano
Marzelline • soprano
Pizarro, Don • bass-baritone
Rocco • bass

Fierrabras (Schubert)
Florinda • soprano
Maragond • mezzo-soprano

Figlia del reggimento, La
   [La Fille du régiment] (Donizetti)
Maria [Marie] • soprano
Sulpizio [Sulpice] • baritone
Tonio • tenor

Fille du régiment, La
   [La Figlia del reggimetno] (Donizetti)
Marie [Maria] • soprano
Sulpice [Sulpizio] • baritone
Tonio • tenor

Filosofi immaginari, I (Paisiello)
Giuliano • baritone
Petronio • bass

Finta Giardiniera, La (Mozart)
Belfiore • tenor
Sandrina • soprano

Flaminio (Pergolesi)
Checca • soprano
Vastiano • bass

Fledermaus, Die (J. Strauss)
Eisenstein • tenor
Rosalinde • soprano

Fliegende Holländer, Der (Wagner)
Daland • bass

Erik • tenor
Holländer, Der [The Dutchman] • baritone
Senta • soprano

Forza del destino, La (Verdi)
Alvaro, Don • tenor
Carlo di Vargas, Don • baritone
Guardiano [Padre] • bass
Leonora • soprano
Melitone, Fra • baritone

Frau ohne Schatten, Die (Strauss)
Amme, Die [The Nurse] • mezzo-soprano
Barak • bass-baritone
Falcon • soprano
Kaiser, Der [The Emperor] • tenor
Kaiserin, Die [The Empress] • soprano
Weib, Sein [Wife of Barak] • soprano

Freischütz, Der (Weber)
Agathe • soprano
Ännchen • mezzo-soprano

Gazza ladra, La (Rossini)
Fernando Villabella • bass-baritone
Giannetto • tenor
Ninetta • soprano
Pippo • contralto

Gioconda, La (Ponchielli)
Alvise • bass
Barnaba • baritone
Enzo • tenor
Gioconda, La • mezzo-soprano
Laura • mezzo-soprano

Giovanna d'Arco (Verdi)
Carlo VII • tenor
Giacomo • baritone
Giovanna • soprano

Girello (Stradella)
Girello • bass
Mustafà • soprano

Giuditta (Lehár)
Anita • soprano
Giuditta • soprano
Octavio • tenor
Pierrino • tenor

Giulio Cesare in Egitto (Handel)
Cleopatra • soprano
Cornelia • contralto
Giulio Cesare • bass-baritone
Sesto • mezzo-soprano

Gloriana (Britten)
Earl of Essex [Robert Devereux] • tenor
Elizabeth I • soprano

Gondoliers, The (Sullivan)
Giuseppe • baritone
Marco • tenor

Götterdämmerung (Wagner)
Gunther • bass-baritone
Siegfried • tenor

Goyescas (Granados)
Fernando • tenor
Rosario • soprano

Guillaume Tell (Rossini)
Arnold • tenor
Guillaume Tell • bass
Mathilde • soprano

Hamlet (Thomas)
Hamlet • baritone
Ophélie • soprano

Hänsel und Gretel (Humperdinck)
Gretel • soprano
Hänsel • mezzo-soprano

Haunted Tower, The (Storace)
Adela • soprano
Elinor, Lady • soprano

Hercules (Handel)
Dejanira • mezzo-soprano
Iöle • soprano

Hérodiade (Massenet)
Jean [John the Baptist] • tenor
Salomé • soprano

Hippolyte et Aricie (Rameau)
Thésée • bass
Tisiphone • tenor

Huguenots, Les (Meyerbeer)
Marcel • bass
Raoul • tenor
Valentine • mezzo-soprano

Idomeneo (Mozart)
Idamante • tenor
Ilia • soprano

Imeneo (Handel)
Rosmene • soprano
Tirinto • mezzo-soprano

Incontro improvviso, L' (Haydn)
Ali • tenor
Rezia • soprano

Incoronazione di Poppea, L' (Monteverdi)
Damigella • soprano
Lucano • tenor
Nerone • mezzo-soprano
Poppea • soprano
Valletto • tenor

Infedeltà delusa, L' (Haydn)
Nanni • bass
Vespina • soprano

Iolanta (Tchaikovsky)
Iolanta • mezzo-soprano
Vaudémont • tenor

Iphigénie en Aulide (Gluck)
Achille • tenor
Agamemnon • baritone

Iris (Mascagni)
Iris • soprano
Osaka • tenor

Italiana in Algeri, L' (Rossini)
Isabella • contralto
Lindoro • tenor
Mustafà • bass
Taddeo • bass

Jérusalem (Verdi)
Gaston • tenor
Hélène • soprano

Knyaz' Igor' [Prince Igor] (Borodin)
Igor' • baritone
Konchakovna • contralto
Vladimir • tenor
Yaroslavna • soprano

Lakmé (Delibes)
Gérald • tenor
Lakmé • soprano
Mallika • mezzo-soprano

Linda di Chamounix (Donizetti)
Antonio • bass-baritone
Carlo • tenor
Linda • soprano
Pierotto • contralto

Little Sweep, The [I Lituani] (Ponchielli)
Aldona • soprano
Walter • tenor

Lituani, I [The Little Sweep] (Ponchielli)
Aldona • soprano
Walter • tenor

Lohengrin (Wagner)
Elsa • soprano
Lohengrin • baritone

Lombardi, I (Verdi)
Giselda • soprano
Oronte • tenor

Louise (Charpentier)
Julien • tenor
Louise • soprano

Lucia di Lammermoor (Donizetti)
Arturo • tenor
Edgardo • tenor
Enrico Ashton • baritone
Lucia • soprano

Lucio Silla (Mozart)
Cecilio • mezzo-soprano
Giunia • soprano

Lucrezia Borgia (Donizetti)
Gennaro • tenor
Lucrezia • soprano

Luisa Miller (Verdi)
Federica • contralto
Luisa • soprano
Miller • baritone
Rodolfo • tenor
Walter, Il Conte di [Count] • bass
Wurm • bass

Lustige Witwe, Die (Lehár)
Danilo Danilowitsch, Graf [Count Danilo] • baritone
Hanna Glawari • soprano

Lustigen Weiber von Windsor, Die (Nicolai)
Anna Reich [*Anne Page*] • soprano
Falstaff • bass
Fenton • tenor
Fluth, Frau [Mrs. Ford] • soprano
Fluth, Herr [Mr. Ford] • baritone
Reich, Frau [Mrs. Page] • contralto
Reich, Herr [Mr. Page] • bass

Macbeth (Verdi)
Banco • bass
Macbeth • baritone
Macbeth, Lady • soprano

Madama Butterfly (Puccini)
Cio-Cio-San [*Madama Butterfly*] • soprano
Pinkerton • tenor
Sharpless • baritone
Suzuki • mezzo-soprano

Mädchen aus der Feenwelt, Das (Drechsler)
Fortunatus Wurzel • tenor
Youth • soprano

Manon (Massenet)
Des Grieux [Le Chevalier] • tenor
Manon • soprano

Manon Lescaut (Auber)
Des Grieux • tenor
Manon • soprano

Manon Lescaut (Puccini)
Des Grieux, Chevalier • tenor
Lescaut • baritone
Manon Lescaut • soprano

Maria Stuarda (Donizetti)
Elisabetta [Queen] • soprano
Leicester • tenor
Maria Stuarda • soprano
Talbot • bass

Martha (Flotow)
Harriet Durham, Lady • soprano
Lyonel • tenor
Nancy • mezzo-soprano
Plumkett • bass

Masnadieri, I (Verdi)
Amalia • soprano
Carlo • tenor
Francesco • baritone
Massimiliano [Count Moor] • bass

Matrimonio segreto, Il (Cimarosa)
Carolina • soprano
Geronimo • bass
Paolino • tenor
Robinson, Count • bass

Médée (Chérubini)
Créon • bass
Jason • tenor
Médée • soprano

Medium, The (Menotti)
Baba [Madame Flora] • contralto
Monica • soprano

Mefistofele (Boito)
Elèna [Helen of Troy] • soprano
Faust • tenor
Margherita • soprano
Mefistofele • bass

Meistersinger von Nürnberg, Die (Wagner)
Eva • soprano
Hans Sachs • baritone

Midsummer Marriage, The (Tippett)
Jenifer • soprano
Mark • tenor

Mignon (Thomas)
Lothario • bass
Mignon • mezzo-soprano
Philine • soprano
Wilhelm Meister • tenor

Mireille (Gounod)
Mireille • soprano
Vincenette • soprano
Vincent • tenor

Mitridate (Mozart)
Aspasia • soprano
Sifare • tenor

Molinara, La (Paisiello)
Pistofolo [Notaio] • bass
Rachelina • soprano

Mondo della luna, Il (Haydn)
Clarice • soprano
Ecclitico • tenor

Muette de Portici, La (Auber)
Alphonse • tenor
Elvire • soprano
Masniello • tenor
Pietro • bass

Nabucco (Verdi)
Abigaille • soprano
Nabucco • baritone

Norma (Bellini)
Adalgisa • mezzo-soprano
Norma • soprano
Pollione • tenor

Nozze di Figaro, Le (Mozart)
Almaviva, Il Conte di [Count] • baritone
Almaviva, La Contessa di [*Rosina*] • soprano
Cherubino • mezzo-soprano
Figaro • bass
Marcellina • mezzo-soprano
Susanna • soprano

Oberon (Weber)
Fatima • mezzo-soprano
Sherasmin • baritone

Oreste (Handel)
Ermione • soprano
Oreste • mezzo-soprano

Orfeo ed Euridice [Orphée et Eurydice] (Gluck)
Euridice [*Eurydice*] • soprano
Orfeo [*Orphée*] • contralto

Orlando Paladino (Haydn)
Angelica • soprano
Eurilla • soprano
Medoro • tenor
Pasquale • baritone

Orphée et Eurydice [Orfeo ed Euridice] (Gluck)
Eurydice [*Euridice*] • soprano
Orphée [*Orfeo*] • tenor

Otello (Rossini)
Desdemona • mezzo-soprano
Iago • bass-baritone
Otello • tenor
Rodrigo • tenor

Otello (Verdi)
Desdemona • soprano
Iago • baritone
Otello • tenor

Paganini (Lehár)
Anna Elisa • soprano
Paganini • tenor

Pagliacci (Leoncavallo)
Nedda • soprano
Silvio [*Campagnuolo*] [*A Villager*] • baritone
Tonio • bass-baritone

Paride ed Elena (Gluck)
Elena • soprano
Erasto • soprano
Paride • tenor

Parsifal (Wagner)
Gurnemanz • bass
Parsifal • tenor

Patience (Sullivan)
Grosvenor • baritone
Patience • soprano

Pêcheurs de perles, Les (Bizet)
Leila • soprano
Nadir • tenor
Zurga • baritone

Pelléas et Mélisande (Debussy)
Golaud • baritone
Mélisande • mezzo-soprano
Pelléas • tenor

Pénélope (Fauré)
Eumée • baritone
Pénélope • soprano
Ulysse • tenor

Périchole, La (Offenbach)
Périchole, La • mezzo-soprano
Piquillo • tenor

Peter Grimes (Britten)
Balstrode, Captain • bass-baritone
Peter Grimes • tenor

Pikovaya dama [Pique Dame] [The Queen of Spades]
(Tchaikovsky)
Liza • soprano
Milovzor [*Daphnis*] [*Pauline*] • contralto

Pimpinone (Albinoni)
Pimpinone • bass
Vespetta • mezzo-soprano

Pique Dame [Pikovaya dama] [The Queen of Spades]
(Tchaikovsky)
Daphnis [*Milovzor*] [*Pauline*] • contralto
Liza • soprano

Pirata, Il (Bellini)
Ernesto • bass
Gualtiero • tenor
Imogene • soprano

Poliuto (Donizetti)
Paolina • soprano
Poliuto • tenor

Pomo d'oro, Il (Cesti)
Ennone • soprano
Paride • tenor

Pont des soupirs, Le (Offenbach)
Baptiste • tenor
Cornarino Cornarini [*Doge of Venice*] • bass

Porgy and Bess (Gershwin)
Bess • soprano
Porgy • bass-baritone

Postillon de Lonjumeau, Le (Adam)
Chapelou • tenor
Madeleine • soprano

Pré aux Clercs, Le (Hérold)
Girot • tenor
Nicette • soprano

Prince Igor [Knyaz' Igor'] (Borodin)
Igor' • baritone
Konchakovna • contralto
Vladimir • tenor
Yaroslavna • soprano

Prodaná Nevěsta [The Bartered Bride] (Smetana)
Circus Master • tenor
Esmeralda • soprano
Jeník • tenor
Kecal • bass
Mařenka • soprano
Vašek • tenor

Puritani, I (Bellini)
Arturo • tenor
Elvira • soprano
Giorgio • bass
Riccardo • baritone

Queen of Spades, The [Pikovaya dama] [Pique Dame] (Tchaikovsky)
Liza • soprano
Pauline [*Milovzor*] [*Daphnis*] • contralto

Rake's Progress, The (Stravinsky)
Anne Trulove • soprano
Baba • mezzo-soprano
Nick Shadow • bass-baritone
Tom Rakewell • tenor
Trulove • bass

Rienzi (Wagner)
Adriano • mezzo-soprano
Irene • soprano
Rienzi • tenor

Rigoletto (Verdi)
Duca di Mantua, Il [*The Duke of Mantua*] • tenor
Gilda • soprano
Rigoletto • baritone

Ritorno d'Ulisse in patria, Il (Monteverdi)
Eumete • tenor
Eurimaco • tenor
Melanto • soprano
Telemaco • tenor
Ulisse • baritone

Robert le Diable (Meyerbeer)
Alice • mezzo-soprano
Bertram • bass
Isabelle • soprano
Raimbaut • tenor
Robert le Diable • tenor

Rodelinda (Handel)
Bertarido • contralto
Rodelinda • soprano

Roi d'Ys, Le (Lalo)
Mylio • tenor
Rozenn • soprano

Roi malgré lui, Le (Chabrier)
Alexina • soprano
Henri de Valois • baritone

Roméo et Juliette (Gounod)
Juliette • soprano
Roméo • tenor

Rondine, La (Puccini)
Magda • soprano
Ruggero • tenor

Rosenkavalier, Der (Strauss)
Annina • contralto
Feldmarschallin Fürstin Werdenberg, Die [*Marie Thérèse*] • soprano
Ochs auf Lerchenau, Baron • bass
Octavian, genannt Quinquin [*Count Rofrano*] • mezzo-soprano
Sophie • soprano

Salome (Strauss)
Jochanaan • bass-baritone
Salome • soprano

Samson et Dalila (Saint-Saëns)
Dalila • contralto
Grand Prêtre du Dagon, Le [*The High Priest of Dagon*] • baritone
Samson • tenor

Sant'Alessio (Landi)
Curtio • soprano
Martio • soprano

Sapho (Massenet)
Fanny [*Sapho*] • soprano
Irène • mezzo-soprano
Jean • soprano

Schöne Galathee, Die (Suppé)
Galathee • soprano
Ganymede • mezzo-soprano

Schweigsame Frau, Die (Strauss)
Aminta • soprano
Henry Morosus • tenor

Scylla et Glaucus (Leclair)
Glaucus • tenor
Scylla • soprano

Semele (Handel)
Juno • contralto
Somnus • bass

Semiramide (Rossini)
Arsace • contralto
Assur • bass
Semiramide • soprano

Serva padrona, La (Pergolesi)
Serpina • soprano
Uberto • bass

Simon Boccanegra (Verdi)
Amelia [Maria Boccanegra] • soprano
Fiesco • bass
Gabriele Adorno • tenor
Simon Boccanegra [The Doge of Genoa] • baritone

Sonnambula, La (Bellini)
Amina • soprano
Elvino • tenor

Sorochinskaya yarmarka
[Fair at Sorochintzï, The] (Musorgsky)
Cherevik • bass
Kum • baritone

Sosarme (Handel)
Elmira • soprano
Sosarme • contralto

Stiffelio (Verdi)
Lina • soprano
Stankar • baritone
Stiffelio • tenor

Straniera, La (Bellini)
Alaide [La Straniera] • soprano
Arturo • tenor
Valdeburgo, Baron • bass

Street Scene (Weill)
Rose • soprano
Sam • tenor

Tabarro, Il (Puccini)
Giorgetta • soprano
Luigi • tenor
Michele • baritone

Telephone, The (Menotti)
Ben • baritone
Lucy • soprano

Thaïs (Massenet)
Athanaël • baritone
Thaïs • soprano

Thomas and Sally (Arne)
Sally • soprano
Squire, The • tenor

Tiefland (Albert)
Marta • soprano
Pedro • tenor
Sebastiano • baritone

Tolomeo (Handel)
Seleuce • soprano
Tolomeo • contralto

Torquato Tasso (Donizetti)
Eleonora • soprano
Tasso • baritone

Tote Stadt, Die (Korngold)
Marietta • soprano
Paul • tenor

Traviata, La (Verdi)
Alfredo Germont • tenor
Giorgio Germont • baritone
Violetta Valéry • soprano

Tristan und Isolde (Wagner)
Isolde • soprano
Tristan • tenor

Troilus and Cressida (Walton)
Cressida • mezzo-soprano
Troilus [Prince] • tenor

Trovatore, Il (Verdi)
Azucena • mezzo-soprano
Leonora • soprano
Luna, Il Conte di [Count] • baritone
Manrico • tenor

Troyens, Les (Berlioz)
Anna • contralto
Cassandre • mezzo-soprano
Chorèbe • baritone
Didon • mezzo-soprano
Énée • tenor

Turandot (Puccini)
Calaf • tenor
Turandot • soprano

Turco in Italia, Il (Rossini)
Fiorilla • soprano
Geronio, Don • bass
Selim • bass

Undina (Tchaikovsky)
Hulbrand • tenor
Undina • soprano

Vanessa (Barber)
Anatol • tenor
Vanessa • soprano

Vêpres siciliennes, Les (Verdi)
Hélène [Elena] • soprano
Henri [Arrigo] • tenor
Montfort [Montforte] • baritone

Vera costanza, La (Haydn)
Errico • tenor
Rosina • soprano

Verschworenen, Die (Schubert)
Isella • soprano
Udoline • soprano

Vespri siciliani, I (Verdi)
Arrigo [Henri] • tenor
Elena [Hélène] • soprano
Montforte [Montfort] • baritone

Vestale, La (Spontini)
Julia • soprano
Licinius • tenor
Pontifex Maximus • bass

Villi, Le (Puccini)
Anna • soprano
Roberto • tenor

Virineya (Slonimsky)
Pavel • bass-baritone
Virineya • soprano

Vogelhändler, Der (Zeller)
Adam • tenor
Marie, Electress • soprano

Walküre, Die (Wagner)
Brünnhilde • soprano
Sieglinde • soprano
Siegmund • tenor
Wotan • bass-baritone

Walzertraum, Ein (Straus)
Franzi • soprano
Hélène • soprano
Lothar, Count • bass
Montschi • baritone
Niki • tenor

Werther (Massenet)
Albert • baritone
Charlotte • mezzo-soprano
Werther • tenor

West Side Story (Bernstein)
Maria • soprano
Tony • tenor

Wildschütz, Der (Lortzing)
Baculus • bass
Gretchen • soprano

Yeomen of the Guard, The (Sullivan)
Elsie Maynard • soprano
Jack Point • baritone

Yevgeny Onegin [Eugene Onegin] (Tchaikovsky)
Ol'ga • contralto
Tat'yana • soprano
Yevgeny Onegin [Eugene Onegin] • baritone

Zaïde (Mozart)
Gomatz • tenor
Zaïde • soprano

Zaparozhets za Dunayem [A Cossack beyond the Danube] (Gulak-Artemovsky)
Karas • bass
Odarka • soprano

Zar und Zimmermann (Lortzing)
Ivanov • tenor
Marie • soprano
Van Bett • bass

Zarewitsch, Der (Lehár)
Sonja • soprano
Zarewitsch, Der [Tsarevich] • tenor

Zauberflöte, Die (Mozart)
Pamina • soprano
Papagena • soprano
Papageno • baritone

Zazà (Leoncavallo)
Dufresne • tenor
Zazà • soprano

Zoroastre (Rameau)
Amélite • soprano
Zoroastre • countertenor

Composers
to Operas

This section is a cross-reference to the duets selected for this volume. It is not intended to represent all of the operas written by the composers. For a complete list of operas by each composer, please consult The Groves Dictionary of Music and Musicians.

Adam, Adolphe (1803-1856)
Le postillon de Lonjumeau (Opéra comique)

Albert, Eugen d' (1864-1932)
Tiefland (Musikdrama)

Albinoni, Tomaso Giovanni (1671-1751)
Pimpinone (Comic intermezzos)

Arne, Thomas Augustine (1710-1778)
Thomas and Sally (Dramatic pastoral)

Auber, Daniel-François-Esprit (1782-1871)
Manon Lescaut (Opéra comique)
La muette de Portici (Grand opéra)

Barber, Samuel (1910-1981)
Antony and Cleopatra (Opera)
Vanessa (Opera)

Beethoven, Ludwig von (1770-1827)
Fidelio (Oper)

Bellini, Vincenzo (1801-1835)
Beatrice di Tenda (Tragedia lirica)
Bianca e Fernando (Melodramma)
I Capuleti e i Montecchi (Tragedia lirica)
Norma (Tragedia lirica)
Il pirata (Melodramma)
I Puritani (Melodramma serio)
La sonnambula (Melodramma)
La Straniera (Melodramma)

Berlioz, Hector (1803-1869)
Béatrice et Bénédict (Opéra)
Benvenuto Cellini (Opéra semi-seria)
Les Troyens (Opéra)

Bernstein, Leonard (1918-1990)
West Side Story (Musical)

Bizet, Georges (1838-1875)
Carmen (Opéra comique)
Les pêcheurs de perles (Opéra)

Boieldieu, Adrien (1775-1834)
La dame blanche (Opéra comique)

Boito, Arrigo (1842-1918)
Mefistofele (Opera)

Bononcini, Giovanni (1670-1747)
Astarto (Dramma per musica)

Borodin, Alexander Porfir'yevich (1833-1887)
Knyaz' Igor' [*Prince Igor*] (Opera)

Britten, Benjamin (1913-1976)
Gloriana (Opera)
Peter Grimes (Opera)

Cesti, Antonio (1623-1669)
Il pomo d'oro (Festa teatrale)

Chabrier, Emmanuel (1841-1894)
L'étoile du Nord (Opéra bouffe)
Le roi malgré lui (Opéra comique)

Charpentier, Gustave (1860-1956)
Louise (Roman musical)

Chérubini, Luigi (1760-1842)
Médée (Opéra comique)

Cilea, Francesco (1866-1950)
Adriana Lecouvreur (Opéra)

Cimarosa, Domenico (1749-1801)
I due supposti Conti (Dramma giocoso)
Il matrimonio segreto (Melodramma giocoso)

Cornelius, Peter (1824-1874)
Der Barbier von Bagdad (Komische Oper)

Debussy, Claude (1862-1918)
Pelléas et Mélisande (Opéra)

Delibes, Léo (1836-1891)
Lakmé (Opéra)

Dezède, Nicolas (c1740-1792)
Blaise et Babet (Comédie mêlée d'ariettes)

Donizetti, Gaetano (1797-1848)
Anna Bolena (Tragedia lirica)
Belisario (Tragedia lirica)
Caterina Cornaro (Tragedia lirica)
Dom Sébastien (Opéra)
Don Pasquale (Dramma buffo)
L'elisir d'amore (Melodramma giocoso)
La favorita [*La favorite*] (Opera)
La favorite [*La favorita*] (Opéra)
La figlia del reggimento [*La fille
    du régiment*] (Opéra comique)
La fille du régiment [*La figlia
    del reggimento*] (Opéra comique)
Linda di Chamounix (Melodramma semiserio)
Lucia di Lammermoor (Dramma tragico)
Lucrezia Borgia (Melodramma)
Maria Stuarda (Tragedia lirica)
Poliuto (Tragedia lirica)
Torquato Tasso (Melodramma semiserio)

Drechsler, Joseph (1782-1852)
Das Mädchen aus der Feenwelt
    (Romantisches Zaubermärche)

Fauré, Gabriel (1845-1924)
Pénélope (Poème lyrique)

Flotow, Friedrich (1812-1883)
Martha (Romantische-komische Oper)

Gershwin, George (1898-1937)
Porgy and Bess (Folk opera)

Giordano, Umberto (1867-1948)
Andrea Chénier (Dramma istorico)
Fedora (Opera)

Gluck, Christoph Willibald von (1714-1787)
Alceste (Tragedia)
Alceste (Tragédie opéra)
Armide (Drame héroïque)
Echo et Narcisse (Drame lyrique)
Iphigénie en Aulide (Tragédie)
Orfeo ed Euridice [*Orphée et Eurydice*] (Azione teatrale)
Orphée et Eurydice [*Orfeo ed Euridice*] (Tragédie opéra)
Paride ed Elena (Dramma per musica)

Gounod, Charles-François (1812-1893)
Faust (Romantische Oper)
Mireille (Opéra)
Roméo et Juliette (Opéra)

Granados, Enrique (1867-1916)
Goyescas (Opera)

Gulak-Artemovsky, Semyon (1813-1873)
Zaparozhets za Dunayem [*A Cossack
    beyond the Danube*] (Singspiel)

Handel, George Frideric (1685-1759)
Acis and Galatea (Masque)
Giulio Cesare in Egitto (Opera)
Hercules (Musical drama)
Imeneo (Opera)
Oreste (Opera)
Rodelinda (Opera)
Semele (Opera)
Sosarme (Opera)
Tolomeo (Opera)

Haydn, Joseph (1732-1809)
L'anima del filosofo (Dramma per musica)
Armida (Dramma eroico)
L'incontro improvviso (Dramma giocoso)
L'infedeltà delusa (Burletta per musica)
Il mondo della luna (Dramma giocoso)
Orlando Paladino (Dramma eroicomico)
La vera Costanza (Dramma giocoso)

Henze, Hans Werner (1926-)
The English Cat (Story)

Hérold, Ferdinand (1791-1833)
Le Pré aux Clercs (Opéra comique)

Humperdinck, Engelbert (1854-1921)
Hänsel und Gretel (Märchenspiel)

Kálmán, Emmerich (1882-1953)
Die Csárdásfürstin (Operette)

Korngold, Erich Wolfgang (1897-1957)
Die tote Stadt (Oper)

Lalo, Edouard (1823-1892)
Le roi d'Ys (Opéra)

Landi, Stefano (1587-1639)
Sant'Alessio (Dramma musicale)

Leclair, Jean-Marie (1697-1764)
Scylla et Glaucus (Tragédie en musique)

Lehár, Franz (1870-1948)
Giuditta (Musikalische Komödie)
Die lustige Witwe (Operette)
Paganini (Operette)
Der Zarewitsch (Operette)

Leoncavallo, Ruggero (1857-1919)
Pagliacci (Dramma)
Zazà (Commedia lirica)

Lortzing, Albert (1801-1851)
Der Wildschütz (Komische Oper)
Zar und Zimmermann (Komische Oper)

Lully, Jean-Baptiste (1632-1687)
Amadis (Tragédie en musique)
Armide (Tragédie en musique)

Martín y Soler, Vicente (1754-1806)
Una cosa rara (Dramma giocoso)

Mascagni, Pietro (1863-1945)
L'amico Fritz (Commedia lirica)
Cavalleria rusticana (Melodramma)
Iris (Melodramma)

Massenet, Jules (1842-1912)
Cendrillon (Conte de fées)
Le Cid (Opéra)
Don Quichotte (Comédie-héroïque)
Hérodiade (Opéra)
Manon (Opéra comique)
Sapho (Pièce lyrique)
Thaïs (Comédie lyrique)
Werther (Drame lyrique)

Menotti, Gian Carlo (1911-)
Amahl and the Night Visitors (Television opera)
The Medium (Tragic opera)
The Telephone (Opera buffa)

Meyerbeer, Giacomo (1791-1864)
L'africaine (Grand opéra)
Il crociato in Egitto (Melodramma eroico)
Les Huguenots (Grand opéra)
Robert le Diable (Grand opéra)

Millöcker, Carl (1842-1899)
Der Bettelstudent (Komische Operette)

Monteverdi, Claudio (1567-1643)
L'incoronazione di Poppea (Dramma musicale)
Il ritorno d'Ulisse in patria (Dramma per musica)

Mozart, Wolfgang Amadeus (1756-1791)
Bastien und Bastienne (Singspiel)
La clemenza di Tito (Opera seria)
Così fan tutte (Opera buffa)

Don Giovanni (Opera buffa)
Die Entführung aus dem Serail (Singspiel)
La finta Giardiniera (Dramma giocoso)
Idomeneo (Dramma per musica)
Lucio Silla (Dramma per musica)
Mitridate (Dramma per musica)
Le nozze di Figaro (Opera buffa)
Zaïde (Singspiel)
Die Zauberflöte (Singspiel)

Musorgsky, Modest Petrovich (1839-1881)
Boris Godunov (Opera)
Sorochinskaya yarmarka [*The Fair at Sorochintzi*] (Opera)

Nicolai, Otto (1810-1849)
Die lustigen Weiber von Windsor (Komische-fantastische Oper)

Offenbach, Jacques (1819-1880)
Barbe-bleue (Opéra bouffe)
Les contes d'Hoffmann (Opéra fantastique)
La Périchole (Opéra bouffe)
Le pont des soupirs (Opéra bouffe)

Paisiello, Giovanni (1740-1816)
Il barbiere di Siviglia (Dramma giocoso)
I filosofi immaginari (Dramma giocoso)
La molinara (Commedia per musica)

Pepusch, Johann Christoph (1667-1752)
The Beggar's Opera (Ballad opera)

Pergolesi, Giovanni Battista (1710-1736)
Flaminio (Commedia musicale)
La Serva Padrona (Intermezzo)

Ponchielli, Amilcare (1834-1886)
La Gioconda (Dramma lirico)
I Lituani [*The Little Sweep*] (Dramma lirico)

Puccini, Giacomo (1858-1924)
La Bohème (Opera)
Edgar (Dramma lirico)
La fanciulla del West (Opera)
Madama Butterfly (Tragedia giapponese)
Manon Lescaut (Dramma lirico)
La rondine (Commedia lirica)
Il Tabarro (Opera)
Turandot (Dramma lirico)
Le villi (Opera-ballo)

Purcell, Henry (c1658-1695)
Dido and Aeneas (Tragic opera)

Rameau, Jean-Philippe (1683-1764)
Les Boréades (Tragédie en musique)
Castor et Pollux (Tragédie en musique)
Hippolyte et Aricie (Tragédie en musique)
Zoroastre (Tragédie en musique)

Ravel, Maurice (1875-1937)
l'Enfant et les sortilèges (Fantaisie lyrique)

Rossini, Gioachino (1792-1868)
Il barbiere di Siviglia (Commedia)
La Cenerentola (Dramma giocoso)
Le comte Ory (Opéra)
La donna del lago (Melodramma)
Elisabetta (Dramma)
La gazza ladra (Melodramma)
Guillaume Tell (Opéra)
L'italiana in Algeri (Dramma giocoso)
Otello (Dramma)
Semiramide (Melodramma tragico)
Il turco in Italia (Dramma buffo)

Saint-Saëns, Camille (1835-1921)
Samson et Dalila (Opéra)

Schubert, Franz (1797-1828)
Fierrabras (Heroisch-romantische Oper)
Die Verschworenen (Singspiel)

Slonimsky, Sergey Mikhaylovich (1932-)
Virineya (Opera)

Smetana, Bedřich (1824-1884)
Dalibor (Opera)
Prodaná Nevěsta [*The Bartered Bride*] (Comic opera)

Spontini, Gaspare (1774-1851)
La vestale (Tragédie lyrique)

Storace, Stephen (1762-1796)
The Haunted Tower (Mainpiece dialogue opera)

Stradella, Alessandro (1639-1682)
Girello (Dramma musicale burlesco)

Straus, Oscar (1870-1954)
Ein Walzertraum (Operette)

Strauss, Johann (1825-1899)
Die Fledermaus (Komische Operette)

Strauss, Richard (1864-1949)
Arabella (Lyrische Komödie)
Ariadne auf Naxos (Oper)
Capriccio (Konversationsstück für Musik)
Daphne (Bukolische Tragödie)
Elektra (Tragödie)
Die Frau ohne Schatten (Oper)
Der Rosenkavalier (Komödie für Musik)
Salome (Musikdrama)
Die schweigsame Frau (Komische Oper)

Stravinsky, Igor (1882-1971)
The Rake's Progress (Opera)

Sullivan, Sir Arthur (1842-1900)
The Gondoliers (Operetta)
Patience (Operetta)
The Yeomen of the Guard (Operetta)

Suppé, Franz (1819-1895)
Boccaccio (Operette)
Die schöne Galathee (Operette)

Tchaikovsky, Pyotr Il'yich (1840-1893)
Iolanta (Lyrical opera)

Pikovaya dama [*Pique Dame*]
  [*The Queen of Spades*] (Opera)
Undina (Opera)
Yevgeny Onegin [*Eugene Onegin*] (Lyric scenes)

Thomas, Ambroise (1811-1896)
Hamlet (Opéra)
Mignon (Opéra comique)

Tippett, Sir Michael (1905-)
The Midsummer Marriage (Opera)

Verdi, Giuseppe (1813-1901)
Aida (Opera)
Alzira (Tragedia lirica)
Attila (Dramma lirico)
Un ballo in maschera (Melodramma)
La battaglia di Legnano (Tragedia lirica)
Il corsaro (Opera)
Don Carlo [*Don Carlos*] (Opera)
Don Carlos [*Don Carlo*] (Opéra)
I due Foscari (Tragedia lirica)
Ernani (Dramma lirico)
Falstaff (Commedia lirica)
La forza del destino (Opera)
Giovanna d'Arco (Dramma lirico)
Jérusalem (Opéra)
I Lombardi (Dramma lirico)
Luisa Miller (Melodramma tragico)
Macbeth (Opera)
I Masnadieri (Melodramma)
Nabucco (Dramma lirico)
Otello (Dramma lirico)
Rigoletto (Melodramma)
Simon Boccanegra (Opera)
Stiffelio (Opera)
La traviata (Opera)
Il trovatore (Dramma)
Les vêpres siciliennes [*I vespri siciliani*] (Opéra)
I vespri siciliani [*Les vêpres siciliennes*] (Opera)

Wagner, Richard (1813-1883)
Der fliegende Holländer (Romantische Oper)
Götterdämmerung (Bühnenfestspiel)
Lohengrin (Romantische Oper)
Die Meistersinger von Nürnberg (Musikdrama)
Parsifal (Bühnenweihfestspiel)
Rienzi (Grosse tragische Oper)
Tristan und Isolde (Handlung)
Die Walküre (Bühnenfestspiel)

Walton, Sir William (1902-1983)
Troilus and Cressida (Opera)

Weber, Carl Maria von (1786-1826)
Abu Hassan (Singspiel)
Euryanthe (Grosse heroisch-romantische Oper)
Der Freischütz (Romantische Oper)
Oberon (Romantische Oper)

Weill, Kurt (1900-1950)
Street Scene (Broadway opera)

Zeller, Carl (1842-1898)
Der Vogelhändler (Volksoperette)

Bibliography

Balthazar, S.L. "The *Primo Ottocento* Duet and the Transformation of the Rossinian Code." *Journal of Musicology* vii (1989), 471-97.

Becker, H. "Das Duett in der Oper." *Musik, Edition, Interpretation: Gedenkschrift Günter Henle* (Munich, 1980), 234-60.

Cook, E. *The Operatic Ensemble in France, 1673-1775.* Diss., University of East Anglia, 1989.

Dent, E.J. "Ensembles and Finales in Eighteenth-Century Italian Opera." *Sammelbände der Internationalen Musik-Gesellschaft,* xi (1909-10), 543-69; xii (1910-11), 112-38.

McClymonds, Marita; Cook, Elisabeth; and Budden, Julian. "Duet." *The New Grove Dictionary of Opera,* ed. Stanley Sadie (New York, 1992), I, 1268-70.

Wallace, Mary Elaine, and Wallace, Robert. *Opera Scenes for Class and Stage.* (Carbondale, IL, 1979).